THE FACE OF THINGS

SUNY series in Contemporary Continental Philosophy

Dennis J. Schmidt, Editor

THE FACE OF THINGS

A DIFFERENT SIDE OF ETHICS

SILVIA BENSO

State University of New York Press

Published by
State University of New York Press, Albany

Printed in the United States of America

For information, address State University of New York Press, State University Plaza, Albany, N.Y., 12246

Production by Diane Ganeles
Marketing by Fran Keneston

Library of Congress Cataloging-in-Publication Data

Benso, Silva.
The face of things : a different side of ethics / Silva Benso.
p. cm.—(SUNY series in contemporary continental philosophy)
Includes bibliographical references and index.
ISBN 0-7914-4573-9 (alk. paper)—ISBN 0-7914-4574-7 (pbk. : alk. paper)
1. Ethics, Modern—20th century. 2. Lâvinas, Emmanuel—Contributions in ethics. 3. Heidegger, Martin, 1889–1976—Contributions in ethics. I. Title. II. Series.

BJ319 .B467 2000
170–dc21 99-043441

10 9 8 7 6 5 4 3 2 1

To Brian, Ulysses, and Clio
Faithful companions of all my joys and sorrows

◆ Contents

And therefore as a stranger give it welcome.
There are more things in heaven and earth, Horatio,
Than are dreamt of in your philosophy.

Shakespeare, *Hamlet* I.i.165–7

❖ Acknowledgments

Over the years and across various landscapes, many faces (and not all of them human) have left marks of their passage in the folds of the thing which is now this book. Some of these faces remain unnamed—pure, anonymous presences that have enriched my work with the warmth of an essential moment, the gift of a shared thought, or the joy of a sudden inspiration. Some other faces have become unnameable—changes in the circumstances of life now forbid naming what once was close, dear, and memorable. Still, other faces should be named, and I gladly do so, in thankful gratitude for their precious presence by my side, in friendship and love, even when at a distance.

My intellectual gratitude goes to my former teachers in the Italian academia—Giuliana Giachino, Ugo Perone, Maurizio Pagano, Claudio Ciancio, and Gianni Vattimo—who first aroused my love for philosophy, my passion for ethical questions, and my interest in Levinas and Heidegger. The same intellectual gratitude goes to my more recent teachers in the graduate program in philosophy at the Pennsylvania State University—Veronique Foti, Al Lingis, Carl Vaught, Dan Conway, and Joe Flay—who nourished my initial love of philosophy, gave it rigor and discipline, refined my knowledge, and supervised in various ways the writing of the original core of this work in the form of a dissertation. To this list I gratefully add the name of Adriaan Peperzak. I would also like to thank John Caputo, who read an early version of this project and, despite its roughness and approximation, gave me advice and encouragement to proceed. Many thanks go to my colleagues at Siena College—Ray Boisvert, John Burkey, Fr. Julian Davies, Dick Gaffney, Jenny McErlean, Paul Santilli, Fr. John VanHook—who supported my project, accommodated a demanding teaching schedule to my research needs, and discussed many of the themes of this work in our monthly colloquia. My philosophical and emotional gratitude goes to some wonderful friends—Dennis Beach, Alessandra Fussi, Alfredo Ferrarin, Shannon Winnubst, Mark Tanzer, Tamsin Lorraine, Tom Thorp, and Gary Scott among others—with whom many hours were spent, at different times and in different places, in passionate discussion of various important philosophical issues, some of which have found their way into this book. And finally, I wish to thank Jane Bunker and Diane Ganeles, editors at SUNY Press, who, with patience, professionalism, and good humor, helped bring this project to completion.

Beyond philosophy lies the concreteness of everyday life. Deep thanks go to my longtime spiritual companion, Monica Gargano, whose philosophical acumen and intellectual restlessness barely match the tenderness of her heart and the gentleness of her person. I would like to express my affectionate and everlasting gratitude to Alberto Marcone, mathematician, bird-watcher, and dearest friend, with whom many of the dreams and visions which nourish this work were first conceived. I owe a special debt of recognition and appreciation to Ermanno, Rosanna, Patrizia, Massimo, and some other Italian friends, who, in the radical simplicity of their choices and in the brave routine of their daily existence, live their relation with things with that love and tenderness of which this book speaks. My infinite and ineffable gratefulness is for my father and mother—Umberto and Arriga—and for my brother—Richi—who have first taught me how to love life with passion, patience, and perseverance. The person I should like to thank the most is Brian Schroeder, philosophical friend, travel companion, and life partner, who has given new meaning and love to my existence; without him, this would be a much worse book. Finally, I am indebted to the very things of life—objects, plants, flowers, animals, landscapes I have visited, situations I have encountered; in the endless variety of their constant and yet discreet presence, they have been the major, and yet gratuitous, source of wonder and inspiration for the themes of this work.

To all of these individuals, to those I have named and to those I have left unnamed, I wish to express my gratitude. The traces of their faces constitute the story and texture of this book.

❖ Abbreviations

For complete bibliographical reference, see the Bibliography at the end of the volume.

1. Works by Levinas

AT *Alterity and Transcendence,* trans. M. Smith (New York: Columbia University Press, 1999)

BPW *Emmanuel Levinas: Basic Philosophical Writings,* ed. A. Peperzak, S. Critchley, and R. Bernasconi (Bloomington: Indiana University Press, 1996).

CPP *Collected Philosophical Papers,* ed. A. Lingis (Dordrecht: Nijhoff, 1987).

DF *Difficult Freedom: Essays on Judaism,* trans. S. Hand (Baltimore: Johns Hopkins University Press, 1991).

DL *Difficile Liberté. Essais sur le judaisme* (Paris: Albin Michel, 1963).

DVI *De Dieu qui vient à l'idée* (Paris: Vrin, 1982).

EE *Existence and Existents,* trans. A. Lingis (The Hague-Boston: Nijhoff, 1978).

EI *Ethics and Infinity,* trans. R. Cohen (Pittsburgh: Duquesne University Press, 1985).

OBBE *Otherwise than Being or Beyond Essence,* trans. A. Lingis (The Hague-Boston: Nijhoff, 1981).

OS *Outside the Subject,* trans. M. Smith (Stanford: Stanford University Press, 1994).

PN *Proper Names,* trans. M. Smith (Stanford: Stanford University Press, 1996).

SF "Sécularization et faim."

TH "Transcendence and Height," in *Emmanuel Levinas: Basic Philosophical Writings,* ed. A. Peperzaak, S. Critchley, and R. Bernasconi (Bloomington: Indiana University Press, 1996), 11–31.

TI *Totality and Infinity: An Essay on Exteriority,* trans. A. Lingis (Pittsburgh: Duquesne University Press, 1969).

TO *Time and the Other,* trans. R. Cohen (Pittsburgh: Duquesne University Press, 1987).

ToO "The Trace of the Other," trans. A. Lingis, in *Deconstruction in Context: Literature and Philosophy,* ed. Mark Taylor (Chicago: University of Chicago Press, 1986), 345–359.

WO "Wholly Otherwise," trans. S. Critchley, in *Re-Reading Levinas,* ed. R. Bernasconi and S. Critchley (Bloomington: Indiana University Press, 1991), 3–10.

2. Works by Heidegger

BDT "Building, Dwelling, Thinking," trans. A. Hofstadter, in *Poetry, Language, Thought* (New York: Harper & Row, 1971).

BPP *The Basic Problems of Phenomenology,* trans. A. Hofstadter (Bloomington: Indiana University Press, 1988).

BT *Being and Time,* trans. J. Macquerrie and E. Robinson (New York: Harper & Row, 1962).

BW *Basic Writings,* ed. David F. Krell (New York: Harper & Row, 1977).

DT *Discourse on Thinking,* trans. J. Anderson and E. Freund (New York: Harper & Row, 1966).

FCM *The Fundamental Concepts of Metaphysics,* trans. W. McNeill and N. Walker (Bloomington: Indiana University Press, 1995).

HCT *History of the Concept of Time: Prolegomena,* trans. T. Kisiel (Bloomington: Indiana University Press, 1985).

IM *An Introduction to Metaphysics,* trans. R. Manheim (New Haven: Yale University Press, 1959).

L "Language," trans. A. Hofstadter, in *Poetry, Language, Thought* (New York: Harper & Row, 1971).

LH "Letter on Humanism," trans. F. Capuzzi, in *Basic Writings* (New York: Harper & Row, 1977), 189–242.

OM "Overcoming Metaphysics," trans. J. Stambaugh, in *The End of Philosophy* (New York: Harper & Row, 1973).

OWA "On the Origin of the Work of Art," trans. A. Hofstadter, in *Poetry, Language, Thought* (New York: Harper & Row, 1971), 17–87.

OWL *On the Way to Language,* trans. P. Hertz (New York: Harper & Row, 1971).

PA "La provenance de l'art et la destination de la pensée," trans. J. Chrétien and M. Reifenrath, in *Cahier de l'Herne: Heidegger,* ed. Michel Haar (Paris: Ed. de l'Herne, 1983), 365–380.

PLT *Poetry, Language, Thought,* trans. A. Hofstadter (New York: Harper & Row, 1971).

QCT "The Question Concerning Technology," trans. W. Lovitt, in *The Question Concerning Technology* (New York: Harper & Row, 1977).

S *Plato's Sophist,* trans. R. Rojcewicz and A. Schuwer (Bloomington: Indiana University Press, 1997).

T "The Thing," trans. A. Hofstadter, in *Poetry, Language, Thought* (New York: Harper & Row, 1971), 165–186.

TB *On Time and Being,* trans. J Stambaugh (New York: Harper & Row, 1972).

WCT *What Is Called Thinking?,* trans. F. D. Wieck and J. Gray (New York: Harper & Row, 1972).

WM "What Is Metaphysics?," in *Existence and Being,* ed. W. Brock (South Bend: Regnery, 1979).

WPF "What Are Poets For?," trans. A. Hofstadter, in *Poetry, Language, Thought* (New York: Harper & Row, 1971).

WT *What Is a Thing?* (Chicago: Regnery, 1970).

❖ Preface

Philosophical Laughters

According to an anecdote, retold in Plato's *Theaetetus* (174a), the beginning of philosophy is marked by a threefold presence: a philosopher, a well, and a servant girl—neat and witty, according to Plato's story. Absorbed in the contemplation of celestial entities, the first philosopher, whom the tradition recognizes as Thales, does not notice terrestrial things. The victims of his negligence, however, take their revenge on him when, because of his lack of attention, he inadvertently falls into a well. At this, the young maid, unintentional spectator to a scene whose seminal significance probably remains obscure to her, bursts out into what we can presume is a hearty laughter. In the apparent innocence of this ingenuous anecdote, often retold and interpreted throughout the history of philosophy, is inscribed the destiny of the entire Western philosophical tradition in its relation to things (but not only).[1]

The story, in the manner Plato has transmitted it to us, condemns, in the spontaneity of the laughter of the maid, the ignorance of the *vulgus*, which relies on the immediacy of sensations. Trapped in the realm of opinions to which sensory perception gives raise the *vulgus* does not understand the beauty, fascination, and primacy of intellectual speculation and pure theory. The laughter of the maid is therefore only the prefiguration of the less laughable, more fatal incomprehension that will accompany the trial of Socrates, model and martyr of philosophical investigation, and will lead to his death. What is comedy for the *vulgus* is tragedy for philosophy, confirming Socrates' intuition in the final scene of the *Symposium* that "the fully skilled tragedian could be a comedian as well" (223d). Thus, by retelling the story, Plato invests philosophy with a mandate of which it will never be oblivious: that of "investigating the universal nature of everything that is, each in its entirety, never lowering itself to anything close at hand" (*Theaet.* 173e). Indifferent to the laughters that its endeavor provokes among the nonphilosophers, Western philosophy, with few exceptions, has accepted Plato's legacy and has made of intellectual speculation its major reason for pride. The philosopher is the one at whom the masses necessarily laugh.[2] From a philosophical perspective, however, such a laughter retains no philosophical value whatsoever. Rather, ignorance is its instigation.

The servant's Thracian origin situates her at the margins of philosophy, closer to the world of *mythos* still incontaminated by the power of *logos*. In her servile but, Plato remarks, witty eyes, which are bowed downward toward the lowly, toward the earthly, toward what is close to the ground; in her feminine sensitivity, which, because of the everyday activities to which she has been consigned, is accustomed to the patience and attention for the little things, the maid has good reason to laugh. Some of these reasons are of a deeply philosophical nature, although they do not appear as such to the logocentric eyes of Western tradition.

It is Nietzsche who, indirectly and without even mentioning the episode, exposes the truth of the story, and retrieves the philosophical meaning of the laughter and the wisdom that lies behind it. In a famous section of *Twilight of the Idols,* devoted to the description of "How the Real World at Last Became a Myth," Nietzsche confirms, via its criticism, the progressive process of idealization of reality accomplished in Western philosophy by retracing what he considers "the history of an error." Which error? The error of "mistaking the last for the first,"[3] which accompanies the other idiosyncracy of philosophy: its "hatred of even the idea of becoming," which Nietzsche stigmatizes as a "lack of historical sense."[4] As the servant girl had already intuited in the person of the first philosopher, Socrates—the seminal champion of rationality—was a buffoon who, rather than being laughed at, got himself taken seriously[5] precisely by those who should have laughed at him, and who, by not joining in the wisdom of the servant girl, confirmed their own rootedness in ignorance nevertheless. Although Nietzsche does not say so, the maid, with the spontaneity of her own laughter which stems from a prerationalistic, sensualistic contact with reality, had very good reasons to laugh. Hers is not the laughter of popular ignorance, as Plato would like his readers to believe. Rather, it is the laughter of a prelogocentric, *embodied* wisdom. Unfortunately, Western philosophy has not taken up the invitation of her laughter.[6] Instead, it has let itself be dominated by centuries of idolizing rationality and believing in otherworldly realities, which it called absolutes.

Both Nietzsche's exposure of the truth, which for him reveals itself as an untruth, a "*moral-optical* illusion,"[7] and the story itself, even in Plato's reproduction, do not speak only of the possible objects of philosophy and of the different path Western thinking might have followed if it had indulged in the embodied laughter of the maid. More fundamentally, the story tells of the radical misplacement of things that takes place within the philosophical inquiry the way it has constituted itself ever since its Greek origin. What is encapsulated in the anecdote is the representation of the ambiguous relation philosophy entertains with the notions of nearness and farness, or, in more traditional terms, immanence and transcendence.

What Thales does not notice, that to which he pays no attention, is precisely what is nearest to him: not simply the things, but the abysmal depths of things, exemplified by the well into which he falls, by which he is, in the story, captured. Were he to look more carefully, the well might disclose to him a more profound, nocturnal, mysterious reality than that revealed by the shining surface of things (to which, however, he pays no attention). The inversion of reality of which philosophy is responsible, and of which the maid is, philosophically or not (but has the maid ever been allowed to philosophize?), aware, marks the philosophical inability to discern that the farness to which the philosophical mind is so powerfully attracted is not situated in a world distant and unreachable (if not through the mystification of a theoretical enterprise that brings near only through its illusory categorizations). Rather, transcendence is paradoxically located in what is nearest, common, and evident, in that embodied immediacy from which the laughter of the maid surges. The mask with which reality protects its own truth is different from the Mayan veil of illusion through which rationality mystifies its own creative fantasies.

In its raising from the depths of her belly, from a wisdom that has remained in closer contact with the depths of the earth into which the well too is excavated, in its embodied origin, the laughter of the Thracian maid, so despised by Plato's elitism, is not merely a manifestation of popular ignorance. Rather, it resonates with the silent laughter of the things themselves, whose arcane profundity could not be obliterated by their transfiguration into the eternal world of essences, whether formal, mathematical, or ontological. In their apparent impenetrability, which envelops the absent-minded and neglectful philosopher, things silently laugh at the illusory vanity of abstract philosophical speculation, which in its act of grasping irremediably loses exactly that which it thought it would be accessing. Concerned with the practices of the world, ancient naturalists knew that it is only from the abysses of the well that one can achieve the best vision of the stars, in their transcending, unreachable reality. One could argue, then, that it is not the stars that mirror themselves in the deep water of the well. Rather, it is the deep, mirroring water of the well that brings the stars, and the trembling luminescence of a light that may no longer be there the moment it is looked at, closer, and, in a sense, makes them real.[8] By looking at the stars, philosophy neglects the well; but by looking at the reflections in the depths of the well, philosophy might be able to get an even better vision of the stars (if it only bothered to look).

The nonvocal laughter of things situates itself at a distance from human beings, thus appointing things to be the silent spectators and witnesses of human actions and interactions with other humans, and with the things themselves. Yet, such a laughter has never found legitimation within philosophical discourse. Ignored, set aside, ridiculed; prized, priced, appropriated; controlled, manipulated, violated; feared, fought against, subjugated; revered, glorified, fetishized, things have been constructed as objects set against the field of the subject's action. Strolling by a stream, the young Narcissus is more attentive to things than his cultural compatriot, Thales. Narcissus stops and looks. Yet, bent on the surface of the water, he does not see the depth of the brook, the powerfulness of the stream, the ceaseless flow of the water. He sees himself. In his action, he exemplifies the attitude toward things of Western philosophy as a whole.

What is near becomes far, what is far becomes mistakenly near, and what is truly far in the near—that is, the depths of things—becomes irretrievably lost and inaccessible. Maybe because accessible to anyone, the multidimensionality of reality that the depths of things protect and enshrine has been accessed by no one. The laughter of the maid has been laughed at by the philosophers, who have read it as a sign of ignorance, and laughed with by the nonphilosophers, who, out of sincere ignorance, have interpreted the philosopher as a comic character. In the general laughter that ensues, what has been forgotten is the possibility that the only genuinely philosophical laughter may be that of the maid, in her "joyful wisdom" that remains attentive to things.

Breaching the Tradition

The contemporary philosophical scenario is marked by the awareness of a break with its past. The break within the tradition has also characterized other philosophical epochs, for example, those of the transition from the Middle Ages to the Renaissance, or from the Renaissance to the movements of the Reformation and Counter Reformation. In our contemporary horizon, however, the break within the tradition becomes a breach *of* the tradition. The philosophical consciousness has become aware of the impossibility of situating itself on a line of continuity with that philosophical past to which it still owes its origin.

In the mind of all major continental philosophers, there is no doubt that, although philosophy may not have reached its end, as some thinkers have announced and claimed,[9] nevertheless it has entered a condition of uncertainty and uneasiness that has been named, among other denominations, "postmodernity." According to Lyotard, postmodernity can be defined as "incredulity toward metanarratives," the condition in which "the grand narrative has lost its credibility, regardless of what mode of unification it uses, regardless of whether it is a speculative narrative or a narrative of emancipation."[10] It is in this sense of epoch of crisis of *grand récits* that the term "postmodernity" is presently employed. Along similar lines, Jean-Luc Nancy speaks of "today" as the epoch in which "there is something like a general loss of *sens*."[11] Regardless of its definition, postmodernity is, and knows itself as, a period of crisis—breach, difference, turn. The message that Nietzsche's madman was anxious to announce, but without the comfort of a successful reception among its audience, has finally reached its hearers, or at least its philosophical hearers: "God is dead! God remains dead."[12] The easy and consolatory faith in any otherworldy reality, be it God, the Good, the absolute under any of its forms (political, social, religious, moral, or even scientific) cannot be seriously entertained after the radical criticism to which the hermeneuticians of suspicion (Marx, Freud, and Nietzsche) have submitted notions such as the truth, the good, and even the self.

As in Hegel's image, however, the owl of Minerva appears only after dusk. The philosophical awareness of the breach with/of the tradition follows the occurrence of a historical event which, whether understood as a *unicum* or as the last episode in a long history of persecutions and violences, signals the destructive potential of which Western culture, despite its humanism, is capable. Such an event is Auschwitz. Levinas explicitly commemorates it as a philosophical inspiration by dedicating one of his major works, *Otherwise than Being or Beyond Essence,* "to the memory of those who were closest among the six million assassinated by the National Socialists, and of the millions and millions of all confessions and all nations, victims of the same hatred of the other man, the same anti-semitism" (OBBE V). Ever since Auschwitz, the necessity, formulated without hesitations by Adorno, to think in such a way that Auschwitz may not occur again,[13] seems to have gotten a firm hold of philosophy, at least in its continental tendency.

The theme, which has imposed itself more frequently to philosophy in its situation of destabilization called postmodernity, is that of the "other" (sex, gender, race, culture), of which the Jews and the Jewish tradition, in their being situated always at the margin of Western culture and philosophy, are an epiphany. Correlatively, such a reflection has taken the form of a meditation on the nature of the subject, self or same, and the possibility that it may enter an intersubjective relation with the other that does not deprive the other of her or his own power of signification.

To many philosophers, Auschwitz appears not merely as an accidental degeneration in the history of Western thought, a deviation from the norm that a more scientific, coherent employment of rationality could have rectified, corrected, and thus avoided. Rather, Auschwitz appears as the ultimate, but direct consequence of a way of thinking that deeply informs the Western philosophical tradition.[14] Such thinking is characterized by the supremacy of the subject (and its reason) as the only authority capable of granting reality—conceived in oppositional terms as the object, or the other-than-the-subject—its truth and meaning. Hegel's highest achievement, the elaboration of dialectics and the system which it originates, has been understood as the most complete formulation of the theoretical movement of reduction of the other to the same—that is, to the subject that has undergone a process of self-identification precisely through and at the expense of the other.

Hegel may bear the most burdensome responsibility in conceptualizing the reduction of the other to the structures of signification of the same. Yet, the nature of philosophy has been discovered to be Hegelian even *ante litteram*. Nietzsche, Adorno, Horkheimer, Heidegger, and Levinas, among others, ascribe to Socrates—the very "father" of Western philosophy, that model of argumentation which Nietzsche characterizes as one of the primary idols of Western culture—the origin of the totalizing attempt to give order and systematization to reality at the expense of the other, whose nature is betrayed and turned into a function of the system.[15]

Before Auschwitz, the reductionist move maintained itself at the level of theory, although covertly substantiating many phenomena of intolerance. With the event of Auschwitz, reductionism goes beyond the theoretical realm of knowledge to reach the very ground of material existence. Confronted with Auschwitz, the question is no longer that of Western philosophy being a philosophy of the subject in the sense of the theoretical constitution of the epistemological self-identity of the subject. Physical annihilation of the other in the person not of *a* Jew, not of *some* Jews, but of *all* Jews is displayed as its truth.

If Auschwitz constitutes a crisis, it does so in the sense of provoking not only a breach, but also a turn. Auschwitz is contemporarily end and beginning, condemnation and obligation, rejection and promise. After Auschwitz, philosophy has become aware of the ideological nature of any position that pledges theoretical allegiance to the path of reductionist thinking. The price philosophy should have to pay to proceed on its old steps, and which it cannot afford to pay, despite the dissolution of the notion of all absolute truths, is that of its transformation into sophistry, in a relinquishment of its claim to be loyal to the truth, be it the truth of the earth and its masks, rather than the truth of a god and its simulacra. If philosophy is to remain faithful not simply to its own nature and self-definition, but, more radically, to the possibility of its own existence, a different path of thinking is needed, in which the otherness of the other is celebrated and maintained in its separation. Hence the obligation, shared by most contemporary thinkers, to explore the theme of the other, and to do so in a nonreductionistic manner.

Although often unacknowledged and unthematized, such an obligation has directed philosophy toward an attempt at a reformulation of the notion of subjectivity in terms that minimize, if not eliminate, the possibility of phenomena of extreme violence and annihilation (what the religious and moral traditions would call absolute evil) witnessed during the years of Nazi Germany, and which philosophy, at least in the vestige of one of its major representatives, Martin Heidegger, has been and is still unable to counteract. The theoretical tool to operate a move away from subjectivity and its violent categorizations, unable to be efficacious in avoiding destruction, has seemed to be that of a (non)thematization of otherness as a disruptive entity that refuses itself to, and thus possibly escapes, the categorization of the same. Ethics is the name that has been given, primarily by Levinas, to the field where a meaningful intersubjective relation with the other can happen, a relation that does not annihilate the possibility that the other be the source of its own signification.

The Primacy of Ethics

Possibly as a response to the horrors of this century, the return to ethics has become one of the major themes characterizing the postmodern scenario. However, again possibly as a consequence of Nietzsche's devastating critique of Christian morality,[16] and of all moral systems gravitating around the notion of an absolute, transcendent referent, in contemporary philosophy, ethics seems to have folded upon itself. The great ethical inspirations of the past, which aimed at embracing and encompassing all aspects of existence (Aristotle, Kant, Mill, even Spinoza), have been reduced to murmurs and whispers. The project of a great ethics has regionalized itself. It has turned itself into the creation of a sequence of small ethical approaches, each appointed with the task of finding minimal common principles to regulate a specific, territorialized area of that reality which the collapse, end, and prohibition of all great metaphysical systems prevents from approaching in its entirety. Now that the ancient faith in metaphysics has been criticized and rejected, because it has been unveiled as an illusion, ethics has been consigned to being a *locus minimus*.

Nourished by the passion coming from the life-threatening experience of one who has witnessed the final destination of both traditional great ethics and the denial of all such ethics,[17] Levinas's philosophical project summons its readers to a renewal of the primacy of ethics. Levinas's invitation to an ethical renewal, however, is not the suggestion of a nostalgic return to the ethical categories developed by Western philosophical tradition. Deliberately neglectful of ethical imperatives grounded on a notion of rationality that theorizes respect for the other only as another form of respect for the self, and which by so doing has not been able to prevent the occurring of Auschwitz, Levinas retrieves the ancient, metaphysical tradition of the Platonic Good as that which is located *epekeina tes ousias,* and couples it with Descartes's notion of the Infinite as that which escapes and overflows the power of conceptualization of subjective rationality.

The result of this difficult union between metaphysics, epistemology, and ethics is the (non)thematization of the notion of the "face" of the Other (*Autrui*)[18] as the (non)experience in which the transcendence of the Infinite, in its goodness beyond being and absolute otherness, reveals itself. Ethics becomes for Levinas the name for this very special metaphysical relation between the self and an Other that is always beyond conceptualization, and yet is the ultimate origin of all meaning, truth, and reason. Rather than being informed by the same and its rationality, Levinasian ethics is directed and oriented by the heteronomy of the appeal of an Other whose face can never be conceptualized, thematized, and thus is left undeconstructed by any hermeneutics of suspicion. In its absolute, infinite, over- and everflowing transcendence, the other becomes the ungrounded and ungroundable ground of Levinas's project. The great ethical inspiration which had instigated pre-Nietzschean ethical systems is thus regained, but on the side of the other. Therefore, without the potentiality for the destructive excesses and totalizations to which the notion of subjectivity that sustained such ethical systems opened the way.

Facialities

The project that I elaborate in the present work, and whose movements I will outline in the next pages, situates itself within this more general background of a rethinking of ethics as the realm within which the other can meaningfully speak to and address the I. However, mindful of the philosophical truth encrypted in the laughter of the Thracian maid, the work has the ambitions of being a contribution to, and a broadening of the ways in which otherness has been thematized. Not only the formulation of an ethics of the Other, but also of an ethics of the other of the Other, an ethics of things, is the provocative novelty that this work wants to propose.

Despite the title, in the singular, the project is located under the sign of multiplicity. Not a face but faces is what this book is about, in homage to, and an affirmation of, irreducible plurality, variety, difference, and differentiation. Moreover, not "faces" but "facialities" is the most adequate term to relate to the subject matter of the work. Faces express a specific content, a defined contour, an individuated existence. Facialities invoke the intimation of signification of a face, and yet the vagueness of a cluster of meaning the demarcation of which remains blurred, fluid, porous to a continuous, osmotic exchange between inside and outside that mobilizes boundaries, and therefore definitions; that runs the risk of a continuous slippage away into the night of the indistinct, undifferentiated, anonymous; that creates zones of shadows, ambiguities, perplexities, contradictions, and therefore richness. Facialities evoke the possibility of the existence of faceless faces, which, despite their facelessness, are yet endowed with the intimating power of the face to demand an ethical response.

Such are things, to which this book is devoted in an attempt to retrieve them from the realm of oblivion to which the ignorance of their facialities has condemned them; in an attempt to retrace in them the possibility of ethical signification; in an attempt to consign them to tenderness as to the philosophical category capable of a recognition of and meaningful response to their ethical appeal; briefly, in an attempt to relate to them as tendered facialities in the dimension of festivity. Not to anthropomorphize things, but, if a somewhat awkward neologism is allowed, to "thingize" ethics is the project of this book. Levinas has suggestive words *à propos*: "in a study of Homeric comparisons M. Snell (as quoted by Karl Löwith) points out that when in the *Iliad* the resistance to an attack by an enemy phalanx is compared to the resistance of a rock to the waves that assail it, it is not necessarily a matter of extending to the rock, through anthropomorphism, a human behavior, but of interpreting the resistance petromorphically. Resistance is neither a human privilege, nor a rock's, just as radiance does not characterize a day of the month of May more authentically than the face of a woman. The meaning precedes the data and illuminates them" (CPP 78). Taking up the echoes resonating in Levinas's quotation, this work asks a daring question: What if ethics revealed a meaning preceding, transcending, and illuminating its application in the sphere of interhuman relations? More dramatically stated, what if things were capable of expressing an ethical signification, an alterity that goes beyond the structures of meaning within which things have been enframed—an alterity that demands the resoluteness of an ethical response on the side of human beings?

The Face of Things plays then with the ambivalence of meaning present in the word "tendered." The prevailing economy of exchange within which things have been inserted condemns them to the status of faceless entities to be offered in payment, compensation and reward, as if they were quantified and quantifiable currency to be tendered among humans. Beyond such an economical meaning of "tendered," *The Face of Things* aims at restoring things to a preeconomical horizon of festive appreciation and celebration within which things can be encountered in their facialities and tendered—that is, treated with tenderness—because of the generosity of their self-giving, as if their alterity were a gift.

The Unfolding of One Story

The unfolding of the project follows a threefold movement. Levinas's philosophy constitutes the dialogical counterpart to the first part of the work, comprised of four chapters. The first chapter explores how, out of a nontotalizing love for the other, who becomes the erotic intention of his philosophy, Levinas advances a path of thinking which situates itself in radical alternative to the course followed by Western thought in its Parmenidean aspiration to unity. As thematized in the notion of filiality, the strength of Levinas's project consists in its ability to accomplish the movement of distancing and differentiation from the philosophical tradition of Greek descent by taking its bearings from elements present in that very tradition. The origin of philosophy, although compromised, is not rejected or denied, but rather, broken open by a different inspiration: that of the other in its radical separation. Yet, the question remains: Does Levinas's project duplicate the totalizing movement that it wants to disrupt?

The nonlocative place within which the encounter with the Other in his or her otherness comes to pass is, for

Levinas, ethics. As chapter 2 indicates, it is within such a space that the ontological subject is called into question by the Other, and opened up to a movement of self-transcendence that transforms it into an ethical subjectivity. Beyond the transcendental foundationalism of ontology and epistemology, ethics is for Levinas the space of a face to face, in which the I and the Other remain separate despite their relation. Ethics is not a place of foundations, but of transformations, a place of love meetings within which ambivalences and differences are allowed to flourish and thrive.

The present essay is greatly and gratefully indebted to Levinas's thematization of ethics as the dimension within which a nonviolating encounter with otherness can come to pass. However, its aspiration reaches further than the limits that Levinas's philosophy has imposed on itself, and thus registers the limitations into which such limits incur. By investigating who is the other whom Levinas places at the core of his philosophy, this essay advances beyond Levinas, offering a critique that primarily intends to be a supplement to his own position. For Levinas, the face of the other that interrupts and disrupts the economy of the same and summons it to ethics is always the human face, certainly the face of the other man, hopefully—and arguably—also the face of the other woman and child. A human presence is what is required, according to Levinas, for the same to be placed in the position of transcending itself and enter the space of ethics.

Levinas's configuration of ethics takes place if not at the expense, at least in the deliberate ignorance of another form of exclusion that such a formulation of the relationship between the I and the Other brings about: the exclusion of nonhuman presences. Levinas's ethics arrests itself in front of the entire realm of nature, animate or inanimate, which is deprived of any notion of otherness. The present project understands things, at least initially, undifferentially as vegetal, mineral, artificial (and maybe even animal) entities. As such, for Levinas, things do not have a face. Therefore, they cannot place any ethical demands on the subject that confronts them. Human ethics, Levinas is not weary of repeating, is the archetype. A discourse about the face of animals, plants, or things, if possible at all, would be only as derivative and as the result of the transference from one realm, which remains privileged, to another. The question with which chapter 3 concludes is thus: Does Levinas's ethics remain, along with the very tradition other aspects of which he so successfully contributes to disrupt, an anthropocentric humanism?

Accessible through the hand that handles and manipulates them in labor, things are pure presence, for Levinas, whose mystery briefly glimmers in the enjoyment to which the subject abandons itself, but which is immediately recuperated through the awareness of one's own sensibility and sensory perception. If things, as gifts, are important, they are so as functional to the annunciation of the relationship between the same and the Other. They serve the possibility of the donation of the self's world to the Other, thus contributing to the dimension of intersubjectivity and, eventually, of social justice. Despite the laudability of the service rendered by things, service which is oriented to the Other rather than to the same, as chapter 4 reveals, in Levinas things are not other, not even in a sense divergent from and incongruous with the sense in which the other person is Other.

Casual Analogies

Several scholars have suggested that there be a more than casual analogy between mass destruction in the form manifested at Auschwitz, and mass production in the form exhibited by modern technology with its deliberate denial of the depth of things, which become the objects of an endless reproduction and confirmation of the manipulative abilities of the subject. According to this trend of thought, Auschwitz and modern technology constitute the culmination of the Western way of thinking, the revelation of the highs and the lows to which modern rationality can rise.

Heidegger himself, otherwise so stubbornly silent on the topic, established a comparison, regarded by many as outrageous, between the mechanization of agriculture and mass murder.[19]

This is not the place to discuss the legitimacy of the accusations of irreverence and insensitivity moved against Heidegger. Nevertheless, granted all due differences, it remains true that an analogous structure of predominance of the subject over what surrounds it is at work in both of the practices mentioned by Heidegger. In the case of Auschwitz, the primacy of the subject asserts itself on other human beings. In the case of technology, it operates on things, which an entire philosophical tradition has constructed mainly as objects deprived of all otherness in the Levinasian sense of the notion. An object is what is cast against the subject, what stands in front of it, what limits, by its sheer presence, as a source of either awe or wonder, the possibility of expansion of a subject, which, to exist, has to be omnivorous—ontologically, epistemologically, and practically. Therefore, the kingdom of things becomes the field of conquest and domination.

The contemporary environmental discussion has alerted philosophy to the connection existing between environmental issues, which the epoch of postmodernity faces with a gravity unprecedented in the (known) history of the planet, and the categories of thought through which we, as contemporary subjects, structure our lives. The modes of relation to things mirror the way in which we think in general. Environmental challenges are not primarily a matter of science and technology. Rather, they ask the more fundamentally philosophical questions of how we live our lives, how we define ourselves, what kind of values we entertain, what kind of beings we are. Ultimately, the question they ask is the question of how we think, and more specifically, of how philosophy thinks and structures the world. To avoid the environmental catastrophe to which technological rationality seems to have consigned the age of postmodernity, it seems therefore necessary to explore, and espouse, ways of relating to things that do not reduce them to objects, but rather recognize in them the possibility of their own signification, of their own difference, of their own alterity.

Levinas's philosophy provides a forceful response to one side of Heidegger's analogy, offering theoretical instruments to develop a notion of subjectivity which, to be meaningful at all, must be respectful of and responsive to the otherness of the other as a human being. Levinas's ethical thought, however, arrests itself in front of the presence of things, to which no alterity is recognized, thus occluding the possibility of entering ethical relations with them. It is with regard to the issue of the otherness of things, referred to as their alterity, to mark the difference between various forms of otherness, and especially between human otherness and thingly otherness, that this essay supplements Levinas.

The Unfolding of Another Story

The second part of the work unfolds in dialogue with Heidegger, somewhat paradoxically because of the lack of ethical concern which allegedly permeates his thought. Yet, Heidegger offers a thematization of things in terms that are amenable to the recognition of their own alterity. Therefore, Heidegger's thought proves itself capable of resetting in movement Levinas's philosophy at the point where it had arrested itself: on the threshold of the alterity of things.

As remarked in chapter 5, Heidegger recognizes the destinal relevance and urgency of the question of things ever since his philosophical beginning. It is in fact as a "return to the things themselves" that Heidegger's phenomenological project develops, as indicated in chapter 6. However, the path that leads to the disclosure of theoretical elements enabling the possibility of a discourse on things in terms of their alterity unwinds slowly and throughout the entire course of Heidegger's philosophical meditation. It is this path that the second part of the present work follows, with attentiveness and care, to discover indications of the correspondence of Heidegger's thought to the appeal coming from the way of being of things. Such a path will come to a rest in Heidegger's later works.

It is here, as argued in chapter 9, that the orientation toward things, initially directed by Dasein's concern, as revealed in chapter 7, and subsequently interpreted from the perspective of artistic disclosure, as noticed in chapter 8, is finally intimated by the very things. According to the later Heidegger, things are the place where the gathering of the Fourfold (the mortals, the gods, the earth, the sky) occurs. None of the dimensions whose nearing constitutes the very nature of things can ever be mastered completely, or reduced to any structure of categorization, thereby revealing the fundamental alterity that nourishes the way of being of things. In a move that turns around the entire tradition in its relation to things, Heidegger grounds the fact of being a human being on the ability to listen, and correspond, to the inner appeal of things. The possibility for an ethics of things is opened up, although never explicitly thematized by Heidegger, who arrests himself on the threshold of ethics.

The Unfolding of a Different Story

Whereas the first two components of this work unfold in dialogue with the texts of Levinas and Heidegger, in order to uncover the points of strength and weakness in their respective meditations on the themes of ethics and things, the third part engages in an innovative, original, and daring movement: it takes up Levinas and Heidegger's meditations on things and ethics precisely at the point where they abandon such themes, and brings their thinking further in directions neither set forth.

Moving from the chiasmatic relation, argued for in chapter 10, that a confrontation between Levinas's ethics and Heidegger's concept of things produces, the third part of the work formulates an ethics of things grounded on things, centered on tenderness, and explicating itself in the everyday dimension of festivity as a dimension within which the alterity of things can be encountered, preserved, and celebrated. The phenomenological analysis of tenderness as a philosophical category lets emerge a nonviolating, nonsubjectivistic, other-oriented way of responding to the appeal to existence, thematized in chapter 11, coming from the way of being of things. As indicated in chapter 12, already etymologically, tenderness is connected to a tending-to. It is both a practical attending to something, in the sense of taking care of it, and a movement of thought which, in its being attentive, does not grasp or incorporate, but rather caresses by a light touch. Tenderness is thus deeply rooted in at-tention: the respectful (and humble) attitude of a mind (or body) that waits for the other to make the first move.

Whereas force, power, and strength impose, and weakness succumbs, tenderness welcomes, in its being respect, a sense of limit, and attention to nuances. Yet, in its lack of force, tenderness cannot fulfill soteriological tasks. Declined as sadness, tenderness becomes acceptance, even of death: never with resignation, always, if anything, with the tender firmitude that enables resistance to obliviousness and forgetfulness. Although patient, in its declination as sadness tenderness is not a quietism serving nihilism, but rather an affirmation of life, in its very power of differentiation. As thematized in chapter 13, sadness is the metaphysical mood corresponding to the appeal coming from the vulnerability of things in their alterity.

Such a vulnerability can be celebrated in the time of festivals, whose temporal structure reveals, as argued in chapter 14, profound analogies with the structure of things and with the modality of tenderness through which the alterity of things can be encountered. Excessive, yet not orgiastic; joyful, yet not hilarious; lay, yet not profane; serious, yet not pedantic, festivity, as a practice of life, becomes the everyday dimension within which things can gratuitously give themselves to appreciation and celebration as things, in the alterity of their own facialities demanding a response of tenderness.

Ecology, Ethics, Metaphysics

The overall theme of this work is informed by many ecological preoccupations. The main concern, however, is ethical, or metaphysical, in the Levinasian sense of inviting thought to enter a place of thinking where the voices of alterities can be heard. Only if things are recognized in their own peculiar alterity which does not submit, because it cannot be submissible, to the categories of the subject, can any ecological project be grounded on something more profound and fundamental than the fortuitous occurrence of subjects of good will. The ultimate importance of this project is thus philosophical in a strong sense.

The main issue is the possibility for philosophy to be faithful to its ancient nature in light of contemporary history and its demands: not only to be the love of wisdom, but also, and more fundamentally, as Levinas says, to be the "wisdom of love" (OBBE 162)—that is, wisdom of a truth constituted as ambivalent, multidimensional, multilayered, and differential. Truth necessarily surrenders to ideology if part of it (the truth concerning things) is swallowed up by a human being who, whether as the I or as the Other, claims to be the constitutive ground for the whole truth. The inspiration for this work is the conviction that not only the Other, but also the other of the Other—things—must become the (nonthematic) theme of love of philosophical discourse. Ethics is the place where the Other can enter philosophy, Levinas suggests. An ethics of things, centered on tenderness, becomes the place where the other of the Other can be approached, in festivity, as a tendered faciality.

I ❖ Levinas: Love without Things

1 ❖ Out of Love: The Break with Parmenides

On s'amuse mieux à deux![1]

Ever since its beginning in the Greek colonies in Asia Minor, philosophy has defined itself, already ethymologically, as an act of love: love of knowledge, love of wisdom, love of truth, according to different suggestions resonating in the word *sophia*. Despite the clarity of the erotic implications, a question remains: Whom has philosophy really loved behind the multiplicity of masks with which its beloved has disguised its face?

The erotic intentions of Levinas's philosophy are disclosed without hesitation in a booklet published under the title *Time and the Other:* "it is toward a pluralism that does not merge into unity that I should like to make my way and, if this can be dared, break with Parmenides" (TO 42). His intentions of love result in an intimation of separation, then. Why is Levinas so vehement? Certainly not for personal reasons, since, as he asserts in *Totality and Infinity,* "it is not the I who resists the system, as Kierkegaard thought; it is the Other" (TI 40).[2] It is out of love for the other that Levinas embarks on his philosophical project.[3] The departure from Parmenidean philosophy does not gratify need, born in the I (Levinas's own self) as an exigency whose possibility of satisfaction confirms the economy of the I (TI 114–15, ToO 350–52)—Levinas's own pride and fame. Rather, it responds to a desire which, in its being directed by the other (the victims to whom *Otherwise than Being* is dedicated), cannot be recompensed by thought (TI 33–34), thus excluding any possibility of satisfaction.[4] Despite all possible rationalizations, Levinas's life has remained haunted and "dominated by the presentiment and memory of the Nazi horror" (DF 291). Inspired by a desire that remains infinite, Levinas's philosophy establishes the impossibility of a complete accomplishment of its task, and the necessity of a continuous un-saying of its said. No word about the victims will ever be accurate enough to portray their suffering. In its infinite inspiration, Levinas's love can only be a love that never ends, an infinite love offered as a homage to the victims.

There is more, however, in Levinas's claim of a breach with Parmenides. Levinas's vehemency is not personal also in the sense of the lack of an argument *ad hominem*. It is neither Parmenides (who is never confronted on a textual ground) nor specific philosophers (although they are individually criticized on several accounts) with whom Levinas contends. Rather, his contention is with a recurrent Parmenidean inspiration which permeates the development of Western philosophy and spurs to read being in terms of unity—that is, in terms of a reassembling of differences within the circularity of thought. Levinas indicates Ulysses as the literary model that best expresses the activity of Western thought.

In agreement with a philosophical tradition to which he objects, but which he never disclaims, Levinas identifies the perhaps "too general and rather empty" task of philosophy as a quest for truth (CPP 47). It is the content of such truth that is at stake in Levinas's philosophy. At the origin of philosophy, Parmenides had perceived the philosophical dilemma as a choice between being and nonbeing, with truth on the side of being and unity. At the farther extreme of that same tradition Levinas reads the great dilemma within which philosophy has unfolded its story as an amphibology between autonomy and heteronomy. On the one end of the dichotomy, truth is understood as the result of a free search, in which the nature of the inquiring self remains the same despite the tantalizing adventures to which it submits. This is the Ulyssean itinerary that Western philosophy, Greek by birth and nature, has preferred, thereby solving the amphibology in favor of autonomy, freedom, and identity.

At the other end, truth is understood as "the outcome of a movement that leaves a world that is intimate and familiar, even if we have not yet explored it completely, and goes toward the stranger, toward a *beyond,* as Plato puts it" (CPP 47). The path thus suggested is that of the transcendence of the self to itself—transcendence that does not yet mean exteriority, but which reveals a tension toward the ideal, the beyond, the other. Such an "equally ancient" (CPP 53) tradition, although minoritarian and submerged, is not completely absent from the history of Western philosophy. As Levinas readily recognizes (AT 50), it surfaces in Plato's notion of the Good beyond being; in Aristotle's remarks on the active intellect coming from outside (TI 49); in Plotinus' One being located beyond being (ToO 347; 358); in Kant's categorical imperative signifying independently from the proofs for the existence of God and the immortality of the soul (OBBE 129, DMT 70-78); in Bergson's duration as continuous source of novelty ("Transcendence et intelligibilité" 20–21).

If the first perspective reveals philosophy as ontology, the second defines philosophy as metaphysics.[5] Abraham is the metaphorical figure which Levinas poses as an escort for the philosophical mind on its path toward heteronomy. Abraham is the model which Levinas claims for himself when, in "The Trace of the Other," he writes: "to the myth of Ulysses returning to Ithaca, we wish to oppose the story of Abraham who leaves his fatherland forever for a yet unknwon land, and forbids his servant to even bring his son to the point of departure" (ToO 348).

What is so peculiar about Ulysses that turns him into not a, but *the,* paradigm of Western philosophy? For Levinas, as for Horkheimer and Adorno before him,[6] it is the fact that, despite all his roamings, the prow of Ulysses' ship always points toward his native island, whereas "all of [his] adventures are but the accident of a return" (TH 92). As true already for Parmenides and his identification of being and thinking, the unity of the project is what is essential also to Ulysses' journey. Levinas retraces the similarity between Ulysses and the philosophical conscience in the monotony of an itinerary whose return is granted even before departure, so that "action recuperated in advance in the light that should guide it—is perhaps the very definition of philosophy" (ToO 347). Socrates' maieutic exercise teaches that in the soul is already present everything that can be experienced, thus establishing the freedom, autonomy, autarchy of the soul. At least since him, consciousness is self-consciousness: immanence of the self to itself, that is, presence to oneself, transparency, atheism. Modelled on the unifying project of self-recognition, philosophy results in a philosophy of identity, which Levinas qualifies as an egology. It is the full coincidence with itself of an I which recognizes itself as same so that "we call it 'the same' because . . . the I precisely loses its opposition to its object; the opposition fades, bringing out the identity of the I despite the multiplicity of its objects, that is, precisely the unalterable character of the I" (TI 126).

The success of the project of self-recognition has its metaphysical cost, however. It is accomplished at the expense of Levinas's infinite beloved, the Other, through a process of neutralization, called representation, which reduces the other to the categories of the same. To proceed in a nonrhetorical manner, philosophy requires an encounter with some other, which is philosophy's object and concern. Yet, in its exotism, an other irreducible to the self[7] engenders the risk of alienation and dispossession. The self might not remain the same. To check the threat and maintain its own security, the philosophy of identity resorts to an act of wit; in representation it contemplates the other that it needs, but always already as another *from* the self, so that the status of the absolutely other—the metaphysical Other—is neglected in favor of a relative, ontological otherness, an otherness that dialectically remains within the horizon from which it stems.[8] In the move, the same and the other do not achieve separation. Rather, they constitute a system, share a common totality, like the

Hegelian masters and slaves, who need each other to exist.[9]

Although generalizing, insofar as he neglects most of the medieval tradition, and interprets the Greek legacy in terms of selected texts of Parmenides, Heraclitus, Plato, Aristotle, and Plotinus, Levinas asserts that "one can see this nostalgia for totality everywhere in Western philosophy, where the spiritual and the reasonable always reside in knowledge. It is as if totality had been lost, and that this loss were the sin of the mind. It is then the panoramic vision of the real which is the truth and which gives all its satisfaction to the mind" (EI 76). The benefits of totality and system are, for the same, immense: the self remains within itself, maintains its identity as limited by nothing, that is, free; the other, although spurious, is present to the same in a nonreversible determination.

The metaphysical unreality of the other is compensated by the same with the accordance of epistemological existence, by which the other becomes objective, transparent, intelligible. But the concession is subdolous. First, there is fraud: objectivity is not exteriority. It is still immanence of the other in the same, since objectivity is already in opposition to the subject, to which it offers a side—its objectivity—to grasp. Through a process of mediation and recurrence to neuters, which at once are and are not—the quality of the objects for Berkeley (TI 44), the horizon for Husserl and phenomenology, the Being of beings for Heidegger (TI 45, CPP 52-53)[10]—the I reduces the distance between itself and the other, and discharges the non-being of the other into its own being. Second, the magnitude of the fraud is augmented by the humiliation of the insult. The apparent alterity of the epistemological other is a service rendered by the other to a same whose cognitive activity gets thereby absolved from the charges of formalism, since thanks to the presence of the other to know is not to enact the empty tautology of "A is A".[11] As suggested in the expression "know thyself," under whose auspices Western philosophy is born and develops, the self does not know itself from the beginning. Rather, it needs an activity of self-retrieval that can be performed by the I through the act of representing, that is, of "suspending the very alterity of what is only at first other, and other relative to me" (TI 38).

Levinas admits that the other can refuse itself to possession. But he also remarks how in the history of Western philosophy, because of its receiving its determination from what it opposes, such a resistance is merely the reversal of an affirmation of identity and, therefore, still within the domain of identity. Epistemology is thus the cunning of reason, which, because the concession serves the system of identity, within the cognitive arena grants the other what it has already denied to it more powerfully at the metaphysical level. "The *outside of me* is *for me*" (ToO 345), synthesizes Levinas, thereby retracing in the idealism of the subject the truth of Western philosophy, while legitimizing Descartes's concerns in the *Meditations* that the world, things, the *res extensa* could be the production of the I, merely its ideas.

According to Levinas's analysis, the path of the unity of being (and thinking) that Parmenides has indicated leads to the autism of the I,[12] which denies the absolutely other and turns it into a negative always recuperable within the system. Rather than being "a situation . . . where the alterity of the other appears in its purity," "a relationship with alterity, with mystery" (TO 85; 88), the act of love by which philosophy has proceeded has been a solitary pleasure, an activity of intellectual masturbation in which the beloved figures as a toy serving the onanism of the I. As in Aristophanes' myth in Plato's *Symposium* (189e–193d), fusion with the other is nostalgia for one's own wholeness. But for Levinas love is neither a unifying nor a complementary relationship. Rather, "the pathos of love . . . consists in an unsurmountable duality of beings . . . lies in the fact of being two" (TO 86), whereas "the very value of love is the impossibility of reducing the other to myself, of coinciding into sameness. From an ethical perspective, two have a better time than one" (Face to Face 22). Thus, in *Otherwise than Being,* Levinas offers a different definition of philosophy, still erotic in nature, though inspired by a different kind of eroticism: not love of wisdom, but "wisdom of love" (OBBE 162). To perform its act of love, philosophy "is called upon to conceive ambivalence, to conceive it in several times" (OBBE 162). The first place where the ambivalence is to be conceived[13] is in the notion of truth to which philosophy devotes itself. No longer the *adaequatio intellectus ac rei,* in which the *res* disappears in its adherence to the categories of the *intellectus,* but "the aspiration to radical exteriority, thus called metaphysical, the respect for this metaphysical exteriority which, above all, we must 'let be,' constitutes truth" (TI 29). It is not forgetfulness of being (Heidegger), then, but insensitivity to the other that has characterized Western philosophy. In its Abrahamitic inspiration, it is to such an insensitivity that philosophy must now obviate.

Several questions arise at this point, though. If philosophy has to be "wisdom of love," and to do so it has to "conceive of ambivalences," how can Levinas conceive of the path of philosophy in terms of antinomies without falling back in the ontological model from which he wants to depart? To love the other, to conceive of ambivalences, Levinas must break with Parmenides, and follow Abraham. And yet, to love the other, to conceive of ambivalences, should not Levinas also love Parmenides? Should not the love of the other also love the same?[14]

The question is not otiose. What resonates in it are echoes of a much broader spectrum of questions encompassing the relation between the Greek and Jewish roots of Levinas's thought, or, more broadly stated, between Greek philosophy and Jewish thinking, or even more broadly, between philosophy and religion.[15] Or, deflecting the question in a different, although related, direction, the issue becomes that of the possible configurations of the relation between Levinas's own thought, by his admission a philosophy, and the other thinkers in the Western tradition in dialogue with whom Levinas's own philosophy unfolds, but whom he often criticizes. Levinas recognizes the influence such a tradition had on his own formation when praising Kant's *Critique of Pure Reason,* Hegel's *Phenome-*

nology of Spirit, Bergson's *Time and Free Will,* Heidegger's *Being and Time* as some "of the finest books in the history of philosophy" (EI 37). Yet, as he readily admits, not all these thinkers are impermeable to the accusation of ontologism that causes Levinas to break with Parmenides.

Out of love of the other, Levinas's philosophy wants to break with Parmenides and abandon the path of being and identity, which privileges unity and communion over communication and community. Still out of love of the other, however, the departure cannot situate Levinas on the path of a nonbeing implying loss of speech and communication, and resulting into silence, as the Parmenidean dichotomization of the two ways of research (between being and nonbeing) would suggest. Coherently, then, Levinas indicates at several junctures how proximity to the other is precisely through language, defined as "a contact across a distance" (TI 172) in which the other manifests itself in "a mastery that does not conquer, but teaches" (TI 171).

For reasons analogous to those that bring to a rejection of the path of silence, the break with Parmenides cannot situate Levinas on the path of *doxa* (a complication of the path of nonbeing). The doxic route annihilates the I in the night of opinion, legitimizing all rhetorical violence, because rhetoric "approaches the other not to face him [or her], but obliquely" (TI 70). In an act of love toward the other, which is simultaneously an act of love toward Parmenides, Levinas must thus accept Parmenides' indication and move against sheer nonbeing. Accordingly, even if performed by the most powerful mind, no *epoche* from being can completely free the I from the "horror and panic" (EI 49) of existing. "Let us imagine all things, beings and persons, returning to nothingness. What remains after this imaginary destruction is not something, but the fact that there is [*il y a*]. The absence of everything returns as a presence, as the place where the bottom has dropped out of everything, an atmospheric density, a plenitude of the void, of the murmur of silence" (TO 46), Levinas writes describing the *il y a,*[16] pure being without nothingess, which does not allow for exits or escapes, not even suicide (TO

50).[17] Nevertheless, out of love for the other, Levinas's act of love toward Parmenides cannot duplicate Parmenides entirely.

The ontological status of nonbeing had already been vindicated by Plato who, in the *Sophist,* proscribes the path of pure being because of the *aporiai* and *aphasia,* to which it leads, as illustrated in the *Parmenides*. But Plato, and the tradition after him, love themselves more than they love the other. Therefore, after the spiritual homicide of Parmenides that dignifies (recuperates?) nonbeing within the five *genera* of being, they invent a dialectic of being able to recomprehend nonbeing totally within itself. Multiplicity is thus achieved only as an illusion. Conversely, Levinas loves Parmenides and the other more than he loves himself. Therefore, he accepts Parmenides' proscription of nonbeing; yet, he reinscribes that very nonbeing within the philosophical discourse not as nonbeing, but as otherwise-than-being.[18] Contrary to what Derrida suggests, Levinas abandons Parmenides but without killing him.[19] Multiplicity, denied by Parmenides and his homicides, is thus maintained.

This complex relation toward Parmenides, the Greek philosophical tradition, and the other is described by Levinas himself in *Totality and Infinity* under the name of filiality, which is not only "the converse" (TI 278) of paternity, but the othering of the father in the child through fecundity as seen from the other side, from the side of the other. Filiality, Levinas says, "designates a relation of rupture and a recourse at the same time" (TI 278). As rupture, the child expresses the discontinuity of an otherness that cannot be recapitulated. Out of love for the other, love that gets multiplied infinitely, the other subtracts itself to the same. "Repudiation of the father, commencement, filiality at each moment accomplishes and repeats the paradox of a created freedom" (TI 278)—that is, of a creature that, as in the creation *ex nihilo,* certainly involves a passivity with respect to being, but which is also there, standing on its own, solitude, distance from its creator, atheism, independence in its dependency, otherness (see TI 105).[20] However, the child "is, without being 'on his [her?] account'" (TI 278),[21] since the child lives an existence "which still subsists in the father" (TI 278), thus echoing the transcendence of paternity in filiality. In this sense, filiality is a recourse in which its other, paternity, its past "is recaptured at each moment from a new point, from a novelty that no continuity . . . could compromise" (TI 278). Levinas explicitly qualifies filiality as "a way of resuming the thread of history" (TI 278). In this case, the thread is that of the Parmenidean tradition, which is however broken open by filial possibilities exceeding paternal possibilities, and nevertheless remaining possibilities of the father. And, Levinas comments, "I would like to underline the upheaval—that this signifies—of the ontological condition and also of the logic of substance, on the one hand, and of transcendental subjectivity, on the other" (EI 70).

Neither an inclusive *and* which assimilates differences (Parmenides and Levinas), nor an exclusive *or* which precludes discourse between differences (Parmenides *or* Levinas), could not this *and/or,* possibility indicated by filiality and not contemplated by the traditional logic of noncontradiction, in its maintaining contradictory movements, be the way to conceive of ambivalences? The way for philosophy to express its love? But if that is the case, what to do of the opposition between Ulysses and Abraham which Levinas so clearly sets up? And who is Abraham, whom Levinas proposes to the reader as the model of heteronomy under which philosophy should risk its future adventures?

Although the children of Abraham's child(ren) may be nomadic *ab origine,* neither Abraham nor his child(ren) are homeless wanderers since the beginning of their time, as Levinas seems to suggest. If Levinas's reading of a nomadic Abraham constitutes the truth of the ethical Abraham, the chronological Abraham (philosophy on its way to become Abrahamitic, perhaps Levinas himself) would be better described as a Ulysses who, after having come back year after year to a home of ontological richness and satisfaction, one day lets himself be othered by the other, welcomes the appeal of the other, and abandons his home forever, without nostalgia or hope for a return. In his journey toward the other, Abraham carries on himself the stigma of his origin as the memory of what cannot be remembered, the Immemorable, an other that must not be recuperated, but must be forbidden from memory, even that of his son, in a complete separation between present and past.

In this chronological reading, Abraham is not a non-Ulysses (negation in which the other is constituted in terms of the same), but a Ulysses whose circular nature has been perforated and othered by the insertion of the other, which now ethically constitutes him; Abraham is an otherwise-than-Ulysses. Levinas may have resisted this reading, and proposed to his readers the figure of Abraham *after* his departure has been consummed, as the model of a radical going out toward the other as toward what is not recuperable. But this reading, which also considers Abraham's relation to his past, must be put forth, if Levinas wants to allow philosophy, still Ulyssean, to become Abrahamitic, and yet remain philosophy, that is, at least marked by its Greek, Ulyssean character. As Levinas asserts very clearly, "there is nothing to be done: philosophy speaks Greek" (DVI 137). Out of love for the other and ambivalences, philosophy must love both Ulysses and Abraham, where the *and,* as is the case in filiality, as is the case in *Totality and Infinity,* expresses separation as much as it expresses conjunction.[22]

In "Philosophy and the Idea of Infinity," Levinas confirms the puzzling, ambivalent, paradoxical move between conjunction and separation when speaking of truth as of the place where the two directions of research, the ontological and the metaphysical, Ulysses and Abraham "interact" (CPP 447). The puzzling interaction, the *and* which coexists with the *or*, is reaffirmed by Levinas when he says that he "would maintain, against Heidegger, that philosophy can be ethical as well as ontological, can be at once Greek and non-Greek in its inspiration."[23] Understanding the meaning of the paradoxical interaction is crucial to understanding Levinas's confrontation with the ontological tradition of Parmenidean descent.

From the Ulyssean side of the interaction—that is, from the side of the ontological tradition, from the *au-deça,*—Ulysses, in its ontological itinerary, may pursue Abraham. Yet, he will never be able to coincide with him, to bring him back home, because the path on which Abraham moves in its nomadism at the service of the other is tangential, touches the circularity of Ulysses' journey only at one point: that of Abraham's departure, which marks the alterity between him and Ulysses. From the Ulyssean perspective, it can only be Ulysses *or* Abraham, because to choose Ulysses means to integrate, recuperate, murder Abraham. The ontological tradition of Parmenidean descent cannot renounce its project without renouncing itself. To become Abraham, Ulysses must step radically ouside the ontological circle. That is why the tradition lives the choice between Abraham and Ulysses as a dilemma, an ambiguity that requires its solution. And, when he sets up the opposition between Abraham and Ulysses, it is the language of the dilemma that Levinas uses to address the tradition. Levinas must break with Parmenides, philosophy must break with the Greek tradition.

On the side of the other, however, on the side of the metaphysical tradition that Levinas reveals as ethics, and to which he assimilates himself, from the *au-delà,* the situation is more complex: the ambiguity presents itself as an ambivalence, and to conceive of the ambivalence, Abraham must love Ulysses.

Abraham's interaction with Ulysses, however, cannot indulge in memories about his own having been like Ulysses without this remembrance becoming a betrayal of the spirit of his journey, which is not his, but the journey dictated by the other. Abraham is no longer like Ulysses. The conjunction, which may sound as Abraham and Ulysses, for Abraham, too, as for Ulysses, means Abraham or Ulysses, separated by the diachrony of time, by the absence of a common land, whereas the lack of nostalgia distancing Abraham from Ulysses constitutes the asynchronicity of their relation. Again, Levinas must break with Parmenides. And yet, if he does not want to repeat the murderous unity (although this time in the name of the other), Abraham must carry on himself the stigma of his having once been similar to Ulysses as the memory of a past for which there is or can be neither recuperation nor longing for recuperation, and for which, yet, there is responsibility—the immemorial past.[24] This time the conjunction remains faithful to its grammatical nature. Therefore, it means Abraham *and* Ulysses, conjoined not by one of them (ontological autism and recuperation within the same), but by the distance that separates them, by the absence of symmetry between them. Levinas cannot reject Parmenides; he must carry the Parmenidean mark as the memory of what must be banned. The lack of a univocal possibility, the presence of an ambivalence in the *and* between *and* and *or,* mark exactly the move outside of fusion and unity.[25] The discrepancy between the ambiguity (only possibility affordable by Ulysses) and the ambivalence (faced by Abraham) is a trace of the asymmetry characterizing the ethical relationship.

In his being ethically appealed by a tradition different from the egological path of Western philosophy, Levinas desires the nomadism of the children of Abraham's child(ren). Nevertheless, although convinced that, on an ethical level, ethics is prior to ontology, chronologically, Levinas is an (even if perhaps illegitimate) son of Parmenides. Therefore, it is always Levinas *and* Parmenides, Levinas *and* the Greek tradition, Levinas *and* the Western ontological thinkers, as it is Abraham *and* Ulysses. While philosophy remains a quest for truth, like Abraham it cannot renounce, although it must dismiss, its origin in the ontological tradition, its Greek birth, nature, language. As already recalled, "there is nothing to be done: philosophy speaks Greek" (DVI 137). Yet, in its differing from that father with whom Levinas wants to break, it is also Levinas *or* Parmenides. Parmenides is the home from which metaphysics, like Abraham, should depart, so that Parmenides must be abandoned. Again, however, not to reenact unity something of the abandonment must be preserved, although not celebrated, because "in Greek philosophy one can . . . discern traces of the ethical breaking through the ontological,"[26] and such ethical traces demand to be loved. Yet, since, like Abraham, metaphysics cannot remain attached to the nostalgia for that home whose memory has been banned, the reinscription of the traces within philosophy must do away with the ontological tradition. This implies that, to be faithful to its inspiration, metaphysics must allow for a negative which remains such without recuperation.

Levinas's confrontation with the tradition thus gestures in a direction which does not assume the negative upon itself. In its exposure to the Abrahamitic journey, the traditional notion of truth by which philosophy operates is undone, unsaid, thereby re-defining the very role and nature of the philosophical inquiry.[27] In its becoming a performance "at the service of love" (OBBE 162)—that is, at the service of the other—philosophy serves heteronomy, thus abandoning its initial Ulyssean spirit in content if not in expression, which remains Greek as a mark of the absence of the Greek content. In this service rendered to the other, philosophy might be able to accomplish the break with Parmenides, and realize the departure from all sites that not Abraham, but the children of Abraham's child(ren) enact.

Yet, in the break which Levinas not only desires, but also claims to have accomplished, it remains to be seen whether he has had the courage to move radically to the *au-delà* and live the life of the children of Abraham's child(ren). It remains to be seen whether the *and* and the *or* can be extended to all aspects of his philosophy, or whether the *and* and the *or* reach points of effacement of each other, whereas Levinas, turned into an Abraham still nostalgic of his Ulyssean home, remains on the threshold of the *au-delà,* and lets the ontological tradition lurk on the background of his ethical project. In other words, has Levinas really loved the other in all his, her, and its ambivalences? And who is the other whom Levinas loves?

2 ❖ In Love: Ethics as the Meeting Place

According to Levinas, the history of Western philosophy is the story of the unfolding of an identity that, like Ulysses, never gets lost in the adventures that it generates. This description seems to be even more accurate after Descartes, considered by many the father of modernity as subjectivism, the most appropriate appellation for the philosophy of identity. Yet, in accordance with his philosophical love of ambivalences, it is precisely in Descartes that Levinas finds traces of the presence of the other, that neglected existence in the history of Western thought.[1]

Descartes's Third Meditation tells an admirable story of misery and splendor. It is the story of the finite in its relation to the infinite. Certain of itself and of its own existence, the Cartesian *ego cogito* is in a situation of despair about the rest of its representations, which might be merely phantasms of a too imaginative spirit. Among the innumerable dubious ideas that crowd its trembling mind, one, however, presents itself as undoubtable. It is the idea of God, an idea that, for its magnitude and nobility, in its glory which signifies the "growing surplus of the Infinite" (CPP 169), cannot be the product of the finite and limited mind of the *ego cogito.* Upon this idea, which functions as an epistemological foundation, Descartes reconstructs his lost faith in the truth of the external world. But, according to Levinas's highly idiosyncratic reading of Descartes,[2] the idea of God implies more than an epistemological possibility: "the idea of infinity is exceptional in that its ideatum surpasses its idea" (CPP 55). That is, the idea of infinity indicates something which remains external, absolutely other, transcendent to the conceptualizations with which the mind tries to imprison it. The idea of infinity comes as a "trauma which cannot be assumed" (CPP 166), as the surprise of a "hyperbolic demand [coming 'from the face of a neighbor'] which at once exceeds [the] response" (CPP 169). And yet, the idea of the Infinite is something that is welcomed (but not contained) in that very mind which it overflows and elevates by opening it up to new possibilities. This formal movement, which Descartes sees at work in the case of God, for Levinas characterizes the relation with the other (CPP 53–55), so that for him "the idea of infinity is the social relationship" (CPP 54). It is the exit from the solipsistic egology defining the ontological I to enter an intersubjective relationship with what remains other.

The social relationship is a relation of a peculiar kind, however, as already suggested by Levinas's description of it as of a "relation without relation" (TI 295): a relationship between the I and the other in which the two terms, confimed in their separation, absolve themselves from each other without thereby destroying the possibility of the relation itself.[3] Such a demanding situation cannot be realized at the level of epistemology, which inevitably accomplishes a totalization of the other through correlation, representation, intentional consciousness. But the Other escapes epistemological constraints, because, properly, the Other is not the content of any ideas, which he or she surpasses in his or her infinity, thus rendering the very notion of phenomenology impossible.[4] On the contrary, the Other, in his or her transcendence, possesses an intentionality of his or her own alien to all cognitive analysis. It is the intentionality of desire, "which does not long to return, for it is desire for a land not of our birth, for a land foreign to every nature" (TI 34).

Distinct in this from need, desire, which Levinas qualifies as metaphysical, cannot be satisfied because of the infinite, unbridgeable distance which always separates the desirer from the desired, which makes all adequation impossible, and which continuously nourishes the hunger, in the desirer, for the desired. In its peculiar intentionality, desire intends, and maintains, "the remoteness, the alterity, and the exteriority of the Other" (TI 34). Further from being what Hegel would call a bad infinite, because for Levinas desire is born in a subject which does not lack anything, the positivity of desire consists precisely in the remoteness, the separation which puts distance between the I *and* the Other, where "the conjunction *and* . . . designates neither addition nor power of one term over the other" (TI 39), but rather proximity (CPP 115), a spatial dimension made of verticality and height in which the I and the Other can be face to face, without assimilation.[5]

The "space" in which this "relation without relation," characterized by the intentionality of desire, occurs is indicated by Levinas as ethics. Ethics is defined as "a field outlined by the paradox of an Infinite in relationship with the finite without being belied in this relationship" (OBBE 148). Or, in a different formulation, "a relationship between terms such as are united neither by a synthesis of the understanding nor by a relationship between subject or object, and yet where the one weighs or concerns or is meaningful to the other, where they are bound by a plot which knowing can never exhaust nor unravel" (CPP 116n6). The exact place where the mutation of cognitive intentionality into ethics happens is the face of the Other. Ethics, which "situates man's first breath not in the light of being but in the relation to a being, prior to the thematization of that being" (PN 137), is the place of a face to face, of an encounter with an alterity that remains other.

A few words need to be said about the peculiar type of spatiality characterizing ethics. The place of ethics cannot be understood as a neutral field, coextensive or co-present with the I and the Other, in which the I and the Other meet with no danger for either. The resort to a neuter, the weapon by which ontology annihilates alterity, would imply the introduction of a third perspective from which the relation between the I and the Other could be recorded, and thus reunited in a unifying gaze. But "the radical separation between the same and the other means precisely that it is impossible to place oneself outside of the correlation" (TI 36). The place of ethics is rather the space opened up by the relation itself.[6] Since the other is located in a dimension of height that is also the anachronistic dimension of a past which has never been present (CPP 68), such a place challenges the coextensiveness of the I and the other in the present, thus realizing a "curvature of space" (TI 291) signifying "the divine intention of all truth" (TI 291)—that is, signifying the exteriority characterizing ethics.[7] In this curvature of space, which redefines the nature of ontological spatiality, "the strangeness of the Other, his irreducibility to the I, to my thoughts and my possessions, is precisely accomplished as a calling into question of my spontaneity" (TI 43).[8] This calling into question is what Levinas names ethics (TI 43): a curved space in which the other can be encountered in his or her majestic exteriority; the space of an intrigue which discovers the I and the Other awoken to a love without lust.[9]

What defines the area of the curved spatiality, of ethics, is discourse which, not a third term but itself the relation, simultaneously resonates with the unicity and particularity characterizing the I and the Other—the Other always speaks to *me*—as well as with the universality of intelligibility—which discourse first makes possible (TI 73)—binding the two together in their separation.[10] It is exactly in the discursive perimeter that the separation of the I and the Other becomes manifest at its utmost degree, since "the relationship of language implies transcendence, radical separation, the strangeness of the interlocutors, the revelation of the other to me" (TI 73). This separation must be present if discourse aims to retain a magisterial quality honoring the Other as teacher, and not be merely rhetorical chatting in which the I folds upon itself in an unrollment of its own convictions. The absolute separation from which discourse proceeds (TI 194) constitutes a challenge to any attempt at viewing the ethical space as the space of a transcendental foundation in which, on the spur of Levinas's claims that "metaphysics preceds ontology"

(TI 42), the Other would function as the ground for the constitution of subjectivity.[11] To be ethical, the curved space can allow no foundationalisms,[12] as an analysis of its primordial discursive expressions will reveal. To proceed any differently would amount to duplicating a totalizing structure whose violating features are not diminished by the mere fact of being performed from the side of the other (ethics) rather than from that of the same (ontology).

Levinas offers two formulations of the primordial words by which the I and the Other institute the space of the "relation without relation": "you shall not commit murder" (TI 199), and "here I am" (OBBE 114, and also 145–46). The former expression is the first, primary because principial, word by which the other expresses itself. Properly, this word coming from the other is not a word, a sentence, an act of speech, the manifestation of a form intelligible to the universality of reason by means of its logical structure. For Levinas, the original language is "without words or propositions, pure communication" (CPP 119) of what has meaning immediately, before any attribution of meaning, before any passing of time which would allow consciousness to recover itself and thematize the message. Language is contact, proximity of the other who expresses itself in the self-signifyingness of a face which, the same moment it presents itself, already expresses itself, in a suspension of vision and representation, thus justifying Levinas's claim that "ethics is an optics," that is, "a 'vision' without image, bereft of the synoptic and totalizing objectifying virtues of vision" (TI 23).

The expression "you shall not kill" (CPP 55) is the immediate signification the face bears engraved on itself. Immediacy without reflection, the face is thus a word of honor, a word that guarantees for itself, with no need for external ratifications of its meaning. On the contrary, it is the self-signifyingness of the face that allows other meanings to appear, and with them reason, thought, and all other sorts of semantic and cultural activities (TI 204–6). Although the face can be said to produce "the commencement of intelligibility" (TI 201), in its signifyingness the face does not speak in the void. The face is a word addressed to an interlocutor, the I, to which it appeals and commands not to proceed on the murderous path of ontology, and to become ethical. This means that the face expresses itself always as a face to face. It is this face to face constituting discourse, and not the face alone, that ultimately "conditions the functioning of rational thought" (TI 204). The Other is not foundational by himself or herself, but only in his or her social relationship with the I.

But what does this signify in terms of a possible foundationalism of the I and the Other? In the desire to break with the Parmenidean tradition privileging the same, the other in Levinas remains completely exterior to the I. Retrieving the ancient tradition of the ontological argument, Levinas reproduces it in terms of the other when he claims that "the exteriority of a being is inscribed in its essence" (TI 196). The Other's first word cannot be understood as a response to a previous question (not even in the form of a threat) formulated by an I existing prior to the Other. The eyes of the Other, by which the Other obliges and questions the supremacy of the same, have always already appeared,[13] before the same, before any threat it may pose to the Other, and will always come back, even if the same were to kill the Other, because the Other, in his or her lack of dialectical constitution, in his or her separation, is always beyond. His or her "ethical resistance" (TI 199) is not resistance to something determinate as the I could be, but it is absolute resistance, the suspension of all powers to be powerful. In his or her first word, the Other is absolved from any constraint, menace, or even any observation of his or her commanding.

What happens to the I, however? Is it, in its interiority, exterior to the Other? Or does it owe its constitution to the Other, in an inversion of the imperialism of the same retaining all the totalizing features of its ontological counterpart? Levinas's answer is very clear. What discourse establishes is "an I . . . capable of society, an I that has arisen in enjoyment as separated, but whose separation [is] itself necessary for infinity *to be*—for its infinitude is accomplished as the 'facing'" (TI 209). The other can address the I in all the signifyingness of his or her face and challenge it to its ethical responsibility only because there is an I there to be obliged, an I that is not only will to power, ontological imperialism, egology, but that has already performed all those activities and has thus reached the richness of self-satisfaction. Almost as if the sacrifice of some otherness (the dialectically constituted otherness) were necessary to the accomplishment of the relation with the absolutely other, only because the I lacks nothing, can it be opened up to the infinity of ethical desire, which is a desire stemming from plenitude, not from need. In this sense, the I is not founded by the Other. This lack of foundation is exactly what Levinas calls a "metaphysical asymmetry" (TI 53): the fact that an absolute transcendence does not only affect the Other, but also the I. Its separation with regard to the other "must result from a positive movement" (TI 53), and not simply as "the reciprocal of the transcendence of the Other with regard to me" (TI 53). The I owes its constitution, its happiness to itself. The Other can affect such constitution, and open it up to discourse rather than to monologue, but to have a discourse the interlocutors must "remain absolute within relationship" (TI 195). As Levinas very clearly asserts, "speech is . . . a relation between freedoms which neither limit nor negate, but affirm, one another. They are transcendent with respect to each other" (CPP 43).

If the I is as separate as the Other within the relationship, what does it mean, then, when Levinas says, with a clarity and determination that do not allow misunderstandings, that ethics precedes ontology (TI 201; DVI 146), or that metaphysics (and ethics is metaphysical) precedes ontology (TI 42); when he accepts the appellation "ethical transcendentalism" for his philosophy (DVI 143)?[14] What needs to be explored is the nature of such a precedence. "What does this *before* mean? Is it the before of an *a priori*?," Levinas himself asks in *Alterity and Transcendence* (AT 31).

Obviously, the precedence cannot retain a chronological character in terms of a before and an after, a cause and an effect, a founder and a founded. This would reject ethics into the very realm of ontology to which history belongs, and which ethics is said to precede. "History . . . ignores a position of the I before the Other in which the Other remains transcendent with respect to me. . . . When man truly approaches the Other he is uprooted from history" (TI 52), Levinas claims. Additionally, chronologically ethics seems to come after ontology, as both Levinas and those philosophers in whom Levinas finds traces of the presence of the other follow Parmenides. As it is the case in Descartes' Third Meditation, "the discovery of [the] metaphysical relation in the *cogito* constitutes chronologically only the second move of the philosopher" (TI 54), so that if there were any chronologically transcendental foundation, it would be of the Other by the I, which is not what ethics means.

Nor can the precedence be ontological, or epistemological. The ontological subject constitutes the world by positing itself, completely autonomous and self-sufficient, at the center of the world, therefore eventually yielding to the epistemological idealism ethics rejects. Still, in Cartesian terms, "the present of the *cogito,* despite the support it discovers for itself *after the fact* in the absolute that transcends it, maintains itself all by itself—be it for an instant, the space of a *cogito*" (TI 54). No matter how brief, that *cogito* lasts long enough to deny an ontological precedence of ethics over ontology. Again, if there were foundationalism, ontologically it would be still of the Other by the I.

The precedence, then, can only be metaphysical. It expresses neither a chronological, ontological nor epistemological foundation, because then one would be forced to say that "the *After* or the *Effect* conditions the *Before* or the *Cause*" (TI 54). Yet this statement, asserting "the posteriority of the anterior," is "an inversion logically absurd" (TI 54). The precedence signifies the very distinction and separation between different orders of temporality: that of synchrony, in which all foundations take place, and that of diachrony (OBBE) or anachrony, in which temporal continuity turns back upon itself in a past that has never been present, with no possibility of a gathering of time in the present.

That ethics precedes ontology does not mean that the other constitutes, or grounds, or is the condition of the possibility of the I, not even the ethical I. Rather, it means that the *separation,* or *transcendence,* of the I and the other, of two modes of temporality, and hence of ethics and ontology themselves, is more primordial than the unity ontology wants to achieve, since transcendence exceeds such a unity. And ontology itself, in the mode of the psychism of the same, in its being a resistence to totalization, as an (although still totalizing) vindication of that transcendence that ethics accomplishes attests a primacy of ethics. Not the Other, then, but the separation within the relation is primary.[15] That is probably what Levinas means when, accepting the appellation "transcendentalism" for his philosophy, he emphasizes that it has to be of an ethical kind (DVI 143).

The absence of foundationalism contained in the first word of the other is confirmed in the second formulation Levinas gives of the primordial expression signifying the access to ethics, "here I am" (OBBE 114). This time the confirmation comes from the side of the I through the difficult language of obsession, persecution, hostage. These are terms that, because of a move into the ethical realm, have replaced separation, whereas the Other has become the neighbor to whom the I relates in proximity (OBBE 100). What provokes the lack of foundationalism is not so much the transcendence, or separation, of the I and the Other, as it was the case in *Totality and Infinity,* but the transcendence of the I to itself through what Levinas calls recurrence (OBBE 102ff.), "the inequality in the oneself due to substitution" (OBBE 115), which for Levinas constitutes the climax of ethical subjectivity.[16]

"Here I am" is the word pronounced by an I who obeys before hearing any command, in a passivity that can never be assumed, because it comes before the self of consciousness can arise to represent to itself the order to which the "here I am" would be the response.[17] Levinas calls this movement of response without hearing any previous appeal "responsibility," the I's being responsible for an other obsessing and persecuting the I before the I even encounters it, before it intends its words, so that the "self is out of phase with itself" (OBBE 115). The metaphor of "the echo of a sound that would precede the resonance of this sound" (OBBE 111; also 106) is used twice by Levinas to describe the subjectivity which, by proclaiming "here I am," contracts itself before the *arche* of consciousness, and thus becomes anarchic, that is, without foundations: "the unconditionality of a subject, which does not have the status of a principle" (OBBE 116). Again, the anachronism of a past never present and from which, despite the diachrony, the other obsesses and inspires the I, which finds itself rejected on the hither side of its own will and consciousness, presents itself to discourse.

The exposure of the I to the other, which Levinas calls inspiration, does not suspend subjectivity. Subjectivity is rather confirmed as irreplaceable (OBBE 105), although in a turn toward exteriority rather than interiority, so that the I is always a me, "an accusative which does not issue out of a declension it would have undergone starting with nominative" (OBBE 112): accused, obsessed, exposed. "I am in myself through the others" (OBBE 112), Levinas says. The I who proclaims "here I am" has already been opened up to the other. But the other who opened it up does not constitute the I, because of the diachrony in which the I and the other live.

Levinas scrupulously stresses the spontaneous arousal of the I's first word, despite its responsive character defying traditional conceptualizations of responsiveness. "The order has not been the cause of my response, nor even a question that would have preceded it in a dialogue. I find the order in my response itself" (OBBE 150), he claims. The constitution of the ethical subject is anarchic because the I retreats on the "hither side" of consciousness, but also because what calls the I to responsibility (the Other in which the trace of the infinite is inscribed) is not present to call. There is no call constituting the ground, the *arche,* of the response (AT 32–34).

Archeology, the establishment of causal connections, in its dealing with a continuous temporality still belongs to the realm of ontology, which the anachronism of ethical subjectivity exceeds. The turn toward exteriority that responsibility demands takes place at a level that is already ethical in its going beyond the linear continuity of synchronic time, which is the temporal modality constituting the ground of foundationalism. "Through the others" (OBBE 112), then, does not imply that the others are the transcendental ground for the me. By proposing a beginning, this move, which amounts to the alienation of an identity, would ignore the fundamental anachronism and lateness to itself of a subjectivity that has no beginning. Rather than a beginning, "strictly speaking the other is the end" (OBBE 128): a for-the-other affecting the me from the distance of an immemorable past, which can therefore never become a ground. "The one affected by the other is an anarchic trauma, or an inspiration of the one by the other, and not a causality striking mechanically a matter subject to its energy" (OBBE 123).

Through different emphases, the two different formulations of the first ethical expressions reveal an identical structure. In their format of pure command and pure answer without antecedences, they go beyond the chronological dimension of anteriority/posteriority characterizing foundationalism, and thus they also exclude the possibility of a grounding soil sustaining either the I or the Other.[18] There can be no subsequentiality of a before and an after in the ethical relationship.[19] The transcendence of the Other to the I is also the transcendence of the I to itself, in a movement that from beyond being goes toward an otherwise-than-being where traditional, essentialistic categories find no place.

In this absence of all foundationalism, ethics remains a place of love, a place whose very space is constituted by relations in which ambivalences are allowed to thrive: the ambivalence of the I and the other in their transcendence, the ambivalence of a me contracting before itself to the point of substituting the Other but without thereby losing its subjectivity, the ambivalence of a temporality in which the present goes back before itself toward a past that can never be reached. Ethics is the space of encounters whose ambivalence does not amount to failure, but to richness. To be ethical is to enter this space of love—space of ambivalence(s), space of otherness(es).[20]

3 ❖ My Love, Who are You? The Face of the Beloved Other

In its Abrahamitic inspiration, Levinas's metaphysics poses itself as the irruption of the absolutely other into Western philosophy, a rupture that lacerates the egoism of the same and forces it to abandon its ontological imperialism and enter the curved space of ethics. The identity of the ontological subject is well known, since, despite the somatic changes of its authors, it has undergone few essential modifications ever since its birth in Greek philosophy. Faithful to its nature, the same has remained the same: the I, the (self)consciousness of Socratic reminescence. But who is this "other" who, for the first time with Levinas, with the resolutedness and dignity of the Master enters the philosophical scene and compels it to a different journey?[1]

The question "who is the Other?" asks for an identity. To burden the Other with the request of an identity, thereby establishing a system of relations thanks to which the other can be ascribed to a family, a gender, a territory, means to reproduce the ontological economy that proceeds in terms of proper, propriety, appropriation. Therefore, the question, which is analogous to asking "what is the Other?" (TI 177; and also OBBE 27), is banned by Levinas already in the description of the Other, who is "not a character within a context" (EI 86). And yet, the unfaithful, ungrateful question "who/what?" needs to be asked, to determine who hides behind Levinas's beloved whom he calls the Other—a truly ambivalent other, or some imposture of the same? —to ensure that no falsification, no betrayal of the Other is taking place. It may be that the only role left to ontology within the ethical domain demanded by the Other is that of exercising a role of skeptical control (see OBBE 165–71): ensure that the said which betrays the Saying is not, rather than an unavoidable betrayal of the Saying, a new imposture of the self. Responsibility for the other, to the point of denouncing one's self: Is this move not in consonance with the figures of ethical subjectivity?

Who/what is the Other, then? A description of "the incomprehensible nature of the presence of the Other" (TI 195) could be offered *via negativa,* as in the beginning of the section of *Totality and Infinity* devoted to "Ethics and the Face." Unnamed and unnameable, inappropriated and inappropriable, the other is nameless, not because of his or her inability to sustain a name like the *il y a,* which would make of the other an impersonal neuter, but because he or she comes before any name, and therefore can sustain them all. "An individual fleeing individuality," (OBBE 190, note 38), the other does not retain the universality of the concept or of the species, nor is he or she the result of an abstraction from a collectivity of I's, as if there were some commonality between the Other and the I. On the contrary, the Other does not depend on the identity of the I as if he or she were an other than the I, an alter ego, whether as a complement or as an enemy of the I. But the nature of the other "is not to be described negatively" (TI 195), in reference to what he or she is not, Levinas warns.[2] The Other "does not simply have another quality than me, but as it were bears alterity as a quality. . . . He is what I am not: he is weak where I am the strong one. . . . What is essential is that he has those qualities by virtue of his very alterity" (EE 94–95). Positively, then, the Other is the one who possesses otherness as his or her own content.[3] In this sense, "*l'absolutement Autre, c'est Autrui*" (TI 39). This fundamental characterization of the Other, not a generic other, otherness, the other, but *Autrui,* the Other in his or her subjective alterity, irreducible to any content of the consciousness of the I, permits shifting the question from "what is the Other?" to "who is the Other?" This is the non-question "prior to every question in search of quiddities" (TI 177), in which "what one asks and he whom one questions coincide" (TI 177), thus suspending the reference to a system of relations. Levinas expresses the complexity of the identity of the Other in his absoluteness, singularity, and irrecuperability to the I in the "notion" of the face (*visage*),[4] special because communication of what is incommunicable, and, in metaphysics, "as fundamental and as universal as quiddity and being and the existent and the categories" (TI 177) are in ontology. To the question "who is the Other?" one should thus respond: *Autrui* is face, where "face" names "the way in which the other presents himself exceeding the idea of the other in me" (TI 50).[5]

Distinct from the corporeality of a nose, a mouth, a chin, a set of qualities forming an image, a representation that the I can portray to itself, reproduce, thematize (EI 85), the face is the expression of the depth of the Other's personal being.[6] Not only then has the Other a face, although not necessarily a biological face, because what is expressed by the face may be expressed by a hand or the nape of a neck (TI 262). More radically, the Other *is* his or her face—uniqueness which distinguishes every Other. "The face is an irreducible mode in which being can present itself in its identity" (DL 20, trans. mine). It is an expression which, in opposition to Heidegger, is neither an appearance nor a disclosure (and this is why a phenomenology of the face is impossible),[7] but an *epiphania*—that is, a "manifestation *kath'auto* consist[ing] in the being telling itself to us independently of every position we would have taken in its regard" (TO 65). The face is the Other exposing, but without giving (TI 202) himself or herself in the immediacy of his or her nakedness without shame. "The face is a living presence; it is expression. The life of expression consists in undoing the form in which the existent, exposed as a theme, is thereby dissimulated" (TI 65–66). In its immediacy, "bearing witness to [it]self and guaranteeing this witness" (TI 201),[8] this nakedness without protection, possibility of any imperialist, ontological violence, is visitation whose mode of presentation consists in "coming toward us, in *making an entry*" (CPP 95). In this sense, "the face speaks," because "speaking is before anything else this way of coming from behind one's appearance, behind one's form" (CPP 96).

The face, then, is already language, discourse, the first word (TI 199) by which the Other, opposing "not some superlative of power, but precisely the infinity of his transcendence" (TI 199), forbids the violation and profanation of his or her being. "To see a face is already to hear: 'You shall not kill'" (DL 21, trans. mine).[9] The Other is thus the one who speaks (TI 198) in a command which is also an appeal, an invocation to freedom and goodness, "a solicitation that concerns me by its destitution and its Height" (TI 200). Trace of the Infinite, paralysis of the powers of the I, obligation for the I to enter the ethical relation, discourse which founds signification, the face expresses itself sensibly in the eyes which observe, accuse, implore the I, thus reversing the scopophilia of the ontological subject, which now finds itself exposed to the Other, judged, and summoned by the Other to its responsibility—the relationship with the face becomes a face to face. That is, the Other is not the one who speaks down to the I, but the one who looks at it.[10]

In the nakedness of the eyes, the Other had expressed his or her destitution, passivity, vulnerability, need for protection in the figures of the poor, the stranger, the orphan, the widow. Now the Other turns into the Judge, the Lord, the Master, the Teacher who, in a suspension of maieutic exercises, brings novelty to the knowledge of the I. The Other's standing before the I, face to face with the I, is not in front, but above the I,[11] in an asymmetry of majesty and authority, which the Other derives not from physical force, but from being the trace of the Infinite.[12] The respectful *Vous* is the only proper way to address the Other who, both in the figures of destitution and in those of height, remains the stranger,[13] the one with whom the I shares no common property, territory, land, the one who comes and disturbs the house of the I and its economy of identity and interiority. As Levinas says, "the Other is the richest and the poorest of beings: the richest, at an ethical level, in that it always comes before me; the poorest, at an ontological or political level, in that without me it can do nothing—it is utterly vulnerable and exposed."[14]

The identity of the Other is captured in this paradox according to which the extremes become proximate, but without coincidence, implying that the Other is never a one, but always intersubjectivity, always society, always pluralism, even in community, always a difference and otherwise than the other, always beyond, transcendence, Infinity. In *Otherwise than Being,* adopting Plato's characterization of the Good and meanwhile hinting at Heidegger's ontology, Levinas asserts that the Infinite "is" in another way than being(s). Its way is not that of "essences," but that of otherness. The life of the Other is a life of paradoxes and ambivalences.

And yet, beyond the suggestions contained in the figures of misery and excellence with which Levinas describes the Other, beyond the ambivalences through which the Other presents himself or herself to the self, who is the Other? Whose faces are expressed in the primary expression that is the face of the Other? Who speaks in the face of the Other? Does the Other express a multiplicity of others? Does the Other express also the otherwise than Other? Is Levinas's love for the Other an act of love toward all others, in their subjective otherness?

Out of loyalty to the erotic inspiration of Levinas's project, out of faithfulness and truthfulness to the other, who invests the self with such truthfulness, the explication of Levinas's philosophy must at this point turn into its criticism—a criticism not inspired by the animosity and resentment of the I, by Levinas divested of its ontological power. Rather, a criticism once again performed "at the service of love" (OBBE 162), in an effort to reduce the said into which the Other, even in Levinas's philosophy, has inevitably elapsed, to the sincerity of the originary Saying. As Levinas remarks in *Otherwise than Being,* "pure criticism" does not lie "in the thematization operated by reflection on itself"—that is, in opening oneself up to the transcendental horizon of consciousness, or to the universality of the "I think." Rather, criticism rests on questioning "the naive spontaneity of the ego" through the passivity of the obsession for the other (OBBE 91–92). Once again, the ungrateful question must be asked: Who is the Other?

Certainly *Autrui* is not God.[15] The other is "indispensable for my relation with God" (TI 78) since "there can be no 'knowledge' of God separated from the relation with men" (TI 78), and "the Other, in his signification prior to my initiative, resembles God" (TI 293). Yet, as Levinas asserts very explicitly in *Totality and Infinity* "the Other is not the incarnation of God" (TI 79). Rather, God is "the *beyond* from which a face comes" (ToO 356), the irreversible past fleeing all revelations and representations.[16] Levinas expresses the difficulty of this notion through the pronoun *Il,* the third person which is neither the impersonal *il* of the *il y a,* which rather corresponds to mythical divinities, "faceless gods, impersonal gods to whom one does not speak" (TI 142), nor the third person of justice, which opens the relation with the other to the immanence of politics. Rather, the *Il* is the third dimension that enables the rectitude and the height of the ethical relation with the Other. Separate, that is, saint, God "is not simply 'the first other,' 'the other par excellence,' or the 'absolutely other,' but other than the other, other otherwise, other with an alterity prior to the alterity of the other, prior to the ethical bond with another and different from any neighbor, transcendent to the point of absence" (CPP 166).

Although different from the Other, God is nonetheless not indifferent to the other, since the Other "precisely by his face, in which [God] is disincarnate, is the manifestation of the height in which God is revealed" (TI 79). God's proximity is thus inscribed in the face of the other as trace, not sign, but presence of what has never been here, of the passage of the one who went by, and therefore is other, transcendence. Despite the fact that the Other is not God, in the notion of the trace which the other bears on his or her face, Levinas's Other gives expression to another other, whose otherness is thus not effaced by the absolutely other as *Autrui*. The Other signifies more than himself or herself so that one could perhaps affirm that *ad infinitum*—that is, ethically speaking—the Other is God.[17]

If the Other is God only *ad infinitum,* the same question is bound to return: Who is the Other? Certainly *Autrui* is the other human being, as explicated by the notion of fraternity, which is "the very relation with the face in which at the same time my election and equality, that is, the mastery exercised over me by the other, are accomplished" (TI 279). It is a relationship whose "original fact" is constituted by "my responsibility before a face looking at me as absolutely foreign (and the epiphany of the face coincides with these two moments)" (TI 214). Since "the third party looks at me in the eyes of the Other" (TI 213), *Autrui* is the presence of the entire humankind, by whom the I is commanded and to whom it commands "thou shalt not kill" (TI 213). But in this humankind which Levinas sees marked by sexual difference as by the situation where "the alterity of the other appears in its purity" (TO 85), thus conditioning "the very possibility of reality as multiple, against the unity of being proclaimed by Parmenides" (TO 85), the woman is *Autrui* only as an ef-faced, forgotten other. That is, the woman is not properly *Autrui.*[18]

A word of caution should be inserted at this juncture. The criticism of Levinas's notion of the feminine should not dwell on the appropriateness of the definition employed to describe the woman, whether it is misogynist, old-fashioned, paternalistic, patriarchal, since such an approach implies that a definition of woman is possible, whereas Levinas himself teaches that essential definitions are a betrayal of alterity. Rather, what should come under scrutiny is the role Levinas assigns to the woman as Other, whether the woman retains any feature of absolute otherness, whether the woman is allowed to play any role as Other. Does the woman express herself as *Autrui*? It would be unfair, and contrary to the ethical mandate not to take the place of the other, to ask Levinas to write *as* a woman.

Yet, a different formulation of the question retains its legitimacy—has Levinas been othered by the woman? In his philosophical love of the Other, has he loved the woman as Other, and philosophically conceived of her in terms of ambivalence, that is, in terms of her otherness? Has he let the woman be *her* otherness?[19]

In *Time and the Other* Levinas asserts that "the absolutely contrary contrary (*le contraire absolutement contraire*) . . . the contrariety that permits its terms to remain absolutely other, is the *feminine*" (TO 85). Her way of being consists in "slipping away from the light . . . withdrawing elsewhere . . . mystery" (TO 86–87) defined as modesty. The same images of the feminine as a discreet, nonconfronting presence are resumed in *Totality and Infinity.* In this work, the feminine—and this time Levinas explicitly says the woman (TI 155), thus thwarting his claims made in *Ethics and Infinity* about participation in the masculine and the feminine as "the attribute of every human being" (EI 68) —makes her first appearance in the intimacy of the home, where she helps the opening up of the virile, masculine I from the immediacy of the world to the solitude and interiority of recollection.[20] There, the presence of the woman is experienced as "a language without teaching, a silent language, an understanding without words, an expression in secret" (TI 155). The modality of the woman's discourse is that of gestures of welcoming and equivocation (TI 264)—rather different than the commanding voice of the Other, which challenges and summons the I to its responsibility. Perhaps to dissipate the latent suspicion that this imagery repeats stereotypical, paternalistic models,[21] Levinas remarks that "this alterity . . . nowise represents a truncated, stammering, still elementary language. On the contrary, the discretion of this presence includes all the possibilities of the transcendent relationship with the Other" (TI 155). It includes, yet one could argue, it does not effect, since what effects a conversion of the I from ontology to ethics, what others the constitution of the I is not the silent language of the woman, but the more powerful word of *Autrui,* the masculine other, the brother, to whose otherness the woman can participate only by suspending her feminine qualities of timidity and modesty.

Levinas admits to this distinction between a more serious, masculine other, *Autrui,* and the feminine, uneffective other when saying that "the Other who welcomes in intimacy is not the *you* [*vous*] of the face that reveals itself in a dimension of height, but precisely the *thou* [*tu*] of familiarity. . . . The I-Thou in which Buber sees the category of interhuman relationship is the relation not with the interlocutor but with feminine alterity" (TI 155).[22] But, as remarked elsewhere, the I-Thou relationship, in which the relationship with the feminine otherness is here enframed, and which can give rise only to the equality of friendship, is not a relationship with the absolutely other—that is, with what alone is a face. Faceless or unfaced because, even when she has a face, her face does not express height, the otherness of the woman is ef-faced from/by Levinas's *Autrui.* To be *Autrui,* the woman should cease being a woman.

While she remains a woman, her function is to help a process of interiorization which, rather than altering the I, serves and confirms it in its economy of sameness and separation. By suspending the I's natural existence, the home, in which the woman is located but which she has not created, favors labor and possession. This move signifies that the (uneffective) otherness of the woman is not absolute, absolved from the context, for herself. Rather, it is functional to the service it performs, recuperated within the system of the ontological I, for the I, constructed from the point of view of virility.[23] Let us assume that the folding of the I onto itself that the woman aids is more than functional, since it is essential to "the dissipation of the virile."[24] Yet, if the voice of *Autrui* is so imperious in its commanding the conversion to ethics, is the silent language of the woman's otherness necessary at all? Or, given that it is overcome by the word of *Autrui,* is it not a forgettable and forgotten discourse? In a word, is it not a neglectable otherness?

Levinas's failure to let the woman play her role as

Other, regardless of the form of otherness she may express, becomes even more evident in the notions of eros and fecundity.[25] In eros, "neither knowledge nor power" (TI 276), the masculine I is in relation with a feminine other, *l'Aimée* (who is never an *aimante,* though), who, as in the interiority of the home, "withdraws into mystery" (TI 276), retreats on the hither side of linguistic expression, thus subtracting herself from the uprightness of the face and its signifyingness which "spreads the light in which light is seen" (TI 261). Whereas in the intimacy of the home the discretion of the woman served hospitality, expectancy, welcome, in eros her inexpressible modesty and secrecy are exposed in an erotic nudity which, equivocal, "hides while unconvering, says and silences the inexpressible, harasses and provokes" (TI 260). In expressing only "this refusal to express, this end of discourse and of decency, this abrupt interruption of the order of presences" (TI 260), the feminine presents an otherness which goes beyond the otherness of *Autrui,* "a face that goes beyond the face" (TI 260), an "inversion of the face" (TI 262), as Levinas puts it. Does not this special kind of otherness, in its signifying otherwise than *Autrui,* signifies also its being other than *Autrui*? Levinas seems to indicate that the woman, although not *Autrui,* might possess an otherness of her own which, since "the pathos of voluptuosity is made of duality" (TI 276), in eros might be offered to "the non-sociality of the society of lovers" (TI 264).

Yet, the possibility of a feminine otherness, a feminine face standing on its own, for itself, is once again effaced in the movement to fecundity. For Levinas, erotic love "seeks what does not have the structure of an existent, the infinitely future, what is to be engendered" (TI 266). What is to be engendered, however, is not the pleasure of voluptuousness the two lovers desire for each other as the always "yet to come." This pleasure might provide the feminine Other with a form of enjoyment intended toward her own femininity. In Levinas, what is to be engendered is rather the child, which replaces, displaces, effaces the feminine Other in itself. Through the child the virile I, or a woman turned virile, and not the feminine Other, achieves its own temporality, the "relationship with the absolute future, or infinite time" (TI 268). In other words, what is sought and accomplished is masculine immortality in the other. To this purpose, "the encounter with the Other as feminine is required in order that the future of the child come to pass from beyond the possible" (TI 267). The feminine is for the child, which is for the masculine.[26] Once again, feminine otherness is only accidental, not for itself but rather constructed so as to serve a sophisticated version of the I's desire for eternity.[27] In erotic love, the I returns on itself through the child thus effacing the feminine other, who is not allowed to other the I on her own terms, who is not even allowed to be other on her own terms. Eventually the face of the beloved, *l'Aimée,* "returned to the stage of infancy without responsibility" (TI 263), fades into animality. "One plays with the Other as with a young animal" (TI 263), Levinas writes. In this return, no specific face is left to the feminine other.[28]

If the woman cannot be *Autrui,* neither can the child be, since the child is not for itself, but for the parent. In the structure of fecundity Levinas describes, the child appears as "the place where the father confers being or existence on himself, the place where he finds the resources to return to himself in relation to this same as and other than himself constituted by the son."[29] Whereas *Autrui,* in his absolute otherness, suspends all intentionality, the child, in its otherness that is also the I, remains the intention of the father's desire for transcendence. When does the son become *Autrui*?[30] "I cannot say at what moment you have the right to be called 'face,'" Levinas replies. Certainly not while one is addressed merely in terms of filiality.

Levinas's failure to conceive both the woman and the child in terms of their otherness reveals how the masculine, his prototype of the human, determines his notion of the Other. The primacy can be detected in two of the metaphorical figures he chooses to describe the Other: the widow and the orphan (TI 215). Granted the biblical origin of such imagery, what can it mean when Levinas chooses to write that the Other takes the face of the widow and the orphan, if neither the woman nor the child can be Other in his philosophy? The imagery, misleading in terms of otherness, is revealing in terms of women and children.

Who is the widow? She is not the unmarried woman, the maiden, who situates herself outside, at the margin of the protective structure of the family and its traditions. She is not the adulterous woman, who evades the closed economy of patriarchal family values and claims for herself those enjoyments and pleasures the masculine self guards as his own privileges. She is not the prostitute woman, who transforms her being an object of diurnal public contempt into being an object of nocturnal masculine desire, thus sublating her being constituted by the masculine into her own richness, exploiting (to an extent at least) what exploits her. In Levinas, the widow needs protection. Her want, however, originates not from the frailty of a separate being, as might be the case for the unmarried, prostitute, or adulterous woman, who may also need protection. Rather, the widow's indigency originates from the loss of her husband, who thus defines her being. The widow is the feminine who receives her identity from the (loss of the) masculine, which, after death as well as in life, defines who the woman is: not an absolutely other, but an other conditioned by the same, by the masculine. In this sense, the metaphor of the widow is misleading as it does not express absolute otherness. Rather, it illustrates what the analysis of the role of the feminine other has already revealed: the woman is not an Other, her otherness is constituted not in relation to herself, but to that possible other the masculine is. Her absolute otherness is betrayed as other of the (other) man, her face is not hers, but what emerges as reflected in the eyes of the other (man).

An analogous move occurs with respect to the child, and is reflected in the metaphor of the orphan, also employed to describe the Other. The orphan is not the child abandoned on the streets who has learned to transform the streets into its source of richness and identity. The orphan is the one who has lost what gives it its proper place—

namely, its parents, and, more precisely, its father, since the widow, who is herself a figure of lack, cannot, by herself, fill the loss of the father. Both the orphan and the widow, as the child and the feminine, derive the destitution which marks the Other not from themselves, but from the masculine which is lacking in them, from that masculine that already defines their identity. Therefore, deprived of their own otherness, the woman and the child are not figures of desire, but of need, not of love, but of lust. In their case, ambivalence is forgotten to the advantage of the univocity of the masculine other.

One reinscription and two effacements, then, determine the identity of *Autrui*. The reinscription: although God is not the Other, he (given the effacement of the feminine other, could God ever be addressed as a she?) is the other than the Other, whose traces are inscribed in the face of the Other. The first effacement: the woman is not the Other, although she possesses an otherness of her own which goes beyond the Other; but rather than being signified in the face of the Other, her otherness beyond the Other is effaced in the movement of fecundity. The second effacement: the child is not the Other as child, although it bears the promises for otherness, when not considered from the point of view of fecundity. The result is that in Levinas's philosophy *Autrui* is not any other, but only a *certain* other: the masculine, which alone possesses the authority to challenge the virility of the same. In this panorama which appears all too masculine, Levinas's love for the other, far from ambivalent, is of a homosexual kind—already a step forward if compared to the onanism of the ontological subject, but still a failure if compared to the heterogeneity the Other should express. As is the case in paternity, where the father finds himself as an I and as an other in the child, Parmenides finds himself as an I and as an other in Levinas: the break with Parmenidean unity, accomplished in terms of the same, whose identity is disrupted by the Other, is not accomplished in terms of the other, whose identity remains masculine, hegemonic, and, ultimately, unitarian and unilateral.

Yet, let us suppose that the woman were recognized by Levinas as Other. Let us suppose that the child (the son and the daughter) were recognized as Other. Let us suppose that these othernesses had been reinscribed, as if their effacement were due to Levinas's accidental carelessness, as if the antitotalitarian, antisystemic, antiunitarian character of his philosophy were more essential than the places of its concretization. And still, let us ask the same initial question: Who is the Other? A betrayal of ambivalence is still revealed in Levinas's philosophy, which loves the other, but not enough to love all his, her, and *its* ambivalences.

Although the subsumption of the Other under the category of person is illegitimate, since the Other escapes any categorization or universalization, it is certain that in Levinas the face of the other expresses itself only in the eyes of the other human being. "It is only man [and one would like to read Levinas, and the translator, say human being] who could be absolutely foreign to me" (TI 73), Levinas writes. The other is always humanly other. The face of the Other is always the human face. Ethically, that is all that matters. This determination implies that the entire realm of nature, animate and inanimate, is deprived of any notion of otherness. Confronted with the question of whether an animal can be considered the Other that must be welcomed, whether an animal has a face, Levinas's answer is resolute. If animals have a face, it is not an ethical face, but only a biological one.[31] A phenomenological analysis, Levinas suggests, may be required to discover traces of the wolf in the dog. Yet, the ethical face, the human face, as Levinas repeats frequently, is not a phenomenon. Since appearance is not its mode of being, the difference between the animal face—if there is one—and the human face could never be bridged by a phenomenological analysis, which would never be able to discover traces of infinity in the dog. As John Llewelyn argues, Bobby, the dog that strayed into the German camp where Levinas and his companions were imprisoned and treated as less than humans, and that welcomed the prisoners every morning and every evening on their way back and forth from work barking and wagging its tail, "the last Kantian in Nazi Germany," as Levinas comments, can never be my neighbor.[32]

If, according to Levinas, not even animals may have an ethical face signifying behind the appearance of their biological face, how could the possibility of an ethical demand ever be granted to entities such as plants, or minerals, or things, which have been denied the gift of even a biological face? How can Levinas's love of the other be the love of any other, of the other than the Other? For him, the face of the other human being remains primary, so that human ethics is the prototype—a fact which renders a discourse about the face of other entities (animal, vegetal, mineral) possible (if possible at all) only by analogy, as derivative, the result of a transference from one privileged realm to another. Levinas's ethics retains anthropologocentric features in its reading life still in terms of an opposition between human and nonhuman,[33] where the human *logos* of ethics is the defining factor, whereas the nonhuman is understood merely as the derivative negation of humanity. In this attitude, Levinas's philosophy does not distance itself from the ontological tradition whose origin is, as Levinas sees it, in Parmenides, and which he criticizes as "imperialism of the Same" (TI 39). Altogether then, the title of one of Levinas's works, *L'Humanisme de l'Autre Homme,* perfectly describes the content and the limitations of Levinas's philosophy. (Nietzschean and Heideggerian) modern antihumanism, in its dissolution of the notion of humanity through a critique of the notion of subject as reified substance or as self-consciousness, also opens up to the murderous excesses witnessed by our century.[34] Against it, Levinas defends a different humanism grounded on the notion of a subjectivity constituted as human only in terms of its being subjected to the other.[35] But, as the very title of the work announces, the other is and remains the other *man.*

Insofar as philosophy, even in its ethical rather than ontological character, is always the activity of a human subject, insofar as philosophy can only be human philosophy, all philosophy is, essentially, anthropocentrism, a humanism devoted to and centered around the promotion of the human being. But need anthropocentrism be anthropologocentrism? The inescapability of the situation, the anthropocentrism to which philosophy is inevitably condemned, would almost be acceptable, in its unavoidability, were the philosopher willing to recognize the inherent danger of its containing violating features, which may exclude and deny the truth of the nonhuman, were she or he willing to take conceptual precautions to minimize the possibility of violation to occur, were she or he willing to dissociate anthropocentrism from anthropologocentrism. That is, were she or he willing to acknowledge that beside the other as human there may be (perhaps) an other which is not human, but which, nevertheless, may be constituted (perhaps) as Other and may place (perhaps) infinite demands on human beings in their attempt to philosophize: infinite demands that possess (perhaps) the authority of the transcendent, that ask (perhaps) from human beings that they transcend themselves, that they become good.

According to Levinas, is not the modality of the perhaps, of the *peut-être* (in its being neither possibility, nor reality, nor necessity) the trace of the passage of the Other, the enigma "irreducible to the modalities of being and certainty" (CPP 71), the "way the Other has of seeking my recognition while preserving his *incognito,* disdaining recourse to a wink-of-the-eye of understanding or complicity, this way of manifesting himself without manifesting himself"? (CPP 66) What if the human being were not the only Other? What if things, too, were Other? Or, perhaps, the other of the Other? Is not Levinas's filiality from Parmenides more obsequious, reverent, subservient than Levinas himself might wish? What if Levinas's anthropologocentric ethics needed to be extended, supplemented by an ethics of things, to be truly that wisdom of love that loves the other more than it loves itself?

4 ❖ Without Love: The Disappearance of Things

The history of things has mainly been a story of neglect and mistreatings. Rejected from the realm of truth (Plato), deprived of any quality other than the mathematical ones (Descartes), declared unknowable if not in their appearances (Kant), things have been the objects thrust in front of a philosophical consciousness more concerned with the achievement of its own identity through a process of reduction of things to itself than interested in unveiling the truth of things in their own reality.

In *Otherwise than Being* Levinas advances a description of philosophy as the "wisdom of love" (OBBE 162), which vividly resonates with the earlier definition of truth offered in *Totality and Infinity:* "the aspiration to radical exteriority, thus called metaphysical, the respect for this metaphysical exteriority which, above all, we must 'let be'" (TI 29). Put together, the two statements lead to a configuration of the philosophical project and task as an amorous act of respect that lets otherness be in its exteriority. With these statements, however, Levinas does more than offer a generic description of philosophy. By announcing his break with the Parmenidean tradition and qualifying his project as ethics, he reclaims such statements as descriptive of his own thought. What better way to assess the legitimacy of Levinas's claim and test the consistency of his philosophy as an act of love than to place it face to face with things? What is the relation Levinas establishes with those entities toward which Western subjectivity has more than often manifested its lack of love? What is the place Levinas assigns to things within his work? Is it an amorous place at all?

Unfortunately, Levinas's account of things is the story of a missed encounter, an account in which no sufficient love is present to retrieve things from the history of ontology. What marks a situation as ethical is, for Levinas, the fact that the I can be situated in a face to face relation with the Other. It is precisely the presentation of the face that suspends the I's temptation of complete negation, and transposes the I from ontology—in which the other appears within a horizon accessible to comprehension—to ethics. Yet, the move toward ethics cannot be performed with respect to things because, as Levinas inequivocably asserts, "things have no face" (TI 140). As explained in *Difficult Freedom,* "things are those which never present themselves personally, and, in the end, they have no identity. . . . Things offer themselves to be grasped, they do not offer a face. They are beings without faces" (DL 20). The facial absence legitimates the proscription of things from ethics and their condemnation to the realm of ontology, to the point that, according to Levinas, "ontology is a relation with things which manifests things" (TI 158). But how can such a manifestation be an act of love, when ontology has been defined throughout as imperialistic and violating, a Ulyssean enterprise performed for the sake of the same?

The reason for the things' facelessness is due to the very nature of things. Whereas no form has been added to the face, since, in its being its own expression, the face immediately signifies its content in its form, thus suppressing the distinction between form and content, "things have a form, are seen *in* the light—silhouettes or profiles" (TI 140). The very presence of a distinct form giving meaning to things deprives things of the possibility of signifying with the same immediacy of the face, which they therefore cannot have. The face to face between Levinas's philosophy and things thus fails miserably, because Levinas is not willing to retrace in things the only condition through which a facing could occur.

Returning to an ontological concept, which he inflects

in a phenomenal direction, Levinas understands things in terms of matter on which a form has been imprinted, what Aristotle would have called formed matter. And neither in the matter nor in the form, and hence not even in their unity, is Levinas willing to find anything which could suggest the presence of an infinite of which the thing would be the expression. On the contrary, Levinas asserts that "the thing evinces . . . ontology" (TI 158). Against all expectations of love for ambivalences, Levinas does not do anything to rescue things from the ontological domain to which they have been condemned.

The matter of which things are made is constituted by raw materiality, the elemental, what elsewhere Levinas calls the *il y a:* pure being, pure existing before all distinctions and supporting the very possibility of existence. An indefinite, nameless, disquieting substratum which menaces with its unforseeable future, the elemental, out of which things are carved, is not able to oppose frontally with the rectitude of a face to face. The elemental can only oppose laterally, "as already abdicating to the hand which seeks its vulnerable point, which, already ruse and industry, reaches for it obliquely" (TI 160). Therefore, as revealed by this fallacious resistance (TI 160), the matter of which things are made cannot resemble the infinite, whose absolute resistance is expressed in the face. On the contrary, what the "fathomless obscurity of matter" (TI 160) brings to manifestation is "the facelessness of the pagan gods whose nothingness is henceforth exposed" (TI 16). The conclusion Levinas draws from the facelessness of matter is rather disheartening, in the absolution it seems to advance of the violence implied in all forms of technological manipulation: "in the last analysis labor cannot be called violence: it is applied to what is faceless, to the resistance of nothingness" (TI 160). As if the only violence worthy of its name and of resistance on the part of the ethical subject were for Levinas the metaphysical violence which aims at killing the Other. As a matter of fact, the Other is "the sole being I can wish to kill" (TI 198), because the Other is the only being to which the notion of killing applies, and the only being that, by expressing itself, by facing me, "says no to me by his very expression" (CPP 21). In their being constituted out of materiality, things inherit the inability to resist characterizing the elemental so that "the thing does not resist acquisition" (TI 162).

Within the indefiniteness characterizing the elemental, the role of the form is to inform the formless, to provide the elemental with a conceptual side that can be grasped and comprehended, so that what the form effects is a suspension of "the independence of the elemental: its being" (TI 158). The traditional attribution to things of a form, which Levinas so lightly undertakes, is already the manifestation of a lack of love toward the things, since, as he recognizes when it comes to *Autrui,* "form . . . alienates the exteriority of the other" (TI 66). The lack of love is aggravated by the modality with which the attribution takes place in Levinas's phenomenological analysis (but how much of it is Levinas's interpretation?), since the imprinting of the form is performed with all the violence characterizing ontological imperialism. Insensitive to an independence that amounts to nothingness because it comes "from an opaque density without origin, the bad infinite or the indefinite, the *apeiron*" (TI 158–59), Levinas does not find anything objectionable in the fact that the suspension of such an independence happens not merely through "*thinking* this suspension or obtaining it by the effect of a formula"—theoretical activities which, in the case of *Autrui,* were violating enough to be condemned as cases of reductivistic egology—but through the more practical, concretely manipulatory acts of "taking possession or labor, the destiny of the hand" (TI 159). It is the hand that operates the primordial grasp on the elemental, thus imprinting a form on matter—the hand which "*comprehends* the thing not because it touches it on all sides at the same time . . . but because . . . [it] is mastery, domination, disposition" (TI 161). While seizing the indefinite being of the elemental and thus separating the object from the milieu in which it is originally located (TI 130), the form impressed through labor posits being as durable (TI 161), makes of an object a thing, lets it appear as a solid "with clearly delimited contour" (TI 160). In this way, the nature of the thing is reduced to its "solidity, offering itself to the hand which takes and takes away" (TI 161). Rather than being defined positively, as if were *kath'auto,* Levinas understands things as objects that have lost their natural existence as part of the elemental, and have assumed another identity through an act of force, effected by the hand in labor, which has thrusted them in a world of identification and identifiability.

Although his analysis of labor lacks a complete and sophisticate account of labor's most modern affiliate, technology, Levinas does recognize the dangers intrinsic in modern technology; as he writes, "nobody is so foolish as to deny the contradictions and miscalculations of technology, its murderous dangers, the new enslavements and mythologies with which it threatens us, and the pollution that follows from it, which poisons—in the proper sense of the term—even the air we breath" (SF 106).[1] However, rather than an act of force, labor is, for Levinas, the way through which a demythologization of the false gods of nature, idolatrically recognized in things, comes to pass. "Technology takes [the] divinity [of the pagan gods and their false and cruel transcendence] away, and, by giving us power over the world, teaches us that these gods belong to the world, that they are things and that things are, after all, no big deal, that there is trickery in their resistance and their objectivity and rubbish in their splendor, and that we must rather laugh in their faces than cry and implore. Through the secularization it achieves, technology participates in the progress of the human spirit" (SF 107).

As formed matter, things are described as fields of conquest. And, in a very phenomenal twist yelding to the imperialism of the I (or of the Other as subjective alterity), the identifiability resulting from the conquest is determined in terms of detachability, that is, graspability for the I. A thing is what can be possessed, in an ontological move which turns being—the elemental—into having. Landscapes, horizons, meadows, mountains, fog, the rain are not considered things by Levinas. They are elemental presences, because in their instability they cannot be seized, conquered, drawn to possession by the I. It is not accidental that the issue of things is addressed by Levinas mainly in the section of *Totality and Infinity* devoted to "Interiority and Economy," within a movement, determined by need rather than by desire, which takes its bearing from the same to return to the same.

The imperialistic twist, performed by the hand through the attribution of a form and denying to things a reality of their own, is paralleled by the phenomenal consideration that, since "objects have no light of their own" (TI 74)—that is, they are deprived of their own signification—they must receive their meaning from the perspective in which they are situated, from the point of view from which they are considered. "They receive a borrowed light" (TI 74), unable, unlike the Other, to present themselves to us "independently of every position we would have taken in regard" (TI 65). Things remain inescapably chained to the perspective on them the I assumes, which the phenomenological analysis calls the horizon, whereas their meaning mutates with the change of the point of view, or of the viewer.

The relativistic approach, turning into subjectivism, is not the least reduced by the fact that the Other makes his or her appearance in the world of the I. When the other presents itself to the I, from objects of labor, resulting into possessions, things become gifts offered to the Other. In this circumstance, the mediation of things is essential for the occurrence of the relationship with the Other, since the I can welcome the Other only because it possesses things which can be donated to cover the Other's nakedness. What constitutes the principle of the donation, however, is the other, and not the things themselves. The appearance of the Other thus does not bring any change in terms of the reality of things, which remains exteriorly constituted, as if things were for humans before being in themselves, as if there were nothing in the piece of bread in itself that would make of it a gift apt to satiate the Other's hunger.

The changeability of the signification of things, which varies according to the light which is cast on them, empties things of a proper identity: "strictly speaking [things have] no identity" (TI 140). In the case of the Other, the impossibility of a determined identity counted in favor of the Other, who could therefore be described as the stranger who escapes and disrupts the territoriality of a home. In the case of things, however, the lack of identity becomes a structural condition accounting for the possessibility of things. Levinas can therefore define the nature of things as mobility: "the thing is a movable (*meuble*)" (TI 161), not what escapes possession, but what, because of its mobility, can be moved from one site to another, even exchanged for other *meubles,* to furnish the unmoveable dwelling which is the interiority of the I. As a result of mobility, the "identity" of things is a precarious notion retrievable only at the crossing of three different movements: labor, enjoyment, and discourse. As already noticed, the world of things described by Levinas is a horizon centered on the human being understood in terms of his or her ability to manipulate matter. Before human labor, ensued by possession, there are no things, but only the elements: "labor . . . draw[s] things from elements and thus *discover*[s] the world. This primordial grasp, this emprise of labor, which *arouses* things" (TI 157), is an activity of institution arranging things in a system of finalities in which they disappear in the function they perform. In labor, oriented by "egoist ends" (TI 159) since it relates "the elemental to the finality of needs" (TI 159) thus enabling the satisfaction of such needs, things appear as exchangeable goods whose value is determined by the situation in which they are located, and whose substance can be stored in the interiority of the I's dwelling to suspend the uncertainty of the future. Things are goods.

The activity of transformation of things, which does not originate in things themselves because there are no things in themselves, renders the nature of things evanescent, despite the durability that labor impresses on them through the imposition of a form. A thing can always be turned into another. A different attribution of meaning is therefore required, a stabilization of identity which Levinas sees happen in language. "The things are fixed by the word which gives them, which communicates them and thematizes them. . . . An earth inhabited by men endowed with language is peopled with stable things" (TI 139). Things appear now as the result of a linguistic act. In the case of *Autrui,* discourse maintained an ethical coloring in allowing the relationship without assimilation of the I and the other. In the case of things, language simply enables the sharing of the ontological constitution of things. In both cases, in labor as well as in language, things are rendered interior. The Levinasian reader has been made aware by the author himself, however, of how any act of interiorization is "not the relation with the other as such but the reduction of the other to the same" (TI 46), prototype of all violence. Yet, with respect to things, the reduction is not problematic for Levinas, because things do not possess any face on which such a violence would be exerted. According to Levinas, "violence consists in . . . ignoring the face of a being, avoiding the gaze. . . . Violence is a way of taking hold of a being by surprise, by taking hold of it in its absence, in what is not properly speaking it." This is not the case for things, though, since "the relationship with things, the domination of things, this way of being over them, consists in fact in never approaching them in their individuality" (CPP 19).

Levinas is willing to recognize that, although it gives form to the elemental, labor is not sufficient to exhaust the meaning of things, as if there were something other in things, an opacity persisting at their bottom and always ready to capture the subject, whether the I or the Other, within the laces of its fascination. The surplus of meaning and being, the something other unaccessible to labor, becomes manifest through what Levinas calls enjoyment, which operates in a direction opposite to that of labor, restoring things to the elementality of their pure matter (TI 134). Enjoyment de-forms things, in its being "an ultimate relation with the substantial plenitude of being, with its materiality" (TI 133). The things which in labor appear as means to satisfy egoist needs, in enjoyment become pure finalities, not the ends of ontology, still related to the representation of their finality, but finalities "without utility, in pure loss, gratuitously, without referring to anything else, in pure expenditure" (TI 133). It is like a game in which the I loses track of its intentions, and bathes in the pure essence of existence. According to Levinas, the intentionality of enjoyment, to which all things submit, whether they are tools like the pen and the hammer, or nontools like the piece of bread, the smoke in the fireplace or the cigarette (TI 133) or even possessions and abstract relations, is constituted precisely by its holding to exteriority, which has been suspended by the transcendental method as well as by labor. Immersed in the object of enjoyment, the enjoyer is conditioned by what is enjoyed.

The possibility that this reversed intentionality might signify "the exteriority of things with respect to man" (TI 130), the possibility that things might reveal some otherness lurking in them, is immediately denied by Levinas, since "enjoyment . . . does not reach [things] qua things. Things come to representation from a background from which they emerge and to which they return in the enjoyment we can have of them" (TI 130). It is no longer the thing that is enjoyed in enjoyment, whose exteriority conditions the enjoyer; rather, it is the thing which has been de-formed, the elemental, which "lies escheat, a common fund or terrain, essentially non-possessable, nobody's" (TI 131). Not the "field cultivated by me, the sea in which I fish and moor my boats, the forest in which I cut wood" (TI 131) are experienced in the intentionality of enjoyment, but wind, earth, sea, sky, air (TI 132)—formless, sideless, indeterminate of an indetermination which, in its coming before the finite and the infinite, "is not equivalent to the infinite surpassing its limits" (TI 132), and therefore cannot express any transcendence, any otherness, any face demanding a move to ethics. If anything, "here we have the eternal seduction of paganism, beyond the infantilism of idolatry, which has been left behind long ago; *the filtering of the sacred through the world.* . . . The mystery of things is the source of all cruelty to humans" (DL 301).

Things exist in a precarious balance between labor, which assigns things a form whose contour itself however needs further stabilization and ultimately dissolves things in their finalities, and enjoyment, which reverts things to the formlessness of elementality. Stabilized only as a linguistic act, the nature of things is therefore always on the edge of disappearing, a fragile presence one can never really capture. The fleetingness of things, their perennial subtraction to the power of conceptualization, which not even in labor can be completely eliminated, and yet the obsessiveness with which things siege the existence of the I presenting it with needs whose satisfaction is essential for the very possibility of the encounter with *Autrui,* might have easily become a mark of otherness, although of an otherness different from the otherness of *Autrui*—the mark of *alterity.*[2] But for Levinas, things do not signify any otherness. If there is any impression of their obsessing the interiority of the I, "it is as possessed by a neighbor, as relics and not as clothed with cultural attributes, that things first obsess" (OBBE 191 n10).

Within the three movements of labor, enjoyment, and discourse, things acquire and lose an identity which is never their own, so that thingness, in its being constituted never in itself, but only for another, whether the I or the Other, or the I and the Other in their relationship, can never become the place of an alterity worth of respect and love. Features present in things, which could be easily read as suggestive of an ethical signification, are retained by Levinas only as ontological concepts. Thus, the move to an ethics of things is precluded. As Levinas writes, "everything in things is exposed, even what is unknown in them. The traces that mark them are part of this plenitude of presence; their history is without a past" (CPP 106).

Captured in what is considered a complete coincidence to their present, a total immanence to the consciousness giving them meaning, not only can things not lead to any past, but they cannot even be said to be passing themselves. The result is that things cannot immediately signify any transcendence. The marks they bear on themselves, which a different analysis might perhaps indicate as traces, are, if not mediated through the activity of human beings, only the marks imprinted by one on the other through a contact that remains causal—that is, ontological and not metaphysical. As Levinas claims, "[things] by themselves do not leave traces, but produce effects, that is, remain in the world. When a stone has scratched another stone, the scratch can, to be sure, be taken as a trace, but in fact without the man who held the stone this scratch is but an effect. It is as little a trace as the forest fire is a trace of the lightning. A cause and an effect, even separated by time, belong to the same world" (CPP 106). To consider the mark left by the lightning as anything more than an effect would be to revert to the animism of mythological gods, which are, however, impersonal gods, faceless gods (TI 142) with which a face to face relationship is impossible.

Analogously, only erroneously can the appearance of nakedness, which things may be thought to manifest, resemble the nakedness expressed by the Other. Whereas the nakedness of the Other is *kath'auto* and signifies before its insertion in any horizon, before the projection on it of any phenomenological light disclosing its meaning, the apparent nakedness of things amounts to the privation of a form in which the thing can be completely absorbed. The thing is naked only by reference to a system of finalities, which it lacks. As Levinas puts it, "for a thing nudity is the surplus of its being over its finality" (TI 74). This poverty of form, which is also an excess of content, is never allowed to turn into ethical destitution. On the contrary, it may be obviated by art, which, by introducing the notion of internal finality, casts a new light on things, thus clothing them with a new signification—their beauty.[3] For Levinas, however, the aesthetic attribution cannot be an ethical gesture, precisely because the perception of beauty is simply a different modality with which things can be discovered, or sometimes placed, within the whole. In art things do not present themselves, they are not by themselves, but only in reference to the concept of beauty, to the nonfinalistic horizon in which they are located.[4]

At least once, when wondering whether things could have a face, Levinas's answer sounds possibilist. *"L'analyse jusqu'ici menée ne suffit pas à la résponse,"* he claims (Entre-nous 22). Nevertheless there is enough evidence in his texts that when it comes to things, there is no possibility of an ethics. Levinas's love, although sincere, does not love enough. In his philosophy, things remain without love. As Levinas himself suggests, to discover the possibility that things may have a face—that is, that they may signify some otherness able to place ethical demands—the project must be carried further, because the actual analysis, in its being limited to the human, all too human domain, is insufficient. To this purpose, however, a wholly otherwise notion of things must be negotiated, a notion that escapes the constraints imposed on things by the ontological categories in which they have traditionally been inserted, and which Levinas has not contributed to undermine. Ironically, suggestions in the direction of a different understanding of things come from Heidegger, whom Levinas confines to the history of ontology,[5] but toward whom, as toward Parmenides, an ultimate act of love may be required, if not by Levinas, at least by his philosophical children, "as if [Levinas's] being, in [philosophical] fecundity—and starting from the children's possibilities—exceeded the possibilities inscribed in the nature of [Levinas' own] being" (EI 70).[6]

II ❖ Heidegger: Things without Love

5 ❖ The Question of Things

> We are plants which—whether we like to admit it to ourselves or not—must with our roots rise out of the earth in order to bloom in the ether and to bear fruit.[1]

The question of things, Heidegger remarks at the beginning of a 1935/36 lecture course later published as *Die Frage nach dem Ding,* is one of the most ancient, venerable, and fundamental problems of metaphysics. By metaphysics one should here understand neither a specific field of philosophical inquiry, as distinct from logic, ethics, or epistemology, nor a deviated, and yet destinal path of philosophy, which needs to be overcome because in it "the oblivion of Being"[2] comes to pass. Rather, metaphysics indicates the constellation of issues which lie at the core of philosophy (WT 4). It is what Heidegger elsewhere defines as "an inquiry over and above what-is, with a view to winning it back as such and in totality for our understanding" (WM 344). That is, despite the enthrallment to reason to which things have been submitted, the question of things, as a fundamental philosophical question which in its interrogative form announces itself as the question "What is a thing?" (WT 4), situates itself at the very center of philosophy, at the very origin of that philosophical wonder which makes one pause to ask, "Why are there essents rather than nothing?" (IM 1), and thus spurs the beginning of philosophy.

In its antiquity, the question about things has often been raised, since "it passes for a known fact that as far back as antiquity, no sooner was the question raised as to what entities are in general, than things in their thingness thrust themselves into prominence again and again as the standard type of beings" (OWA 22). The answers that the philosophical tradition has given to the prominent question of "What is a thing?" can be reduced to three: a thing is the composite of substance and accidents, a thing is the unity of a manifold of sensible properties, and a thing is the fusion of matter and form (OWA 21–22).

None of these descriptions, however, can be deemed satisfactory in terms of unveiling what a thing is. Interpreting the thing as substance and accidents has been regarded as the most "natural" description of things. Yet, Heidegger points out how such an interpretation is not well-founded at all, insofar as "what seems natural to us is probably just something familiar in a long tradition that has forgotten the unfamiliar source from which it arose" (OWA 24). Moreover, what is regarded in this interpretation as proper to things can be used to describe *any* being whatsoever, "hence it cannot be used to set apart thingly beings from non-thingly beings" (OWA 24).

Of no greater advantage is the description of things, greatly accepted in modern philosophy, which conceives of them in terms of the *aistheton,* the sum total of all that the senses of sight, hearing, and touch convey. Although not incorrect, such an interpretation forgets that "much closer to us than all sensations are the things themselves. We hear the door shut in the house, and never hear acoustical sensations or even mere sounds. In order to hear a bare sound we have to listen away from things" (OWA 26). Although for opposite reasons (one sets the things too far off, the other makes them press too hard upon us), in both conceptions "the thing vanishes" (OWA 26).

The third interpretation which the tradition has advanced is that which conceives of things as formed matter. Such a description properly applies to things understood as equipment, from where it has then been extended, whether in its original, Christian, or Kantian interpretation, to the constitution of every entity. But, Heidegger concludes, "matter and form are in no case original determinations of the thingness of mere things" (OWA 28).

In this history of failures, a fundamental truth unveils itself: Western thought infallibly documents "that the thingness of the thing is particularly difficult to express and only seldom expressible" (OWA 32). A fundamental reluctance to disclosedness envelops the nature of things. Nevertheless, once again the question of things must be asked, and as Heidegger remarks, the novelty of the question "is merely that it must be asked again and again" (WT 1). Why, and whence such an obligation to renew an impossible question?

Before venturing any attempt to explore the question, a preliminary issue should be addressed: that of a delimitation of the subject of the discourse. A clarification of what is meant when invoking the name "things" is offered by Heidegger himself in the introduction to the 35/36 lecture course. Appealing to that same common sense which considers useless the question of "What is a thing?," insofar as it belongs to that range of issues with which "one can really do nothing. . . . One can start to do nothing with it" (WT 2), Heidegger retraces three meanings commonly clustered in the word "thing," with the provision that the term has no rigid determination, but rather oscillates among the different significations, as if, already in their average prethematic—that is, prephilosophical—understanding, things resisted all definitions and delimitations: "1. A thing in the sense of being present-at-hand: a rock, a piece of wood, a pair of pliers, a watch, an apple, and a piece of bread. All inanimate and animate things such as a rose, shrub, tree, spruce, lizard and wasp. . . . 2. Thing in the sense in which it means whatever is made but which includes also plans, decisions, reflections, loyalties, actions, historical things. . . . 3. All these and anything else that is a something (*Etwas*) and not nothing" (WT 6). When asked, the question about things (and Heidegger's own interest in the lecture, but also in general) applies to the restricted range of signification, because it is from here that the problem begins, even when one understands things in their broader meaning. "As we ask 'What is a thing?' we . . . mean the things around us"

(WT 7). The questioning about things begins in the *nearness* of things.

What does it mean, then, to ask the question about the things around us? Still in the context of the same lecture, Heidegger observes that the questioning about things cannot be restrained to a scientific definition, description of functions, or catalogue of analogies and differences of the surrounding things. With respect to these discriminations philosophy is always anachronistic, since detailed specifications have already been provided by scientists and technicians. The anachronism of the empirical analysis, limited both in its beginning and in its ending to the sensible character of things (the Aristotelian *to aistheton*), is avoided by philosophy's opening up of the questioning from the surrounding things to what Heidegger here names the thingness of the thing, from the thing as a being to the being of such a being. As he writes, "with our question 'What is a thing?' it obviously is not our purpose to discover what granite, a pebble, limestone or sandstone is but rather what the rock is as a *thing*. . . . In inquiring this way, we seek what makes the thing a thing and not what makes it a stone or wood; what conditions (*be-dingt*) the thing. We do not ask concerning a thing of some species but after the thingness of a thing. For the condition of being a thing, which conditions the thing as a thing, cannot itself again be a thing, i.e., something conditioned. The thingness must be something unconditioned (*un-bedingtes*). With the question 'What is a thing?' we are asking for something unconditioned. We ask about what is all around us and can be grasped by the hand. . . . But we want to pass beyond even these things to the unconditioned, where there are no more things that provide a basis and ground" (WT 8–9). Whereas what is questioned is the things surrounding us, what is in question, what they are questioned about is their thing-being, the mode of being which lets them be what they are—things. The question, then, is one of transcendental conditions: what is the unconditioned condition that lets things be what they are. Things reach further than what the opacity of their shining surface might let one presuppose. If correctly investigated, things point to—in the sense of indicating, referring, and signaling—being.

The orientation of the questioning, directed not to the things but to the thing-being, has important consequences. If the questioning about things is not a question about a thing, but about their mode of being, then the question "What is a thing?" can never receive a direct answer, but only an oblique response. As already clear to Hegel in his *Phenomenology of Spirit,* an apophantic definition of the thing, such as *this* or *that* is a thing, would be unsatisfactory. Beside requiring an endless cataloguing, such a response would still appeal to something conditioned, reducing things to what Heidegger elsewhere calls entities present-at-hand. Instead, Heidegger warns, things cannot be grasped, seized, grabbed, but only approached (WT 27). Therefore, the answer to the question of things will exhibit what it takes for a thing to disclose itself as such, the opening within which things can manifest themselves as things. It will unveil the ungrounded, unconditioned ground of things—that is, being itself.

Since being is never *a* being, it can never become the object of a complete exhibition. Therefore, the answer will never properly be an answer, a certainty, a knowledge. The answer to the question will rather be the renewal of the questioning. As Heidegger suggests in the opening sentences of the 35/36 lecture, the question of things is an ever newly arising question, which, in its questioning, provokes a change of perspective in the questioner and in what is questioned. The answer to the question "What is a thing?," Heidegger continues a few pages later, is "not a proposition but a transformed basic position or, better still and more cautiously, the initial transformation of the hitherto existing position toward things, a change of questioning and evaluation, of seeing and deciding; in short, of the being-there (*Da-sein*) in the midst of what is (*inmitten des Seienden*)" (WT 50).

It is not true, then, as common sense would have it, that the question of things is completely useless (WT 2). Pragmatically useless, it may nevertheless have existential import which goes beyond any commonsensical expectation, insofar as it may provoke a change of perspective not only in the way human beings deal with things around them, but in the very mode of the self-unveiling of things. As Heidegger remarks in *An Introduction to Metaphysics,* having admitted the correctness of the statement about the uselessness of philosophy, "the rejoinder imposes itself: granted that *we* cannot do anything with philosophy, might not philosophy, if we concern ourselves with it, do something *with us?*" (IM 12). Two delicate issues present themselves here: that of the relation which occurs between theory and praxis, the discrepancy and separation of which are, according to Heidegger, a consequence of the departure of philosophy from its origin, and that of the ability of philosophy to appropriate human beings to itself, and therefore affect them (LH 236).

Rather than operating a reunion of what Western philosophy has severed, Heidegger situates originary thinking, and with it philosophy, once it has overcome the oblivion of being to which it has consigned itself, before the separation of theory and practice. In the "Letter on Humanism" he writes that "thinking does not become action only because some effect issues from it or because it is applied. Thinking acts insofar as it thinks" (LH 193). The activism of originary thinking properly distinguishes itself from "action, which grasps hold directly of the real and alters it,"[3] thus constituting the ground for the presentification and manipulation of entities displayed in modern technology. Its activism consists instead in opening, or keeping open, the space in which being can manifest itself—that is, a space in which a resurgence of the questioning can come to pass. This keeping open is itself an activity of thinking under the mode of questioning. Still in the "Letter on Humanism," Heidegger can therefore assert that "such thinking has no result. It has no effect. It satisfies its essence in that it is" (LH 236). Rather than a case of Aristotelian, self-reflective activity, it is a form of thinking which has its own result within itself, it is its result. Therefore, such thinking has no effect, if by such a notion one understands the exteriority which divides a cause from its effect. Thinking is to keep open—that is, to question. To question is "the resolve to be able to stand in the openness of the essent" (IM 22), that is, to let be. And letting be already implies a relation to things which does not cover them up with utilitarian rationalizations. To do so, though, a change of comportment (an existential "effect") is required in the one who does the thinking. According to a more originary perspective, one which situates itself before the separation of theory and practice takes place, the question of things invokes a task, and not simply an answer. The task, accomplishable through the ever-new posing of the questioning, is that of keeping open a space able to "to preserve things in their inexhaustibility, i.e., without distortion" (WT 65).

Whence comes the obligation to keep such a space open? Whence the obligation to even ask the question of things? In a sense, it is a matter of necessity, aroused by the situation itself in which the contemporary *Dasein* finds itself thrown. In *What Is Philosophy?*, Heidegger writes that "the question about the nature of something awakens at those times when that, whose nature is being questioned, has become obscure and confused, when at the same time the relationship of men to what is being questioned has become uncertain or has even been shattered."[4] The question of things might be the question of our times, because these are times when modern natural science and its most direct affiliation, technological calculative thinking, which have become "a universal way of thinking along certain basic lines" (WT 51), "hold us captive and make us unfree in the experience and determination of the things" (WT 51). These are times when the "unshattered preeminence" of "the determination of the thing as material present-at-hand" (WT 52) has obfuscated our relation to things because of their reduction to devitalized, inert, dead entities toward which no relation is in fact possible. The question of things, then, is a destinal question, or as Heidegger qualifies it in *What Is a Thing?*, a "historical question" (WT 52). "To question historically means to set free and into motion the happening which is quiescent and bound in the question" (WT 48). The question of things frees the determination of things which are in question. And yet, why such an obligation?

In the "Letter on Humanism," Heidegger asserts that "thinking . . . lets itself be claimed by being" (LH 194). In other words, the thinker is not at the origin of thinking. Questioning comes from beyond the questioner, from that about which is being questioned. In "The Question Concerning Technology" Heidegger writes that "questioning is the piety (*Frommigkeit*) of thought" (QCT 35). What Heidegger means with these words is explained in another conference, devoted this time to language: "'piety' is meant here in the ancient sense: obedient, or submissive, and in this case submitting to what thinking has to think about" (OWL 72). In the same essay, Heidegger adds that "inquiry and investigation here and everywhere require the prior grant of whatever it is they approach and pursue with their queries. Every posing of every question takes place within the very grant of what is put in question" (OWL 71). As the essays chronologically following *What is a Thing?* reveal, what is announced in questioning, then, is "to listen to that which our questioning vouchsafes" (OWL 72). Granted that Heidegger refers this consideration to *die Sache par excellance,* the question of being, his words seem to retain a broader relevance and hold true for questioning in general. If this is the case; if questioning is in fact a corresponding to what gives itself to question; if, as Heidegger writes, "the correspondence listens to the voice of the appeal,"[5] the obligation to ask the question about things cannot come from anything else but the very things. That is, the possibility that things may send out an appeal, to which human beings are obliged to correspond—the possibility of an ethics—is, if not thematized, at least suggested. But so that the appeal may be heard, a questioning of the mode of being of things is required which lets them be *as* things.

6 ❖ Phenomenologically, Things

In *The Basic Problems of Phenomenology,* Heidegger radically and unequivocally asserts that "*being is the proper and sole theme of philosophy,*" and that "philosophy is not a *science* of beings but of *being*" (BPP 11). These considerations situate philosophy in sharp opposition to what Heidegger calls the "positive sciences" (BPP 13), which "deal with that which is, with beings; that is to say, they always deal with specific domains" (BPP 13). These sciences are subsequently divided into more and more specified fields of inquiry: nature as lifeless and living nature, in turn subdivided into plant and animal world; history as the sphere of historical beings, subdivided into art history, political history, history of science, history of religion; the pure space of geometry, as abstracted from the space of the environing world.[1]

At the beginning of *Being and Time* Heidegger claims, consistent with his later statement about the thematic issue of philosophy, that the aim of his essay is that of raising anew and working out "*the question of the meaning of being*" (BT 19), which, despite "its venerable origin" (BT 29), has not received "a definite answer" nor "any satisfactory formulation" (BT 29), to the point that it "has today been forgotten" (BT 21). And, he warns, his goal is that of "do[ing] so concretely" (BT 19). Such an inquiry that prioritizes the question of the meaning of being in general over the question of specific beings (what will be elsewhere [BPP 17 and FCM 358] called the ontological difference)[2] can be named, at least at this stage of Heidegger's thought, an "ontology," where ontology is "taken in the widest sense without favoring any particular ontological directions or tendencies" (BT 31). As Heidegger explains in a very clear passage in *An Introduction to Metaphysics,* "the word 'ontology' was first coined in the seventeenth century. It marks the development of the traditional doctrine of the essent into a discipline of philosophy and a branch of philosophical system. But the traditional doctrine was an academic classification and ordering of what for Plato and Aristotle and, again for Kant, was a question, though no longer, to be sure, a primordial one. And it is in this sense that the word 'ontology' is used today. Under this title each school of philosophy has set up and described a branch within its system. But we can also take the word 'ontology' in the 'broadest sense,' 'without reference to ontological directions and tendencies' [see *Sein und Zeit,* p.11, top]. In this case 'ontology' signifies the endeavor to make being manifest itself, and to do so by way of the question 'how does it stand with being?' (and not only with the essent as such)" (IM 41).

Yet, despite the clarity of the assertion about the theme of philosophy (being and not beings), a nonindifference to things is present, although in a distanced and oblique manner, precisely in Heidegger's understanding of ontology ever since his first major work, *Being and Time.* Certainly, as remarked both in *Being and Time* and in *An Introduction to Metaphysics,* ontology is not simply a matter of conducting some speculative reflection on some specific field of experience, as it is the case for example for logic, ethics, or even politics. As Heidegger writes, "when . . . we use the term ontology, we are not talking about some definite philosophical discipline standing in interconnection with the others. Here one does not have to measure up to the tasks of some discipline that has been presented beforehand; on the contrary, only in terms of the objective necessities of definite questions and the kind of treatment which 'the things themselves' require, can one develop such a discipline" (BT 49). That is, nothwistanding its thematic provision, ontology is the result of a specific attention paid to the "objective necessities" of the things themselves, which therefore become a fundamental orientating factor in the philosophical discourse. One could here apply to ontology what Heidegger will say years later *à propos* of phenomenology: "it is the possibility of thinking, . . . of corresponding to the claim of what is to be thought."[3] In its midst, there are things. It hardly need be remarked that, having accepted Nietzsche's lesson, when Heidegger mentions "the things themselves" he does not intend any Kantian being the reality of which is located beyond this phenomenal world. The things themselves Heidegger has in mind are the beings, the things of this world, "the things around us" (WT 7), since, consistently with his warning about concreteness, "being is always the being of an entity" (BT 29).

In accordance with the prescription of differential ontology, Heidegger does not turn the ontological project into an ontic endeavor. What is of interest to him in his nonindifference to things is not the entities, the things around, but more properly the being of such entities: the being of things which give themselves to experience. Things cannot be encountered, and related to appropriately, unless they are understood in their being. When inserted into the issue of the question of things, it seems then appropriate to say that "the task of ontology is to explain being itself and to make the being of entities stand out in full relief" (BT 49). The aversion from beings, "the leading back or re-duction of investigative vision from a naively apprehended being to being" (BPP 21), cannot do away with the consideration that the "apprehension of being . . . always turns, at first and necessarily, to some being; but then, *in a precise way, it is led away* from that being *and led back to its being*" (BPP 21). Things are not dismissed by Heidegger's project, although they are reinterpreted from the perspective of an understanding of being.

Accordingly, then, despite the step "forward positively toward being itself" (BPP 21) that the being of things may enable, the theme of things receives only a tangential development in Being and Time, which is instead devoted to the analytic of *Dasein*. The reasons for the lack of a more specific analysis of the way of being of things, and for the precedence assigned instead to *Dasein,* are offered by Heidegger himself in *Basic Problems of Phenomenology,* which takes up, but again without completing it, part of that ontological project which *Being and Time* had itself been unable to complete. There Heidegger writes, reasserting what had already been made clear in *Being and Time,* that "it lies in the circumstance that [*Dasein*] is so uniquely constituted in its very makeup that *the understanding of being* belongs to its existence, an understanding on the basis of which alone all comportment toward beings, toward extant things as well as toward its own self, becomes possible" (BPP 223). Consequently, "ontology has for its fundamental discipline the analytic of *Dasein*" (BPP 19), which therefore becomes "the foundation for all further inquiry, which includes the question of the being of beings and the being of the different regions of being" (BPP 224).[4] Such a foundational analysis, however, Heidegger repeats at several points, is only a "preparatory ontological investigation" (BPP 224). In its preparatory character, it does not aim at a dismissal of Heidegger's interest in the being of things, but at an "illumination of the meaning of being," which will serve "to establish the foundation for a radical ontology" (BPP 224). Such a radical ontology will supposedly have as one of its themes that of the way of being of those entities that are called things.

Unfortunately, after *Being and Time* and its continuation (although not in the initially planned form) in *Kant and the Problem of Metaphysics* and *The Basic Problems of Phenomenology,* the project of a radical ontology is never developed by Heidegger. He nevertheless will continue to ask the question of things, although from reoriented perspectives. However, already in his preparatory work Heidegger displays a fundamental, although unthematized realization, which is determinant in the (later) path Heidegger will follow with respect to an understanding of the ontological nature and signification of things. The question of things understood as the question of the being of things, he realizes, reaches further than one might initially and naively think if one were to conceive of the issue as the trivial question about one particular, specific, and isolated kind of entity. A whole cluster of ontological issues which need to be rethought surrounds the question of the being of things, and it is precisely such a question which opens up the horizon for new questions. To ask the question of things is inseparable, first of all, from asking the question of the meaning of being in general. Consequently, it requires a rethinking of the ontological role of that being which asks such a question (what in traditional ontology, operating through oppositional terms, is called the subject, what Heidegger will rather name *Dasein*). Things do not stand in ontological isolation; in connection with them, the entire horizon of philosophy as questioning is opened up. And yet, according to Heidegger, a distancing from things is required.

The oblique sensitivity to the question of things, which announces itself ever since Heidegger's early works, emerges not only in the issue of the delimitation of the theme—Heidegger states that "entities are in every case our preliminary, and our accompanying theme" (BT 95)—but also in the necessity of a specific method through which to carry out the ontological inquiry: the method of phenomenology, the maxim of which is, according to Husserl's formulation which Heidegger repeats, "to the things themselves!" (BT 50). The ontological project bespeaks faithfulness and loyalty to things.

Yet, in Heidegger the phenomenological maxim assumes a significance of its own.[5] Without entering the complex problematic of Heidegger's relation to phenomenology, or to his former teacher who such a phenomenological project initiated—that is, to Husserl—it will suffice to say that in Heidegger's reinterpretation of the phenomenological saying, the return "to the things themselves" assumes the features of a return "to the being of the things themselves"— that is, ontology and phenomenology are declined together. Heidegger's return, then, is not that of an unconditioned access to things as entities, but rather to their way of being, which alone will be able to disclose their nature as things. Within the provision of the ontological difference, the interrogation on things therefore should not ask: "*What* is a thing?," because the question of the "*what?*" would imply a reduction of things to pure objects of representation, to entities the nature of which has been flattened to their simply being present. Rather, the question to be asked will be, "*How* do things manifest themselves?," which subtracts things to the horizon of simple presence and locates them on a perspective of depth.

To ask the question of the *how?* of things means to ask the question of their coming to be into the light of truth, of their disclosedness. That is, to return to the being of things means to ask the question of their phenomenological manifestation, to understand them not as essences but rather as phenomena. As Heidegger remarks already in *Plato's Sophist,* a lecture course which dates back to the winter semester 1924/25, "the phenomenological way of consideration is distinguished by the determinate respect in which it posits the beings that show themselves and in which it pursues them. The primary respect is the question of the being of these beings" (S 6).

What such an understanding, sought through the method of phenomenology, entails, is explained by Heidegger in the introductory pages of *Being and Time.* The Greek word *phainomenon,* Heidegger writes, "signifies *that which shows itself in itself,* the manifest" (BT 51). Against Kant, and in agreement with Nietzsche, for Heidegger a phenomenon is all that there is; there is no noumenon behind it, no other reality which would give to the phenomenon its own significance and signification. That is, a phenomenon manifests itself by itself without the necessity of a supporting foundation. It is in their self-manifestation as things that the access to their being is opened up. Nevertheless, a phenomenon could not be reduced to an entity simply present, as ontotheological metaphysics has done, since the phenomenon is rather the *movement* of self-manifestation of the entity. This implies that the meaning of things can never be determined in a univocal, absolute, once-forever manner. On the contrary, it always needs to be revised according to the different modalities of the things' coming into manifestation, that is, into being. Since "an entity can show itself from itself in many ways, depending in each case on the kind of access we have to it" (BT 51), fluidity, flexibility, multiplicity are at the roots of Heidegger's understanding of the ontological nature of things. In other words, the thing as an entity (as *a* being) and its self-manifestation (as its being, or thinging) do not coincide in a single concept, so that the possibilities of self-manifestation of a thing always transcend the specific entity which is encountered from time to time. And yet, the specific entity that is encountered is all that there is, precisely in the way in which it is encountered. There is no deeper, truer, hidden reality beyond it.

The distinction between a thing and its self-manifestation, which is merely a varied formulation of the ontological difference, is preserved precisely by the method of phenomenology in the sense understood by Heidegger. "The expression 'phenomenology,'" he writes, "may be formulated in Greek as *legein ta phainomena,* where *legein* means *apophainesthai.* Thus 'phenomenology' means *aphophainesthai ta phainomena*—to let that which shows itself be seen from itself in the very way in which it shows itself. This is the formal meaning of that branch of research which calls itself 'phenomenology.' But here we are expressing nothing else than the maxim formulated above: 'To the things themselves!'" (BT 58). The attention to things declines itself under the form of an attention to the phenomena. Phenomenology is that kind of discourse that lets things become manifest as phenomena, in their being—that is, in their thinging—and not simply as a being or a thing; that lets what has remained hidden, buried-over, or disguised come into the light of its own self-manifestation—that is, into its own *aletheia.*

The theme of a return to the being of things is thus what orients the application of the phenomenological method to ontology, to the point that the two become inextricable: "*only as phenomenology, is ontology possible,*" Heidegger writes (BT 60). The question of the meaning of being is a question which can be addressed properly only through the method of a return to things as phenomena. One way or another, things as the being of things are reserved an unprecedented attention. To ask the question of being means to ask the question of the being of entities, and to ask the question of the being of entities a return to things as self-manifestation is required. "We must first bring forward the entities themselves if it is our aim that being should be laid bare; and we must do this in the right way. These entities must likewise show themselves with the kind of access which genuinely belongs to them" (BT 61). It is the very things which demand the rigor of the phenomenological discourse.

It is in deference to this demand that the notion of truth as *aletheia* is interpreted, already in the 1924/25 lecture course on the *Sophist*. As Heidegger writes, "truth means the same as compliance (*Sachlichkeit*), understood as a comportment of *Dasein* to the world and to itself in which beings are present in conformity with the way they are" (S 17). In this sense, objectivity has nothing to do with universal validity, but rather it has everything to do with *Dasein*'s mode of being in a way that does not distort beings. Perhaps that some ethical resonance might be heard in the Greek concept of truth as *aletheia*? Perhaps that *Dasein* needs to be responsive to things to be truthful? "Truth, unconcealedness, uncoveredness conforms rather to beings themselves and not to a determinate concept of scientificity," Heidegger warns (S 17). The suggestion directs toward an interpretation of conformity as correspondance, rather than epistemological *adaequatio intellectus ac rei*. The truth of phenomenology lies in its returning "to the things themselves."

7 ❖ Instrumental Modes of Disclosure

How do things manifest themselves within the horizon of Heidegger's work, which initially portrays itself as a phenomenological analysis?[1] Despite the obliqueness of the treatment of things in *Being and Time,* Heidegger recognizes the determinant role played by things in terms of the constitution of *Dasein.* In *The Basic Problems of Phenomenology,* Heidegger asserts that without things, *Dasein* cannot properly exist, since "it belongs to the nature of the *Dasein* to exist in such a way that it is always already with other beings" (BPP 157). *Dasein* "never finds itself otherwise than in the things themselves, and in fact in those things that daily surround it" (BPP 159), to the extent that "its own self is reflected to it from things" (BPP 159). Already at the beginning of *Being and Time,* Heidegger explains how every possible mode of *Dasein* is grounded a priori in a constitutive state of being called being-in-the-world.[2]

Despite the suggestion of multiplicity, being-in-the-world "stands for a *unitary* phenomenon" (BT 78), thus excluding the possibility of heterogeneity, exteriority, and more specifically dualism between *Dasein* and the world. The exclusion of a separation fulfills a double purpose. First, given the continuity that has been established between *Dasein* and the world, *Dasein* does not need to pursue a gnoseological conquest of the world, because "the perceiving of what is known is not a process of returning with one's booty to the 'cabinet' of consciousness after one has gone out and grasped it" (BT 89). Second, neither *Dasein* nor the world are to be conceived as substances, "like subject and object, or like I and thou" (BPP 297).[3] Rather, *Dasein* is an intentional being that becomes itself by its being directed to the world. Heidegger names the ontological situation of intimacy existence: *Dasein* is inside itself by being outside *in* the world, it exists in the world, it transcends itself toward the world, so that no abyss exists between inside and outside. In other words, *Dasein* is constitutionally open to the encounter with the world and the entities which manifest themselves within such a world. "Ontologically, 'world' is not a way of characterizing those entities which *Dasein* essentially is *not;* it is rather a characteristic of *Dasein* itself" (BT 92).

It is with reference to the world that the distinction between *Dasein* and things is established: world understood not ontically as the sum total of all beings present within the universe, but ontologically as the prethematic horizon of interpretation, "that which is already previously unveiled and from which we return to the beings with which we have to do and among which we dwell" (BPP 165). Whereas the world "belongs" to *Dasein*[4] in its essential characteristic of being-in-the-world, things do not have a world, but rather belong to a world, which they presuppose to be able to disclose themselves in their being. In this sense, things are rather, at most, intraworldly beings, beings which can be encountered only within-the-world.

And yet, intraworldliness is not a characteristic that belongs essentially and indiscriminately to all things. Things need a *Dasein* to become intraworldy—that is, to disclose themselves in the truth of their being—since "world is only, if, and as long as a *Dasein* exists" (BPP 170). Thus Heidegger observes that, although nature can be also when no *Dasein* exists, it does not have intraworldliness as its necessary way of being, and there is no necessity that it be uncovered. Intraworldliness belongs to nature "*not* as a determination of its being, but as a *possible* determination, and one that is necessary for the possibility of the uncoverability of nature" (BPP 169). That is, for things to be encountered they must become part of a world, they must come into contact with *Dasein* as being-in-the-world. The only truly intraworldly beings are in fact historical entities, Heidegger remarks; that is, "all the things that the human being, who is historically and exists historically in the strict and proper sense, creates, shapes, cultivates: all his culture and works" (BPP 169).

As the remark on truly intraworldly beings suggests, the sphere of the encounter with entities, which lets things be discovered in their intraworldliness, is that of *Dasein*'s *dealing* with, handling of them; that is, it is the sphere of practical knowledge.[5] Not acting randomly, but rather guided by a projective cognition (*Umsicht*), a form of knowledge directing its practical activity, *Dasein*'s virtue is not *episteme* or *sophia,* but *phronesis*—that is, a complication of theory and action.[6] The move to practicality establishes the primacy of contact, of involvement (*Besorgen,* as Heidegger names it), of touch as touching and being touched, meant not as technological manipulation, but as concerned handling.[7] Later characterized as care (*Sorge*), involvement can explicate itself in activities as varied as "having to do . . . producing . . . attending to . . . and looking after . . . making use . . . giving . . . up and letting . . . go, undertaking, accomplishing, evincing, interrogating, considering, determining . . ." but also "leaving undone, neglecting, renouncing, taking a rest" (BT 83). All these variations of touch are united by the fact that, against the scientific prescription of disinterestedness and objectivity, the original encounter with entities within-the-world is never disengaged. Although Heidegger is reluctant to admit a specifically ethical connotation in *Dasein*'s commitment to the world,[8] *Dasein* is always ontologically involved and turns to entities within the world out of the (dis)interest and (dis)passion it has for them.[9]

In the touch-immersion that is its being-in-the-world, *Dasein* touches what is commonly named (but Heidegger will in fact proceed to a proscription of this word) the *things* of the world, *die Dinge*: houses, trees, people, mountains (BT 91). Grounded in the modality of *Dasein*'s touch, grounded in the ways in which *Dasein* deals with them, Heidegger uncovers a variation in the way in which things "can be brought to the light" (BT 51), "in the distinctive way in which [they] can be encountered" (BT 54), in the way in which they manifest themselves as phenomena. Three (at least) are the ways in which things disclose themselves to *Dasein* in *Being and Time:* as *Zuhandene,* as *Vorhandene,* and as the meaningless entities that face *Dasein* in its ontological situation of *Angst.* In conformity with the phenomenological method which prescribes an attention to things themselves, in all three cases to understand things means to understand how they unveil themselves.

According to Heidegger, the manifestation of things as *Zuhandene* is the primordial ontological modality with which things disclose themselves to *Dasein* in its everydayness. It is of no relevance that such a way of being-in-the-world assumes the character of inauthenticity, because such a qualification does not entail a statement of value, but moreover because "*Dasein*'s everydayness is *not nothing,* but a positive phenomenal characteristic of this entity" (BT 69) and it makes up what *Dasein* "*proximally and for the most part*" is (BT 37). In its everyday existence, *Dasein* does not relate itself to things as to material objects, or as to objects of value (BT 96). Rather, it encounters things as "what gets used, what gets produced, and so forth" (BT 95). Not to acknowledge the original primordiality of this fact means to consign oneself to that history of concealment through which tradition has approached the meditation on things as such.

Appealing to the originary authority of the Greek language, Heidegger uncovers an appropriate term to describe the character of being a thing: *pragmata.* The word, used by the Greeks to denote what one would call, in everyday experience, things, refers to *praxis,* so that a thing becomes what "one has to do with in one's concernful dealings" (BT 96).[10] The roots for the primacy of touch are retraced within the original meaning of the word *pragmata,* which the Greeks have "left in obscurity" (BT 197).

Things, touching, concern are here restituted by Heidegger to their inextricable connectedness. Things do not disclose themselves primordially as abstract notions, stiffened by the metaphysical Western tradition into "substantiality, materiality, extendedness, side-by-side-ness, and so forth" (BT 96), but as what is tangible, affecting and affectible (BT 176), what is the intention of *Dasein*'s concern.[11]

As concernful dealing is Heidegger's translation of *praxis,* so is equipment, implement, gear (*das Zeug*) his translation of *pragmata.* A *pragma,* in fact, is qualified primarily by the *use* to which it can be put: a *pragma* is a *Zeug,*[12] and every *Zeug* is a *Zeug* to do something—that is, a thing which is "ready to hand." "The kind of Being which equipment possesses—in which it manifests itself in its own terms—we call 'readiness-to-hand'" (BT 98), that is, at hand, at manual disposition, manipulable.[13] This does not necessarily mean that all things are tools, instruments which *Dasein* effectively uses and exploits, but rather that they disclose themselves to *Dasein* as endowed with some form of significance for its own existence and tasks. *Dasein* is in the world by means of its projecting on it; therefore, things are encountered by it first of all as part of a project, that is, in a broad sense, as ready-to-hand.

In a much later essay, meditating on Greek words in their nearness to a more originary understanding of things, Heidegger explains how, within the functional whole within which equipment is situated, the notion of "use," which characterizes equipment, signifies, rather than an instrumentalist ontology, a letting equipment be what and how it is, a disclosure of something already there in the *Zeug*, and a remittance (*Bewandenlassen*) of each *Zeug* to its proper being, precisely that of *Zeughaftigkeit* (BT 117), in a response to the proper being of the thing. As Heidegger writes, "'using' does not mean the mere utilizing, using up, exploiting. Utilization is only the degenerate and debauched form of use. When we handle a thing, for example, our hand must fit itself to the thing. Use implies fitting response. . . . Authentic using first brings the thing used into its being and holds it therein. Thought in this way, use itself is the summons that something be admitted into its own being and that using not desist from it. Using is: admitting into being, preserving in being" (WCT 187). The necessity of a fitting response implies an attention devoted to things, and the announcement of the possibility of an ontological appeal with which things address *Dasein* in its encounter with them.

In its being-ready-to-hand—that is, in its being ready for use—a *Zeug*'s being reveals itself most adequately: a hammer is for hammering, as a pen is for writing. In other words, things as equipment are endowed with a specific functionality, which "is not a property adhering to the thing, and it is also not a relation which the thing has only on account of the extant presence of another entity" (BPP 164). In an Aristotelian manner, each *Zeug* is defined with reference to its telic function, which gives the *Zeug* its "in-itself," its destination, intentionality, purpose as an "immanent reference to that *for which* it is what it is" (BPP 163). But the *Zeug*'s teleology is not autotelic—hammering does not fulfill, or exhaust, the *telos* of the hammer. On the contrary, the telic structure accounts for the nonsolipsistic nature of the *Zeug*. Never alone, so that properly "there 'is' no such thing as *an* equipment" (BT 97), a *Zeug* is always inserted in a referential structure of equipmental assignments, in a sequence of means and ends where each end is a means for something else. Such a whole, within which equipment can exhibit itself as it is, in its functionality, is always "*pre*-understood" (BPP 164) as the *Umwelt,* the environment, the milieu in which *Dasein* as being-in-the-world is always already thrown.

The teleological structure of functionality of the *Zeug* allows Heidegger to assimilate in a same function not only tools, but also the works to whose production the tools are geared. "The shoe which is to be produced is for wearing; the clock is manufactured for telling the time. The work which we chiefly encounter in our concernful dealings . . . has a usability which belongs to it essentially" (BT 99). Although Heidegger's concern in *Being and Time* is primarily with artifacts, as the notion of *Zeug*, as well as the examples employed, suggests, natural beings are not absent from the range of entities *Dasein* encounters within the world (BT 92). Against any romanticizing, however, nature discloses itself in its necessary relation to equipment, in the referential totality of which it is always co-discovered. Nature can then be encountered in the form of natural products, which, themselves understood as *Zeug*, provide a direction to nature itself: "Hammer, tongs, and needle, refer in themselves to steel, iron, metal, mineral, wood, in that they consist of these" (BT 100). Or nature can be encountered as the environment in which *Dasein* as *Geworfenheit* exists. Again, the ecological conception of nature is disclosed with reference to and through its usability, so that the forest is always the wood usable for timber, the mountain a quarry of rock, the river is for producing water-power, the wind is "wind in the sails" (BT 100). Made public, such a usability refers also to the totality of *Daseins*, for which it exists as such. "A covered railway platform takes account of bad weather; an installation for public lighting takes account of the darkness, or rather of specific changes in the presence or absence of daylight—the 'position of the sun.' In a clock, account is taken of some definite constellation in the world-system" (BT 100–101).[14] An important innovation emerges in the self-manifestation of things as *Zeug*: things never reveal themselves in static isolation. Rather, they are always part of a complicated network of flexible relations to which they provide access through their own disclosure.

And yet, although or perhaps because in its everydayness *Dasein* is always lost (BPP 162) among things as *Zeug*, which thus reveal an arcane power of fascination capable of wrapping and absorbing *Dasein* in it, the "equipmental contexture of things" as they surround *Dasein*, the "unity of an equipmental whole" (BPP 163) which enables things to disclose themselves in their equipmental character remains completely unobtrusive and unthought to *Dasein*, that is, "it is not thematically apprehended for deliberate thinking about things" (BPP 163). This means that, although disclosing themselves as equipment to *Dasein*'s everyday handling of them in a manner which is "so self-evident, so much a matter of course that we are completely oblivious of it" (BPP 165), things resist thematization, withdraw themselves to thought and hold back, as if in an obstinate modesty and reserve which makes them impenetrable to thinking. In their equipmental being, things are invisible, unnoticeable, and unnoticed, taken for granted. And yet, they are there, disclosing themselves as instruments exactly when they are the least thought of as such.

The equipmental character of things is explicitly apprehended *via negativa* when a thing reveals its unusability, or is missing, or "stands in the way" of *Dasein*'s concern (BT 102–3). In these privative cases, what is missing is participation in the structure of referential assignments through which equipment can disclose itself as within-the-world. Equipment lets its equipmentality be thematically apprehended when it loses its functionality. In such an instance, the readiness-to-hand of the thing discloses itself as conspicuous, obtrusive, in its obstinacy (BT 102–3). Although the equipmental character is still there, "holding itself in" (BT 106) and waiting to be restored, what also glimmers in such situations of conspicuousness, obtrusiveness, and obstinacy of the equipment is a different modality of the self-manifestation of things—that of their presence-at-hand. "The presence-at-hand of entities is thrust to the fore by the possible breaks in that referential totality in which circumspection 'operates'" (BT 107).

The presence-at-hand of things is the horizon within which things disclose themselves as *Vorhandene*. Rather than being encountered, things stand in front as *Gegenstände* and *objecta* within a world which is itself simply present-at-hand. Things as *Vorhandene* are entities "which we come across and whose nature we can determine if we discover them in their own right by going through the entities proximally encountered" (BT 121)—that is, through the entities ready-at-hand. The modality of presence-at-hand, Heidegger observes, is ontologically derivative from and founded on the disclosure of things as equipment. In a privative sense, *Vorhandenheit* is in fact the way of disclosing themselves of all entities that have been subtracted from the structure of functionality. Such beings indeed are, but in an unfamiliar way, that is, in a way in which no commerce with them can be entertained, since "familiarity with beings lies *in dealing with them* appropriately" (BPP 301). Consequently, such entities simply confront *Dasein,* which confronts them back, without knowing what to do with them, and turning them instead into the object of its theoretical observation. "When concern holds back from any kind of producing, manipulating, and the like, it puts itself into what is now the sole remaining mode of being-in, the mode of just tarrying alongside. . . . This kind of being toward the world is one which lets us encounter entities within-the-world purely in the *way they look* (*eidos*). . . . In this kind of '*dwelling*' as holding-oneself back from any manipulation or utilization, the *perception* of the present-at-hand is consummated" (BT 88-89). Speculation, in all its forms, as the look of the mind and not necessarily as philosophical or scientific, is the primary mode of encountering entities which are present-at-hand, and which offer themselves to sight rather than to touch as to their sensory correlate.

Although *Dasein* is primarily in the world by means of its pragmatic activities, Heidegger notices how most things nevertheless disclose themselves to *Dasein* precisely in the mode of their presence-at-hand.[15] "It is only in the tiniest spheres of the beings with which we are acquainted that we are so well versed as to have at our command the specific way of dealing with equipment which uncovers this equipment as such. The entire range of intraworldly beings accessible to us at any time is not suitably accessible to us in an equally original way" (BPP 304). The self-manifestation of things as present-at-hand is certainly the way in which things are confronted at first, in the cases when *Dasein* is even prethematically unaware of their functionality, when it is at loss with respect to them (BPP 304). Such a modality is also the way in which nature discloses itself before being uncovered as intraworldly (BPP 169), when nature appears not as natural products, not as the environment, but simply as an extant, "as a being that we come up against, to which we are delivered over, which on its own part already always is. It is, even if we do not uncover it, without encountering it within our world" (BPP 169). The modality of the present-at-hand is thus the modality of things which are worldless.

Lacking a world—that is, a whole constituted as a structure of referentiality—things as present-at-hand are impoverished entities. What is lost in the disclosure of things as present-at-hand is the structure of intentionality that inextricably connects *Dasein* to the world and to the entities-within-the-world, what Heidegger has named the structure of existence or being-in-the-world. Things that appear as present-at-hand are therefore entities that have lost their connections, their web of relations and references. No longer a place of intersections, they are taken in isolation, from *Dasein* and from other things. With the fleeing of the relational structure, the richness of the threefold structure of the ecstatic temporality that discloses itself in the being of equipment also dissolves. What is left is the unidimensionality of the present, which becomes the only temporal dimension of the entities present-at-hand. They are their here and now, cementified in the staticity of an unchangeable, unmoveable appearance.

The modality of the presence-at-hand is what becomes the specific object of theoretical thematization, as it has happened in traditional metaphysics and in the positive sciences. Oblivious of the ontological difference, they concern themselves with beings rather than with the being of such beings. The context within which such disciplines move is dualistic: in their simple presence, things appear as objects cast in opposition to a subject, which represents them to itself by placing them in front of its speculative eyes, and by reducing them to the flatness of its own vision. They become thus things that simply are, opaque because without depths or facets, displaying on the platitude of their surface everything which can be exhibited, inserted in a context of enunciative explanations that makes them penetrable to thought, but meanwhile impoverished, numbed, stiffened. As Heidegger notices in a brief statement *à propos* of nature,[16] in a consideration of nature as simply presence-at-hand "the Nature which 'stirs and strives,' which assails and enthralls us as landscape, remains hidden. The botanist's plants are not the flowers of the hedgerow; the 'source' which the geographer establishes for a river is not the 'springhead in the dale'" (BT 100).[17] Entities that disclose themselves as present-at-hand become still-life objects, entities deprived of the dynamism and vitality coming from the possibility of multiple intersections of references.

The loss of interconnectedness displayed in the thematization of things has double effects, in that it discloses the reduction to presence-at-hand not only of things, understood as objects, but also of the subject which, as is the case for Descartes's *cogito,* cannot be sure of the existence of the world. Within such a horizon of presence, things are disclosed as objects of thematization, classification, categorization. Rather than a movement of self-manifestation, their being becomes what can be ascertained, delimited, fixed in the definition of a what, which is constituted as their essence: "substantiality, materiality, extendedness, side-by-side-ness, and so forth" (BT 96), as things have been described by traditional metaphysics. According to Heidegger's interpretation, traditional metaphysics is precisely a metaphysics of presence, which "tell[s] us what-is by conceptualizing the 'is-ness' of what-is" (WM 351), and which he will deconstruct in many of his following works.

The way of being of things as *Zuhandene,* as well as their derivative mode of disclosure as *Vorhandene,* come, however, to a halt when confronted with *Dasein*'s state-of-mind (*Befindlichkeit*) of anxiety. In their definiteness, entities within-the-world can cause fear, since "we are always *afraid* of this or that definite thing, which threatens us in this or that definite way" (WM 335). No entity within-the-world, however, can be the cause of anxiety, which, as an ontological *Stimmung,* is rather such in face of something that remains completely indefinite: it is the very condition of "being-in-the-world as thrown being-toward-death" (BT 395), which causes anxiety to mount. *Dasein* is anxious in face of and about itself. Yet, despite its self-reflectiveness, anxiety also discloses a peculiar way of being of the entities within-the-world: that of their complete insignificance and irrelevance, which "reveals the nullity of that with which one can concern oneself" (BT 393). In anxiety "the totality of involvments of the ready-to-hand and the present-at-hand discovered within the world, is, as such, of no consequence; it collapses into itself; the world has a character of completely lacking significance" (BT 231).

Faced with its own potentialities for being disclosed to it in its being-toward-death, *Dasein* realizes that the entities within-the-world, among which *Dasein* existed as lost in its everydayness, by which it was completely absorbed to the point of self-forgetfulness, and which constituted its horizon of familiarity, are nothing but a source of fragmentation and distraction from its own self. Entities do not disappear in their being present-at-hand; they are still there, they still surround *Dasein*, but the vanity of its concern with them, whether as present-at-hand or ready-to-hand, is revealed, since they do not "'say' anything any longer" (BT 393). They no longer have any involvement. They simply disclose themselves "in an empty mercilessness" (BT 393). This is the experience of nothingness, in which what-is in totality, things as a system of referential intersections withdraw, slip away. "There is nothing to hold on to" (WM 336).[18]

In this situation, in which things disclose themselves to *Dasein* as insignificant, as nothing, thus signifying the "impossibility of projecting oneself upon a potentiality-for-being which . . . is founded primarily upon one's objects of concern" (BT 393)—that is, the impossibility of being authentic while being lost among things—another possibility is however lit up: that of "an authentic potentiality-for-being" (BT 393), in which *Dasein*'s can-be is projected "by *Dasein* itself from its own most peculiar self, which nevertheless exists, just as it is, always as dealing with things" (BPP 289). This means that by renouncing their own implication in the structure of referentiality, by manifesting themselves as void of meaning and signification, things gain for themselves precisely what they have lost, and in a more authentic manner. They access the possibility of a disclosure according to the ecstatic temporality of being.

The nature of equipment can in fact be encountered only "if we have already *projected this entity upon functionality relation*" (BPP 293)—that is, only in light of a "letting-function" (BPP 293, BT 404). A proper letting-function, however, can happen only when conceived in terms of temporality, the ecstatic nature of which has been revealed precisely through *Dasein*'s being-toward-death, that is, through *Dasein*'s aversion from things. As Heidegger writes, "letting-function, that is, the understanding of the functionality which makes possible an equipmental use at all, is a retentive expectance, in which the equipment is enpresented as this specific equipment. In expectant-retentive enpresenting, the equipment comes into play" (BPP 292). In light of the temporal structure within which things can be disclosed, they are no longer occasion for distraction and fragmentation, but rather they become contingent possibilities for *Dasein*'s temporal being-in-the-world. The relinquishment of things is thus the return to things, which do not disappear from the ontological scene even in the moment of their uttermost irrelevance. As Heidegger remarks in the context of his meditation on Nothing, "the essence of Nothing as original nihilation lies in this: that it alone brings *Dasein* face to face with what-is as such" (WM 339).

What seems to characterize things in Heidegger's oblique meditation on them, what constitutes the difference between *Zuhandene, Vorhandene,* and the things' insignificance, is the presence or absence of a referential structure working as a totality on the background of which things can appear and disclose themselves in their being. "The *understanding of world* . . . is the presupposition for the experience of an intraworldly being" (BPP 175). That is, things disclose themselves as what they are within the horizon of a world, which becomes the mediation for their own disclosure. Heidegger does not grow weary of emphasizing how the world does not coincide with things, or with the totality of things, but rather with a horizon of signification within which things can find their proper location, meaning, and possibility of disclosure. Therefore, there is a sense in which things owe their own way of being, their "truth of being," precisely to the world. The world comes *before* the things within-the-world, although such a "before" does not imply a temporal, but an ontological connotation: the world is the a priori for the disclosure of things.

In addition, entities within-the-world (and their derivative disclosures as present-at-hand or insignificant entities) are such only insofar as there is someone who uses or can use them in their equipmentality; that is, things can disclose themselves as things only insofar as there is a *Dasein* for which equipment has its meaning, its functionality. *Dasein* is at the root of there being a world as a system of referential significations.[19] "World exists—that is, it is—only if *Dasein* exists, only if *Dasein* is there" (BPP 297). Heidegger goes on to say that "only if world is there, if *Dasein* exists as being-in-the-world, is there understanding of being, and only if this understanding exists are intraworldly beings unveiled as extant and handy" (BPP 297). It is certainly true that *Dasein* cannot be if not as being-in-the-world, if not as thrown. But the worldhood of the world is founded on *Dasein*, and not vice versa. This is why Heidegger can state that the world is "a characteristic of *Dasein* itself" (BT 92). In other words, *Dasein* as being-in-the-world constitutes the a priori transcendental ground for the possibility of disclosure of things as entities-within-the-world.[20]

The notion of transcendental here employed should be understood in the sense Heidegger himself gives to the term. Whereas in the traditional philosophical sense, the "transcendent is the being that lies beyond, the otherworldly being" (BPP 298), Heidegger follows "the pattern of the original meaning of the word" (BPP 298) and understands transcendence as "to step over; the *transcendens,* the transcendent, is *that which oversteps as such* and not that toward which I step over" (BPP 299). The overstepping, then, can properly belong only to *Dasein* in its mode of being as being-in-the-world—that is, as being out beyond itself with entities within-the-world and with-others, so that, as Heidegger claims, "the *epekeina* belongs to *Dasein*'s own most peculiar structure of being" (BPP 299).[21] *Dasein* can only understand itself "from a world" (BPP 300), which means that it constitutes the opening within which things within-the-world can disclose themselves in their peculiar mode of being. As Heidegger himself phrases it, "the possibility of understanding the being of intraworldly beings . . . is possible only on the basis of being-in-the-world" (BPP 298). This is exactly what is meant when saying that *Dasein* constitutes the a priori transcendental ground for the disclosure of the being of things: by letting them function, by understanding their significance within the referential structure, *Dasein* lets them come to their proper self-manifestation.

Dasein's transcendentalism, in its ontological significance, does not amount to an ontical consideration aimed at establishing the primacy of *Dasein* over the things within-the-world, as if *Dasein* were the teleological center of the world at the service of which all things had been made. Heidegger's denial of (a certain interpretation of) the biblical book of Genesis, leading to understanding the world in terms of "a purposive contexture" (BPP 295) with *Dasein* as its crown, could not be more clear or severe: "That all functional relations are grounded ontologically in a for-the-sake-of [by which *Dasein* understands itself] in no way decides whether, ontically, all beings are as beings for the sake of the human *Dasein*. The ontological rooting of the ontological structures of beings and of their possible intelligibility in for-the-sake-of-which is still extraneous to the ontical assertion that nature was created or exists for the purpose of the human *Dasein*" (BPP 295). As Heidegger will say in a different context in the later "Letter on Humanism," "man is not the lord of beings" (LH 221). All statements about the purposiveness of the actual world hide an ontic character, whereas *Dasein*'s transcendental function is ontological.

That "*Dasein* is the transcendent being" (BPP 300), whose transcendence, however, is "*founded* in its specific wholeness *on the original ecstatic-horizonal unity of temporality*" (BPP 302), does not introduce a renovation of a subjectivism which opposes a subject constructed as self-consciousness to an object understood as an entity out there cast against the subject (modern philosophy after Descartes). Even less does it reintroduce idealism as the extreme form of a one-sided subjectivism (the philosophies of Fichte, Schelling, Hegel). Heidegger recognizes that idealism is perhaps "not tenable in the form in which it has obtained up to now" (BPP 167). Yet, in the opposition between idealism and realism, Heidegger's sympathies would still side with idealism, first of all because he is unaware of "any infallible decision according to which idealism is false" (BPP 167), but moreover because "it is not an already settled matter whether idealism does not in the end pose the problems of philosophy more fundamentally, more radically than any realism ever can" (BPP 167).[22] This consideration does not equate *Dasein*, or Heidegger's existential analysis, with the position of an idealistic subjectivity, principally because *Dasein* is not a subject at all, at least not a subject understood in the traditional sense of an extant being endowed with self-consciousness as its essential property. The reason is that, whereas the subject-object relation depends on the mode of existence of a subject, and such a subject could "surely forego the relation to objects," *Dasein* could not exist if not as always already relating itself to, in interconnection with other beings. Intentionality, that is, the fact of relating-itself-to, "belongs to the existence of *Dasein*" (BPP 157). This antecedent "transposition" of *Dasein*, which Heidegger names more properly "transcendence" (BPP 162), is not an act by which "*Dasein* . . . 'transport[s]' itself to the things by leaping out of a presumably subjective sphere over into a sphere of objects" (BPP 161). Nor is the world "a piece of myself in the sense of some other thing present in me as in a thing and that I throw the world out of this subject-thing in order to catch hold of the other things with it" (BPP 168).[23] It is the very notions of an "inner" and an "outer" that are dissolved by Heidegger's understanding of the concept of intentionality, as he reformulates it in terms of *Dasein*'s basic unitary structure of being-in-the-world. Such notions in fact, together with the affined concepts of subject and object, obstruct the access to an ontological, rather than ontic, understanding of the modes of being of what are called the subject and the object, but which need not be called so, because the correlation holds true only in terms of itself. As Heidegger notices, an entity is an object only when objectified by a subject; but does an entity have to become an object? "Plainly not," is Heidegger's answer (BPP 156). Therefore, Heidegger reformulates the problem of *Dasein* and the world in different terms: "so far as the *Dasein* exists a world is cast-forth with the *Dasein*'s being. To exist means, among other things, to cast-forth a world, and in fact in such a way that with the thrownness of this projection, with the factical existence of a *Dasein*, extant entities are always already uncovered" BPP 168). *Dasein* has always already stepped out, beyond itself, is always in the thrownness of the projection. Therefore, *Dasein* "is never like a subjective inner sphere" (BPP 170). Idealism, as well as subject-object dualism, is thus averted.

Yet, although the orientation toward the subject is by Heidegger corrected and deconstructed in its traditional formulation, which thinks of it as of a being, is such a tendency truly dismissed and removed? "Philosophy must perhaps start from the 'subject' and return to the 'subject' in its ultimate questions" (BPP 155). Is it not precisely this tendency that somehow vitiates the disclosure of things in Heidegger's early works? If *arche* "names that from which something proceeds,"[24] things are not the *archai* of their own self-manifestation—they do not disclose themselves in and by themselves. Rather, they disclose themselves within-the-world for *Dasein*. As Heidegger notices in his meditation on Aristotle's considerations on *phronesis*, "*Dasein* is the *arche* of the deliberation of *phronesis*" (S 35). The direction of the movement of understanding does not originate from things, as if in an unconditional because unconditioned self-giving gift. Rather, it goes from an although thrown, nevertheless projected *Dasein* toward the way in which things are: as ready-to-hand, present-at-hand, or insignificant.[25] It is *Dasein*, and not the things, which constitutes the "clearing" within which entities are discovered in their truth out of their concealedness (*lethe*). In this sense, the much advocated "return to things" remains only partially a return *to things* as such. "The thingness must be something unconditioned" (WT 9), Heidegger claims. What Heidegger thematizes in *Being and Time* and related works, however, is that *Dasein* is at the origin of the way of being of things. That is, the thingness of things is not truly unconditioned, as the inquiry into the questioning of things had promised. Once again, the question of things needs to be asked.

8 ❖ Artistic Modes of Disclosure

The question "What is a thing?" is asked again by Heidegger in "The Origin of the Work of Art," a lecture dating to the same years in which the antiquity of the very question was acknowledged. Yet again, in the lecture on art Heidegger approaches the question of "What in truth is a thing, so far as it is a thing?" (OWA 20) only tangentially, because of his declared preoccupation with the being of the work of art. Even more radically, Heidegger restricts the legitimacy of a separate inquiry about things when claiming that "the question about the thing's thingly character can be brought into the right course by way of a knowledge of the work's work-character" (OWA 69). As a result, the question of what is a thing is not positively answered in the course of the lecture. Despite its limitations, Heidegger's meditation on art proves itself precious in terms of an articulation of the being of things in their distinction from other types of entities. Moreover, the lecture is suggestive of a novel attitude required from human beings to let things be, that is, to preserve the ontological reality of what has concerned philosophy in its questioning since its origin.[1]

The question of "What is a thing?," Heidegger reminds the reader at the beginning of the lecture, aims at knowing "the thing-being (thingness) of the thing. The point is to discover the thingly character of the thing" (OWA 20). Analogously to art and artworks (OWA 18), and contrary to what traditional interpretations have believed, thing-being is not a quality that some entities (which we call things) possess as a consequence of their being things.

Rather, it is a mode of being in a certain way that eventuates things. This mode of being in a certain way is exactly thing-being, or even better, thinging, so that it is by thinging that an entity is a thing. In other words, the qualification of certain entities as things is an a posteriori classification, consequent to the specific mode of being of the entities under inquiry. The goal is thus that of a determination of the event of thinging. Thing-being is not deducible from things, since in the absence of thing-being we do not know which entities are to be considered things. And yet any consideration of things and their being can only originate from the everyday understanding of things, and from "the sphere to which all entities belong which we have long called by the name of things" (OWA 20). In other words, the discussion must start *in media re,* caught in a circle which is "neither a makeshift nor a defect. To enter upon this path is the strength of thought, to continue on it is the feast of thought" (OWA 18). A festive path guides the adventure into the meditation on things.

In *Being and Time*, all things, that is, all non-*Dasein* entities, were assimilated as *Zeug* or as modalities thereof, and even natural entities were equipment-to-be. In "The Origin of the Work of Art," the discourse on things gains articulation and complexity, becoming less totalizing than previously announced. In a very broad sense, all beings can be considered as things: stones in the road, clods in the field, jugs, wells, clouds in the sky, leaves in the breeze, hawks over the road, as well as the whole of the world, God, death, and judgment (OWA 20–21). As remarked in *Die Frage nach dem Ding* (WT 6), "the word 'thing' here designates whatever is not simply nothing" (OWA 21). The excessive generality of this definition, however, calls for articulation, since it is only hesitatingly that the deer in the forest clearing, the beetle in the grass, the blade of grass can be called "things." The same hesitation holds true for the hammer, the shoe, the ax, the clog, which although commonly called "things" are rather things of use, or what *Being and Time* has taught its reader to recognize as equipment, *Zeug*. The denomination "things," Heidegger warns, should be properly reserved only to the lifeless beings of nature—a stone, a clod of earth, a piece of wood (OWA 21)—which constitute "mere" things, that is, "pure things," but also "that which is only a thing, in an almost pejorative sense" (OWA 22). It is with reference to mere things that the thing-being of things is more likely to be disclosed, Heidegger claims. A tripartition is suggested: there are mere things, equipment (*Zeug*), and works (of art). Mere things attain an ontological status distinct from that of *Zeug* and works, whereas animals and animate beings, which might be considered things, but only in a generic sense, are intentionally left unthematized in the discussion of the thing-being of things (they will be retrieved into the discourse later because of the disclosive power of art).[2]

Within the tripartition, the thing-being of the thing contains more than the spoliation of qualities belonging to entities the thing is *not* (OWA 39). In other words, thing-being is not a privative, derivative concept, whose nature is affirmed through lack or negation, in accordance to an Augustinian ontological tradition of (Neo)platonic inheritance. The tripartition does not establish a hierarchy of perfections arranged as if in a progressive hypostatization of being. Description by deficiency has marked the traditional interpretations of the nature of things, which "attack the thing's thingly character" (OWA 69) by reducing the thing to the bearer of traits, to the unity of a manifold of sensations, or to formed matter (OWA 22–30). All these modes of interpretation, and particularly the predominant view, guided by the matter-form distinction, are for Heidegger totalizations electing equipment as the paradigm whose essential constitution is subsequently extended to things and works in the same way as it is retraced in the piece of equipment itself. The result is the occlusion of the way toward "the thingly character of the thing as well as toward the equipmental character of equipment, and all the more toward the workly character of the work" (OWA 31). Heidegger's concern with the obstruction such a procedure causes in terms of an understanding of the workly character of the work indirectly implies the vindication for things of an autarchic way of being, so that the thing-being of things makes an autonomous and separate claim to existence.

Yet, Heidegger seems to introduce a discrepancy between ontological multiplicity and hermeneutic strategy. Despite the uniqueness of its way of being, thing-being cannot be understood per se, he claims. It can only be retrieved at the end of a questioning that moves from entities different from things (*Zeug*, art works, . . .) and only later discloses the thing-being in them. Such a hermeneutic procedure is legitimized by the fact that, as Heidegger recalls, "even the much vaunted aesthetic experience cannot get around the thingly aspect of art work. There is something stony in a work of architecture, wooden in a carving, colored in a painting, spoken in a linguistic work, sonorous in a musical composition. The thingly element is so irremovably present in the art work that we are compelled to rather say conversely that the architectural work is in stone, the carving is in wood, the painting in color, the linguistic work in speech, the musical composition in sound" (OWA 19). Although hermeneutically plausible, the retrieval of things by a progressive reduction to their thing-being runs the risk, unaccounted for by Heidegger, of the oblivion of their very being. By considering a *Zeug* as *Zeug*, or a work of art as a work of art, the thing-being that lies at their core may be left unthematized, as the progression of discourse in both *Being and Time* and "The Origin of the Work of Art" exhibits.

The key to circumvent the obfuscation of the thing-being of things that traditional interpretations have brought about is to avoid assaulting the thing with the superimposition of essential characters belonging to other entities, and rather "leave the thing to rest in its own self, for instance, in its thing-being. . . . We ought to turn toward the being, think about it in regard to its being, but by means of this thinking at the same time let it rest upon itself in its very own essence" (OWA 31). Out of loyalty to Heidegger's warning, it becomes mandatory to twist Heidegger's hermeneutic strategy in "The Origin of the Work of Art" toward a different focus of discourse, and bring forth a discussion of the thing-being of things as distinct from the entities in which it can be retrieved. Ultimately, it becomes necessary to exert a hermeneutical deflection of Heidegger's meditation, refocusing it not on art and artworks, but on things and their being.

Even so, however, to let the being of things rest upon itself is problematic, because "where there is no language, as in the being of stone, plant, and animal, there is also no openness of beings" (OWA 73). In the absence of language, thinking has no direct access to an immediate understanding and disclosure of the thing-being of things. Read negatively, the inaccessibility amounts to a lack in the things' constitution. Read positively, however—that is, outside the economy of lack that constitutes Western metaphysics as need, not as desire (TI 62)—this difficulty discloses the resistance of things to theoretical intrusions and penetrations: things evade thought. Despite all categorizations, they remain stranger, alien, other to the activity of thinking. Impenetrability, which is not equivalent to the irrationality of matter, since there is nothing irrational in the thing's self-refusal and self-containment, is the closure of the thing upon itself, which arises from the thing's stubborn, almost virginal, unpretentiousness and reticence. The thing closes itself to thought out of modesty, Heidegger claims. To try to penetrate this unsurmountable character by bringing it into the Open amounts to a profanation of the thing-being of the thing, which is not let to rest upon its own being. Consequently, to avoid the violation "we should not force our way to its thingly character" (OWA 32). The refusal of disclosure is recognized by Heidegger as part of the being of the thing, to the point that the being of the thing is defined by such a withdrawal. Heidegger refers to it as to the "earthy character" of the thing. He states that to understand the thing-being of the thing one must "aim at the thing's belonging to the earth" (OWA 69).[3]

As explicated in the context of Heidegger's description

of a Greek temple, the earth is not simply the raw material of which objects are made. Rather, as the ground "on which and in which man bases his dwelling . . . whence the arising brings back and shelters everything that arises without violation" (OWA 42), the earth retains a foundational character. It belongs to the dimension of concealing (*lethe*) that is at the basis of unconcealment. The earth appears as a protective shelter, as a nonhistorical ground that tends to de-historicize the world with which it is at strife.[4] In its belonging to the earth, the thing retains the presence of a hard, dark, solid core burdening its being, impenetrable to the clarity of explication and elucidation. The association of things with withdrawal and concealment implicates that even in the event of their exposure, something remains undisclosed in the things, other than the occurred disclosure. To be a thing means to manifest an alterity which, although impersonal, in its distinction from pure opacity and obscurity refuses itself to possession and penetration by any discursive analysis. It is precisely this reticence that renders the definition of things so problematic.

Self-concealing, the earth is not thereby uniform, homogeneous, and undifferentiated. Conversely, its concealment can assume an "inexhaustible variety of simple modes and shapes" (OWA 47). Since the earth contains within itself the possibility of differentiation, to recognize, as Heidegger does, an earthy character at the core of things does not prejudicate their differing despite the unity of the thing-being that gathers them. The things' belonging to the earth does not totalize things in the undifferentiation of their self-concealment, as if the earthy character were to make the multiplicity of things disappear.

Moreover, although things belong to the earth because, like the earth, they are self-secluded, they are not exhausted in a complete coincidence with the earth. In their resting upon themselves, unlike the earth they do not need to engage in a strife with the world to realize their being. Their self-concealing character is thus ineradicable and absolute. The implication, not carried forth by Heidegger, seems to be that things are such even before their insertion in a world which, by historicizing them, discloses them to the possibility of thematic discourse. In other words, things subsist as de-historicized and de-worlded—which may not amount, however, to their being void of any historical traces, as Heidegger's analysis of a pair of shoes will reveal. In the stubborness of their withdrawal into themselves, things provide the solidity and consistency of the foundation, which traditional philosophy has equated to materiality, thus translating the alterity of things into an (ir)rational concept.

Because of his focusing on art, but also because of the self-refusal of things, ultimately the thing-being of things is not exposed by Heidegger in the course of the lecture. Yet, since all entities retain a thingly character, which legitimizes our generic denomination as "things" of everything that is not nothing (although not everything is a "mere" thing, and some entities, for example a stone, have more "mere thingness" than others, for example a thing of use), it is possible to approach the thing-being of things not in "mere things," but in pieces of equipment, despite the fact that the purity of their thing-being has been lost in favor of their usability. To this purpose, Heidegger chooses a pair of shoes, and offers a suggestive description of what is preserved and guarded in the apparent innocence of their being worn. "From the dark opening of the worn insides of the shoes, the toilsome tread of the worker stares forth. In the stiffly rugged heaviness of the shoes there is the accumulated tenacity of her slow trudge through the far-spreading and even uniform furrows of the field swept by a raw wind. On the leather lie the dampness and richness of the soil. Under the soles slides the loneliness of the field-path as evening falls. In the shoes vibrates the silent call of the earth, its quiet gift of the ripening grain and its unexplained self-refusal in the fallow desolation of the wintry field. This equipment is pervaded by uncomplaining worry as to the certainty of bread, the wordless joy of having once more withstood want, the trembling before the impending childbed and shivering at the surrounding menace of death" (OWA 33–34).

Heidegger's aristocratic intellectualism impedes that the attitude of the peasant woman toward the shoes she wears be recognized as sufficient to accomplish a disclosure of the thing-being of things and of the mystery of the earth that calls from the depth of their thing-being. The lack of disclosure is attributable to two factors. First, as the earth to which it belongs, the thingly character of the equipment refuses itself to the light of discourse, of the clearing, of the Open. Second, the peasant who wears the shoes is not thematically aware of the earthy character of her equipment, since her being is totally absorbed in the use of her shoes. Since her attitude is athematic—that is, she does not *know* about the earth—not only there is not, but there cannot even be any *real* coming forth of the earth into the Open. To come into the Open means to be part of a world. But "a stone is worldless. Plant and animals likewise have no world" (OWA 45). In their worldlessness, things do not disclose their thing-being to those who simply use them.

The consequence Heidegger derives is that the shoes, like the stone, and plants, and animals, need to be assigned to their world. *Being and Time* had taught that this assignation happens through *Dasein* as the *Worum-willen* directing the usage of the *Zeug*. Now Heidegger asserts that that assignation is not enough, because the peasant lacks the proper language (poetic language, *Dichtung*) by which the institution of a world can happen. In the peasant's attitude, a variation of *Dasein*'s instumental attitude in *Being and Time*, the thing-being of the thing goes unnoticed. Heidegger is willing to recognize that the woman's is not a simple, unconscious wearing of the shoes. "When she takes off her shoes late in the evening, in deep but healthy fatigue, and reaches out for them again in the still dim dawn, or passes them by on the day of rest, she knows all this without noticing or reflecting" (OWA 34). Like an animal or an angel, the peasant woman senses the earth without the circular movement of knowledge leading to self-affirmation and self-recognition in the object of one's cognition. Heidegger names the unreflective awareness of the peasant woman *Verlässlichkeit,* reliability, which comes to constitute the equipmentality of the utensil. Through reliability on her shoes the earth is disclosed to the peasant woman, and thus is made part of her world.

Yet, Heidegger insists, all this happens athematically, therefore it cannot be revelatory. To achieve a relation with things that lets them be in their essence, a thematic suspension of the usability of equipment is required, which also implies that the analysis of equipmentality presented in *Being and Time* necessitates a revision. The thematic suspension of instrumentality, necessary to access the thing-being of the thing, yet unaccomplished and unaccomplishable by the peasant woman, is for Heidegger achieved in the work of art.

Through the work of art, the earth, and with it the thing-being of things, is brought forth to thematic exposure. We learn what a pair of shoes is, and what is intrinsic to it, "not by a description and explanation of a pair of shoes actually present; not by a report about the process of making shoes; and also not by the observation of the actual use of shoes occurring here and there; but only by bringing ourselves before Van Gogh's painting. . . . The art work lets us know what shoes are in truth" (OWA 35). The work of art does more than lead to a better understanding of what the shoes are. More fundamentally, it corresponds to a happening of the truth, so that in the work of art disclosure of being occurs—"some particular being, a pair of peasant shoes, comes in the work to stand in the light of its being" (OWA 36). The work of art thus substitutes for *Dasein,* thanks to whose constitution as being-in-the-world, in *Being and Time,* the disclosure occurred.[5]

The "re-production" of the peasant's shoes in Van Gogh's painting, and not the things themselves (the concrete shoes), lets the truth of their being emerge, and with it their thingly character. In the "re-production," which for Heidegger is not simply a *mimesis* of the real shoes (it is the real shoes that are, rather, a copy after a certain pattern of production), the shoes let their being be seen: not as *Vorhandenheit*, as objects in front of us, and not even as *Zuhandenheit*, as *Being and Time* had taught (which is now considered to be the residual of the *Zeug*'s essence), but rather as the novel modality of *Verlässlichkeit*. The artwork displays such a *Verlässlichkeit* better than the shoes themselves could do, and in *Verlässlichkeit* the thingly character of things emerges, too.

If read in relation to things, Heidegger's claim is that, among all other possible disclosive activities, in its being an event in which the truth happens, art preserves the earth best, and therefore is the most adequate to let the thing-being of things be. Thus, he offers a description of how, in a work of art such as a Greek temple, materiality, which can be uncorrectly and yet broadly equated with thingness, is not used but celebrated. When celebration stops—that is, when the loss of the earthy character occurs—the work thus produced is no longer a work of art, but an object of display for a museum. Analogously, Heidegger shows how Van Gogh's painting of the shoes lets the earthy character of the shoes emerge. The description of art as a disclosive event raises a range of questions, the answer to which determines not only the destiny of things, but also of philosophy. Does Heidegger's claim imply that to let things be in their alterity an artistic attitude toward the world is required? Paraphrasing Hölderlin, should human beings artistically dwell in the world to preserve the thing-being of things?[6] Is the artistic approach the best to address not only the ecological concerns preoccupying today's society, but also a philosophy that wants to remain faithful to the earth, and respectful of the things' alterity? Should philosophy turn into an artistic meditation?

The move to artistic disclosure is certainly beneficial to the thing-being of things, if compared to the earlier instrumental account provided in *Being and Time*. First, a nontotalized, articulate, differentiated ontological constitution pointing in the direction of multiplicity and differing is recognized to things. Furthermore, a dark, impenetrable, impermeable resistence is acknowledged at the core of things to resist as other, unconquerable to thought and approachable athematically through *Verlässlichkeit*, thematically through art itself. The thematic disclosure of the earthy character of things performed by art, in its having to do with the way in which materials are employed, does not penetrate and violate, but discloses. In its activity of exposure, the art work does not use the matter from which it is made. Rather, it celebrates such a matter, so that its function is gratuitous and atelic, as manifested by the temple resting upon itself and by the disclosure the temple brings forth. In the usefulness of a tool, the material of which the tool is made disappears in the uses to which it is to be put. In the artwork, however, material is allowed to come forth into the Open of the work's world without its being denied or sublimated for the sake of a higher purpose. The artwork sets forth the material (the thing-being) out of which it is made. In the temple, this setting forth is a setting itself back in the massiveness and heaviness of the stone. The material, exposed and celebrated but not penetrated by the artwork, constitutes the resistance of the earth, its self-secludedness, which is thus preserved in the gratuity of the celebration. At the core of the disclosive activity of the artwork there thus remains a dark core that resists the clarity of thought and weakens the disclosive power of art as if it were undermined from within. It is precisely this dark core of things, inaccessible to art, which will call for a new arising of the question of things.

More fundamentally, though, what is abandoned through artistic disclosure is *Dasein*'s instrumental attitude. As Heidegger maintains, the performance of artistic activity, rather than an act of genial creation on the side of *Dasein*, resembles *physis*. Art abstains from turning things into objects of display, and the world into a museum, which one would then contemplate at aweful and respectful distance. Artistic activity concerns the modes of production, the ways in which production is brought forth. Works of art share with equipment the fact of having been made, and with mere things the fact of resting completely upon themselves, of having arisen by themselves, and of being constrained by nothing. In other words, works of art, although humanly made, are self-sufficient. Their self-sufficiency erases the presence of the artist in them, in order for the work to be released to its pure self-subsistence. "It is precisely in great art . . . that the artist remains inconsequential as compared with the work, almost like a passageway that destroys itself in the creative process for the work to emerge" (OWA 40), Heidegger writes.

The self-denial of the artist represents the annihilation of the Nietzschean will to power, which, in a residual way, somehow still inspires *Dasein* in *Being and Time,* and the overcoming of the metaphysics of the artist prefiguring such a will. Heidegger is certainly ready to admit that createdness constitutes a main character of the work of art, to the extent that the work of art is distinguished by all other products precisely in virtue of its being created (OWA 65). But a qualification must be made with respect to the creator. What properly creates is not the artist, not even as a variation of *Dasein*, but art. Art is the origin, both of the work of art and of the artist. Art is "the creative preserving of truth in the work. *Art then is the becoming and happening of truth*" (OWA 71). That is, a releasement to being is accomplished by the artist in his or her producing. Producing becomes a safeguarding of what comes forth, whereas the artist turns into a preserver. What is preserved is the unconstrained arising, the mystery. In this sense art is an imitation of *physis,* not in the trivial sense of its being a copy, a mimetic reproduction of an already existing given, or of an essence. Art resembles *physis* in the sense of being an unfolding of the truth. Art (not the artist) brings to thematic knowledge the athematic sensing of the peasant woman. Yet, in its corresponding to *physis,* this knowledge does not assault and violate, it rather preserves. What discloses things as such, thus, is not a variation of *Dasein*'s mode of existing; it is art itself.

Yet, despite all the advantages that the artistic attitude brings with itself as opposed to the instrumental environment characterizing *Being and Time*, art is not completely innocent in its exposure of the thingly character of things. Its revelatory power retains the characters of a transcendental performance that annihilates the unconditionedness of things constituting their thing-being (WT 8). The annihilation is best revealed through the consideration of a nonrepresentational artistic work (a Greek temple), and unequivocally emerges in another work written by Heidegger in the same period of the lecture on art—*An Introduction to Metaphysics*. There, Heidegger writes that "it is through the work of art as essent being that everything else that appears and is to be found is first confirmed and made accessible, explicable, and understandable as being or not being" (IM 159). Art retains a foundational character.

At a naive consideration, the Greek temple does nothing but stands.[7] Nevertheless, in this apparently innocuous erectness it "first gives to things their look and to men their outlook on themselves" (OWA 43). The temple inserts things into their world in the sense that it lets the gods be present, and lets human beings relate themselves to the holiness of the god, so that it "fits together and at the same time gathers around itself the unity of those paths and relations in which birth and death, disaster and blessing, victory and disgrace, endurance and decline acquire the slope of destiny for human being" (OWA 42). As a work of art, the temple acts as a transcendental gatherer that brings together the sacred and the profane in the horizon of a world, in a relatedness that involves things as well as human beings. It is only within such relatedness, brought about by the work of art, that not only the thing-being of things, but also the very things are allowed to emerge as things. As Heidegger writes, "standing there, the building rests on the rocky ground. This resting of the work draws up out of the rock the obscurity of that rock's bulky yet spontaneous support. Standing there, the building holds its ground against the storm raging above it and so first makes the storm itself manifest in its violence. The luster and gleam of the stone, though itself apparently glowing only by the grace of the sun, yet first brings to radiance the light of the day, the breadth of the sky, the darkness of the night. The temple's firm towering makes visible the invisible space of air. The steadfastness of the work contrasts with the surge of the roof, and its own repose brings out the raging of the sea. Tree and grass, eagle and bull, snake and cricket first enter into their distinctive shapes and thus come to appear as what they are" (OWA 42). All things, mere things, natural things, animals, together with their thingly character are rendered possible in their own being and gathered into a world through the celebration performed by the work of art, which gives things their location, and only thus lets their thing-being come forth and shine in a world. In a denial of things' autarchy, art becomes the condition for things' appearing as things.

Yet, if the thing-being of things is to be something *un*conditioned, the foundational unveiling accomplished by art cannot be legitimately disclosive of such thing-being without violating its unconditional character. Nor is the conditionness accomplished through artistic foundationalism weakened by the historical—that is, de-absolutized—character of art, which Heidegger emphasizes. Rather, transcendental foundationalism is infinitely multiplied, since every time art historicizes itself, in its archaic character it sets things into a new world. Although nuanced by positive accomplishments in terms of offering things ontological articulation, the transcendentalism underlying *Being and Time* is not overcome in Heidegger's meditation on art, although it assumes a different declination. It is made artistic, and historicized through the epochality of the work of art.

The issue to be addressed, which may bring toward an overcoming of Heidegger's thought at least as manifested at this stage of his philosophical development, is whether the artistic attitude Heidegger suggests, in its although weakened transcendental tendency, is altogether adequate to enact the preservation of things and their thing-being that Heidegger wishes to accomplish, and which traditional philosophy has trespassed and violated. Were preservation possible, transcendentalism might be forlorn. Unfortunately, several objections can be moved to the transition to art suggested by Heidegger.

First of all, Heidegger asserts that it is only *great* art that is capable of bringing forth a happening of the truth. But things are encountered in the context of everyday concerns. Therefore, they require a preservation which must be enacted on an everyday basis. Either everyone can transform him or herself into a great artist in the performance of his or her everyday activities, or some essential part of the thing-being of things will be irreversibly lost in the process of everyday concern with things. Since, according to the description offered in *Being and Time*, *Dasein* is first and foremost lost in the everydayness of the they-selves, the conclusion seems to be that a preservation of the thing-being of things is precluded to most human beings.

Yet, some more substantial considerations, which move beyond the realm of ontic objections, are in order. According to Heidegger, art corresponds to the essence of *physis,* imitates *physis,* not in the sense of being a reproduction of natural objects, but in the sense of attuning itself to the self-disclosing character of *physis.* However, in his reflection on "The Origin of the Work of Art," Heidegger states clearly how the artistic production is an institution, not only of the truth, but also of things. The most evident examplification is, once again, the Greek temple. According to Heidegger's reading of the function performed by the Greek temple as a work of art, things are nothing outside of their being positioned through the work of art itself. In this institution of things lies the violation that art performs to the detriment of the thing-being of things. Art discloses thematically what, according to its inherent nature, intends to remain hidden. The violence lies not so much in the disclosure of this reticent aspect, since the reader has been told how the notion of earth is meaningful only in its relation to the world, with which it entertains an agonic relationship—the veiling needs to be unveiled in its veiling, and that is what art accomplishes. Rather, the violence lies in the fact that the disclosure originates not from within the thing itself, in its earthy, dark, reticent, obscure depth, but from outside the thing, from art. Shoes are not artistic themselves, they need to be made such. The *arche* of their manifestation is outside themselves.

According to Heidegger's interpretation, although part of the earth, things do not have a location of their own. It is art, and, Heidegger insists, only great art which gives things their location, their perspective, their horizon within the world—their home. In other words, it is not only that the art work renders the earth visible. More fundamentally, it directs the earth not from the earth, as *physis* supposedly does, but from art itself. It is the art work that instigates and enacts that strife between earth and world which, according to the description of the earth, should be an urge of the earth itself, as well as of the world. In this sense, although art may strive to correspond to *physis,*it remains external to things, and in so doing it discloses its affinity with the (although desubjectivized) transcendentalism that in *Being and Time* had *Dasein* at its core.

That the potential for violation is inherent in the artistic activity had been understood clearly by the Greeks, which used a same word, *techne,* to express both art and that kind of knowledge which will later give birth to technology and its aberrations.[8] Art is not the self-disclosure of things; rather, it is an external act of disclosing. As a mode of bringing-forth that remains external to the things it institutes, art retains a violating character that cannot guarantee, and therefore safeguard the thing-being of things. The work of art sets the earth and the world in a relation. But this relation should originate from what is already earth—namely, from the thing-being of things. The recourse to art seems to be an unnecessary superimposition in which art acts as a mediator between things and the disclosure of their thing-being. As Levinas has taught his readers, though, like all mediations such an interference endangers the risk of several violations. Among them, misunderstanding, neglect, abuse, betrayal of the thing-being of things.

Contrary to Heidegger's claims in "The Origin of the Work of Art," but in accordance with the future line of development of his meditation on things, a more respectful relation with things, dictated from the very thing-being of things, seems to take place not in Van Gogh's artistic painting of the shoes, but rather in the attitude of the peasant woman—not in the usability to which she submits her shoes, but in her depending on the shoes' reliability. Despite Heidegger's insistance on art, the artist, and especially the poet throughout his entire philosophical meditation,[9] a hidden suggestion resonates in "The Origin of the Work of Art": that the peasant's attitude, and not Van Gogh's painting or the Greek temple as pieces of art, may be close to the thing-being of things, respectful and preservative of their earthy character. According to such resonance, which remains feeble and just whispered, what characterizes the peasant's relation to her shoes is her attitude of *Verlässlichkeit*, which belongs to her not as a demand, but rather as a response to the shoes's inspiration of such an attitude. The peasant relies on her shoes because *they* are reliable. In her reliance on them, she lets herself and her life be ordered and directed by the shoes, on which her life, her death, her worries and concerns, her joys rest. Rather than instituting the shoes as part of her world, she entrusts her world to those shoes in whose earthy essence her dreams, hopes, and aspirations—her being—are guarded.

Certainly, there is no epistemological thematization of reliability in the peasant. And certainly, reliability is forlorn in the usability to which the shoes are subjected. But usability is consequential to reliability as to a more originary character. In other words, it is possible that mere usability of the kind experienced in *Being and Time* is not to take over, that reliability is to be maintained. Were one to consider preethical this relation with things in which reliability is maintained, the suggestion would then be that the ethical relation, and not the artistic one, is the proper approach to maintain and protect the thing-being of things. As for the lack of thematic knowledge, the peasant does not need to thematize things and their thing-being, because, by relying on her shoes, she is already part of them, thus dissolving the distance that thematic knowledge maintains, but that also gives rise to the opposition between theory and practice, and the aberrations thereby implied (for example, the presence-at-hand to which artworks can be reduced). On the other hand, by not thematizing her shoes the peasant lets their thing-being abide in its earthy character, lets it maintain its impenetrability and resistance to the clarity of thought. By relying on her shoes, she lets such an impenetrable thing-being be part of a world—her world (not the world that *she* institutes, but the world which is entrusted to her and to which she entrusts herself).

A final, ontic consideration may be appropriate at this point. Heidegger's claim is that art is the setting into work of the truth. But it is hardly imaginable that the Greeks who built and went to the temple to pray were artists, or had an artistic attitude of the kind expressed by Heidegger. If anything, the attitude of Greeks was more likely to resemble the attitude of the peasant. For the ancient Greek the temple is not an art work which discloses or locates the being of the storm, the sky, the birds. Rather, the temple is a thing of use (to pray to the gods) in which not equipmentality, but reliability, predominates. The Greek, whether as builder or prayer, relied on the temple and entrusted it with his or her hopes, dreams, expectations, so that they became engraved in the stony walls of the temple, and therein, in its earthy character, preserved. It is in the relation between this earthy character and the Greek builder or prayer that the Greek world is disclosed. And the world takes its measure from the earth, that is, from things.[10] Yet Heidegger's ear, tuned to the melody of art, is deaf to the song of the earth and its humble inhabitants. Therefore, a new questioning of the issue of things is in order—the questioning that takes place in Heidegger's essays from the 1950s.

9 ❖ Ethical Disclosure? The Faciality of Things[1]

"Near to us are what we usually call things" (T 166), Heidegger observes in a lecture he delivered in the early 1950s, and, once again, concerned with a renewal of the question of things. Yet, the nearness of things has not facilitated the access to their being, which has remained and remains concealed—to science, which "always encounters only what its kind of representation has admitted beforehand as an object possible for science" (T 170); to philosophy, which conceives of things in terms of *substratum*, materiality, or ideas (OWA 23ff); and, one may add, also to Heidegger, who, despite his preoccupation with things ever since *Being and Time*, has never confronted the issue with conclusive determination because always "on the way" to something else: fundamental ontology, art, *physis*. Yet, possibly as a consequence of the persistence of things which, in their nearness to us, are reluctant to being banished at the margins of philosophy, the question "What is a thing?" (T 166) imposes itself (once again) to Heidegger, more clearly and resolutely than ever, in a series of later conferences ("Building, Dwelling, Thinking," and "The Thing") in which things are finally granted the honor and dignity of a special inquiry, and where a yet unheard word is told with respect to their being. As Levinas might rephrase it, the layers of sedimentation through which, in the things, the Saying of transcendence has consigned itself to the said are finally reduced (AE 208ff); the said is unsaid and broken open through the interruption of the possibility of comprehensive thematization produced by the nearing of the Fourfold.

The unsaying of the said coincides with the novelty of Heidegger's meditation in its standing out against the traditionalism of the example(s) employed. To illustrate the thingness of things, in "The Thing" Heidegger chooses a rather obvious case of things, an artifact—a jug, which in *Being and Time* would have been considered, at best, a piece of equipment, and whose truth, according to "The Origin of the Work of Art," would have been disclosed only through its appearance in/as a work of art. Faithful to what he remarked in "The Origin of the Work of Art," Heidegger admits that, as a container made of a certain type of soil, a jug certainly requires external production. Although a description in terms of "self-supporting independence" (T 166) may help to differentiate things from technological objects (in which case a jug may *not* be considered a thing, but an artificial object), now, however, Heidegger promptly dismisses such a discrimination as unable to reach the essence of things when asserting that "from the product's self-support, there is no way that leads to the thingness of the thing" (T 167). The dismissal, which liberates things from any productivistic determination,[2] indicates their essence to be lying elsewhere—in the case of the jug, in its being a vessel (T 169), whereas its being brought into existence is merely a consequence of this primordial being.

The relinquishment of the productivistic interpretation releases Heidegger from the necessity to consider the affiliation between *techne* and technology in the determination of the nature of things (that is, products *are* things, and not simply objects)—need for differentiation, which has plagued Heidegger in many of his meditations on technology. More fundamentally, though, the obliteration of the productivistic interpretation blurs the traditional distinction between art and *physis*, ultimately allowing for a reinscription within things (whether artworks or artificial products) of characters originally recognized only to natural entities. The differentiation among various types of things (artificial, mineral, vegetal, animal)—that is, the fact that the universe of things does not constitute a homogeneous horizon—is not abolished by Heidegger. Rather, the distinction will be regained later at a level different than, and uncontaminated by a unilateral determination in terms of human agency. Even more importantly, however, a yet unheard suggestion is implied in Heidegger's claim that "the jug is not a vessel because it was made; rather, the jug had to be made because it is this holding vessel" (T 168). It is as if there were something archaically imperative in the essence of things that mandates a course of action; almost as if things were able to place a demand that can go unanswered only at the price of a transgression of their being. The path for an understanding of the thing-being of things according to lines that radically differ from most Western tradition, and even from Heidegger's previous approaches to it, is opened up.

Reverent, as usual, to the fact that "it is language that tells us about the nature of a thing, provided that we respect language's own nature," Heidegger's long-established passion for etymologies retraces the semantic origin of the word *Ding,* the thing, in the high-German term *thing* (BDT 153). The reconstruction, more essential than merely "the accidents of an etymological game" (T 124), reveals that originally the word *thing* denoted a gathering (T 174). The concern with transcendental acts of gathering, which had inspired both instrumental and artistic disclosures in *Being and Time* and subsequently in "The Origin of the Work of Art," is not eliminated from Heidegger's renewal of the meditation on things. Yet, the origin and meaning of such a gathering are declined in a different and novel direction. It is the event of gathering that Heidegger assumes as the being of things. A thing is a thing, rather than an object, insofar as it gathers—when it gathers, the thing things, Heidegger claims (T 174). It is the thing itself that is at the origin of the act of gathering.

The novel, awkward expression, "the thing things," indicates more than a tautology or a duplication of reality, as a naive, unsympathetic reading of Heidegger might suggest. By *thinging,* the thing becomes an event, that is, a being whose nature is dynamic, vibrant, alive. Heidegger offers various illustrations of the eventuation of things—a bridge (BDT), a jug (T), a tree (L),[3] a threshold (again, L). Their eventuation, their becoming alive expressed through the verbalization of the noun, consists in bringing together *das Geviert,* the Fourfold, the "simple oneness of the four" (BDT 150): earth and sky, divinities and mortals.[4] Could it be that this gathering that the thing unveils may be made to resonate with echoes of Levinas's understanding of ethics as the place of encounter of othernesses remaining separate in the relation?

Although the Fourfold is a "*primal* oneness" by which the Four belong together in one (BDT 149), "enfolded into a single fourfold" (T 173), this oneness (*Einfalt*) is not unity (*Einheit*), but rather a preservation and unfolding of the differences of its participants.[5] Possibly in spite of Heidegger's own intentions, the nearing of the Fourfold brought about by the thinging of things discloses a form of alterity comparable to, although necessarily not identical with, the otherness which Levinas retraces in persons, but is unwilling to recognize in things. Heidegger does not thematize it as alterity, neither in persons, nor in things, because uninterested in the thematization of ethical otherness. It is the presence of such alterity that enables a discourse on things in terms of their faciality, therefore allowing for the possibility of the development of an ethics of things.

The alterity of the thing that Heidegger's account discloses is revealed in a signifying that is not exhausted in its signification. In its thinging, the thing is not immediate presence. In its gathering, it intends beyond itself toward a Fourfold, which, by its same nature, indicates beyond itself—multiplicity in oneness; oneness in multiplicity; sky, mortals, and divinities in the earth; earth, mortals, and divinities in the sky; earth, sky, and divinities in the mortals; earth, sky, and mortals in the divinities.[6] As prefigured by the tracing of an earthy character at the core of things in "The Origin of the Work of Art," there is always something other to the thing than what its appearance immediately presents; something which surpasses its immediate signification, is not exhausted by it, remains transcendent, and yet can only emerge in the immanence of that very first appearance. In a variation of the distinction already established in *Being and Time* between entities present-at-hand, exhausted in the platitude of their presentification, and entities ready-at-hand, endowed with the depth offered to them by the referential structure and the ecstatic temporality of time of which they benefit, only in virtue of this signification beyond itself is an entity to be considered a thing, rather than an object. As Heidegger anxiously remarks, however, the description of things in terms of alterity does not reduce the discourse on things to a symbolic order, in which the transference from the signifier to its signified remains external, culturally determined, and ultimately arbitrary. In its intending beyond itself, a symbol "expresses something that strictly speaking does not belong to it" (BDT 153). That is, its essence lies elsewhere than in the symbol, ultimately opening up a space for inauthentic signification, misinterpretation, violence, and betrayal. Conversely, the being of the thing consists precisely in the immanence of its transcendence, in its, so to speak, transimmanence or, to borrow a term from an order of discourse which honors the laughter of the Thracian maid and its philosophical significance, in its embodied transcendence. In other words, alterity is not simply intended by the thing: it *is* the thing—schizophrenia of things, which, in their being near to us and yet far away from us, immanent and yet not reducible to, and exhaustible in, the immanence of simple presence, reveal an idiosyncratic order of signification—the order of things.

Within such an order, things act as the aletheic powers of disclosure of other things, so that, as in Heidegger's example, "the banks emerge as banks only as the bridge crosses the stream" (BDT 152). From being conditioned by the context, the horizon, whether pragmatic (BT) or artistic (OWA), within which they appear, things achieve the new ontological status of conditioners, both of other things and of what is gathered within them, in nearness to them;

in the first place, the mortals. As Heidegger explicitly remarks, "in the strict sense of the German word *bedingt,* we are the be-thinged, the conditioned ones. We have left behind us the presumption of all unconditionedness" (T 181). The suspicion of a transcendental foundation of things, still present in *Being and Time* and in *The Origin of the Work of Art,* is vanished through the achievment of the new perspective on things—a thingly perspective, as Heidegger acknowledges when claiming that "the thing things the world" (T 181). The recognition is striking, if compared to previous meditations, where things were said to be *weltlos,* and where only through the world could the being of things be disclosed. Now, things have become the unconditioned condition of their own thinging.

The conditioning things impose, however, is of a peculiar kind, in its receiving its determination not by the conditioner (the very thing), but by the conditioned (other things, and the Fourfold). Philosophical foundationalism introverts itself undermining the solidity of the foundation, exposing it to the shaling and shattering provoked by the intrusion of alterity, and thereby denouncing, as is the case also in Levinas's ethics, the impracticability of the foundationalist approach. Despite the gathering performed by things, what is disclosed remains itself—the square a square, the castle a castle, and mortals are not transfigured in their standing in front of the divinities. The lack of transfiguration, that is, the absence of a sublimation of the disclosed within an order pre-established by the discloser; the refusal to attribute to things a meaning previous to their own donation of meaning preserves the alterity of that which is thus gathered. Since gathering does not achieve unity or assimilation, it is itself shaped—that is, determined—by the differences that it brings together. The way the bridge gathers and the way another thing, even another bridge, gathers, do not result into homogeneous configurations, Heidegger warns.[7] The landscape which the Fourfold originates remains varied, its lines of flight always directing toward new constellations of gathering of the Fourfold. The gathering is the same, yet the modality and consequently the results of the gathering are different, because "we can only say 'the same' if we think difference. It is in the carrying out and settling of differences that the gathering nature of sameness comes to light" (PMD 219).[8] Alterity is thus preserved throughout: in the gatherers, which are not assimilated into one single kind of entity; in the gathered, which are allowed to be in their own way; and in the modality of gathering, which, although the same, is always different. No two things are the same, in a respectful homage to the alterity of their manifestation.

By staging this complex relation of reciprocal conditioning, the thing brings the Four near to one another in that being that the thing itself is. Yet, the thing is not the relationship. Rather, the relationship has its basis in things. That is, what the thing as gatherer opens up is not reality, but, analogously to Levinas's understanding of ethics, the place of a relationship. As Heidegger himself warns, "we should learn to recognize that things themselves are the places, do not merely belong in space."[9] According to Heidegger, a space is a "place cleared or freed for settlement and lodging" (BDT 154). By opening up a place, things offer a lodging for the gathering of the Fourfold. Analogously to language, as described by Heidegger, things become the abode of being; in their being withdrawn from the penetration of all speculations, they disclose a hollow, a niche in which the Fourfold can nestle (T 180). Rather than transcendental founders, things are topological founders, insofar as they open up a space that allows for a vicinity.[10] Far from abolishing farness, however, "nearness preserves farness" (T 178), because "nearness brings near—draws nigh to one another—the far and, indeed, *as* the far" (T 177–78). In the nearing, none of the participants needs any transcendental foundation, because each of them exists prior to, and separate from, the relation itself.[11] Yet, each can achieve its own signification only within the space described by the relation—space that remains fluid, flexible, unlimitable and unlimited, because not the space defined by geometrical contours and perimeters, but rather the place of ever new configurations and negotiations of the relationship—never a given proximity, always a promised one.[12]

Through the relation which is thus instituted, the earth, the sky, and the divinities renounce the indetermination of what Levinas names the *il y a*, the anonymous being that constitutes the mythical dimension of existence (EE, TO, and TI), and enter a determined relation with mortals and with each other which declines, although does not transfigure, their own previous identity. Thus, in things the earth, the sky, the divinities are not "the impersonal, faceless gods with which it is impossible to speak" (TI 142), as Levinas claims, with direct reference to Heidegger. Rather, they become the gods of the relationship, of the place, of the abode that the thing itself is—pagan gods, maybe, as Levinas maintains. Yet, as several non Judeo-Christian traditions attest, not thereby necessarily faceless, impersonal, indeterminate, impermeable to relations, or fundamentally cruel and "source of all cruelty to humans" (DL 301).

As prefigured in the scission of things from any economy of production, the complexity and multiplicity of relations characterizing the thinging of the thing precludes all classifications of things (whether fabricated, or artistically produced, or naturally grown) established on the ground of the relation (or the lack thereof) human beings entertain with them, as if such a relation were the archaic condition of their being. On the contrary, the differing of things from one another becomes a direct function of their own way of thinging, of their own way of eventuating the relation, whereas all different things are nevertheless gathered in the commonality of the same thingness because of their hosting the Fourfold. Although differing among themselves, the qualification of things can thus be applied to both the jug and the desk, the bridge and the plow. "But tree and pond, too, brook and hill, are things, each in its own way. Things, each thinging from time to time in its own way, are heron and roe, deer, horse, and bull. Things, each thinging and each staying in its own way, are mirror and clasp, book and picture, crown and cross" (T 182), bread and wine (L 205).

That is, things are conceived of broadly enough to encompass, yet without homogenization, not only artifacts, excluded from the consideration of *physis*, but also natural entities, excluded from the consideration of *Zeug* as unfolded in *Being and Time*.[13] Only because of the primordial relation of the Fourfold can things be classified as artifacts or natural entities, which are peculiar modes in which the relation configures itself. Rather than resulting in generality, the denomination "things" enhances and legitimizes the possibility of differences—not the chaotic proliferation of unrelated multiplicities, but rather the fertile richness of differences within the same, because the ground for the determination of what the thing is has become the thing itself in its alterity. Each thing remains other in hosting the Fourfold in its peculiar way: other than the Fourfold, other than any other thing, and other than the mortals. The separatedness of things from one another and from what they gather is the open circle they describe, which traditional metaphysics has mistaken for their extensionality. It is the continuous tending and dis-tending of a difference that cannot rest upon itself, unless it loses itself. When staticity replaces eventuation, the thing undergoes an absolutization, it loses its fluidity, and becomes impermeable to any relation and gathering. The scenario, then, is the well-known panorama of naturalistic realism, which considers things as objects in antithesis to the subjective conscience—the horizon of the *Vorhandene,* as described already since *Being and Time*.

In these later essays which, once again, renew the question of things, the thingness of things has been finally achieved by Heidegger, and has been achieved in its fundamental character of alterity: unconditional alterity, because things are unconditioned; absolute alterity, because the alterity of things does not stem from an oppositional confrontation with mortals, or divinities, which are rather appropriated by and relocated within the alterity of things. Undeniably, the alterity things display according to Heidegger's renewed interpretation of their being lacks the most fundamental feature qualifying Levinas's other (*the* Other *par excellence*) as Other. Despite its signifying beyond itself toward the Fourfold, the alterity of things is not their transcendence, if, as for Levinas, transcendence implies vertical directionality, height, ascension. In "Language" Heidegger states that "the unitary Fourfold of sky and earth, mortals and divinities . . . is stayed in the thinging of things" (L 199), where the preposition in, locating the thinging *in* the thing itself, cannot be ignored. The ringing of the Fourfold is not a unidirectional movement, whether from the bottom upward or vice versa. Rather, the ringing bears closer resemblance to a circular dance (T 180), in which the direction of the ringing moves back and forth, in a deflection that decenters (but does not raise toward transcendence) the origin of the movement itself.

In its ringing, the circle is open, abolishing beginning and end, inside and outside. Things are always open to becoming other than themselves, always resistant to fixation, determination, definition, and therefore, precisely because of the lack of a hard core at their center, vulnerable to appropriation, exploitation, profanation. At any moment the dynamics of the mirroring may privilege one component over the others, in an overflowing of significations rendering the temporalization of the thing varied, and the meaning of each thing continuously open to new configurations and disclosures. Rather than in their being transcendent in the sense of erection and elevation, the alterity of things lies in their perennial difference and differing from themselves and from one another (maybe what, with a Derridian term, could be named their *différance*), which render their nature so evanescent, so frail, and so difficult to reach to any philosophical, even phenomenological, description.

Yet, the absence of the dimension of height, brought about by the de-centeredness of things, is balanced by the presence of another dimension, equally primordial, equally original, equally powerful in signifying the possibility of things' alterity: the dimension of breadth drifting into depth. It is the breadth/depth originating from the temporalization of the ringing of the Fourfold, from the difference and differing of things from the Fourfold and from other things. The open circle the mirror-play of the Fourfold describes, which Heidegger qualifies as a play bonding in freedom (T 179), constitutes the breadth of things, which traditional metaphysics equates with their spatial dimension. In its being a mutual betrothing of its participants,[14] such breadth is traversed by lines of inscriptions recording the temporalization of the Fourfold itself. The elements of the Fourfold enter the thing endowed with stories of their own, coming to them from previous relations, from previous constellations, from previous places of encounter they have entered, from their having witnessed the anarchic past preceding the origin of their relation as Fourfold. These stories do they entrust to the thing in its enabling the intersection of "the onefold Fourfold into a single space-time" (T 174). By thinging, the thing enriches itself with an irretrievable past granting the thing its depth. Things ward the past, becoming the shrine of the past—of the origins. It is this very past, which things bear inscribed in the folds of their breadth, that offers things depth and the possibility of being subjects of narration. As all good storytellers know, things tell stories, as much as they are material for stories. Although there is no height in things, certainly there is the alterity brought by the depth of the irretrievability of the past. Steeped in being, nevertheless things indicate an otherwise-than-being which, inviolable, inviolated, and yet always menaced by violation, is enshrined and expressed within the folds of their being.

The fragility and precariousness of the alterity of things is understood by Heidegger himself, when he notices how, endowed with a modesty and unpretentiousness (T 182) bereaving them of the power to resist domination, things are delicate entities always on the verge of disappearance into objectification—entities whose otherness is dissolved in the heteronomy of their being a representation: a *Gegen-stand* and a *Vor-stellung*.[15] Yet, if let be present in their thinging, things place a demand on mortals to which mortals can only co-respond, releasing the autonomous power of initiative, making themselves passive and responsive. "We are called by the things as things" (T 181), Heidegger claims, acknowledging the reality of their demand, and providing suggestions on how to comply with such an appeal. In connection with such an appeal, he warns, the role of mortals becomes crucial, since things do not appear as things "without the vigilance of mortals." And, he adds, "the first step toward such vigilance is the step back from the thinking that merely represents" (T 181).

However, vigilance cannot be a voluntaristic—that is, subjectivistic—shift of attitude, which would, once again, abandon things to the power and arbitrariness of the good will, or lack thereof, of the human agent. Rather, "the step back takes up its residence in a co-responding which, appealed to in the world's being by the world's being, answers within itself to that appeal" (T 181–82). Since the beginning, vigilance assumes its orientation from an appeal coming from somewhere else than itself. Meditating on this vigilant co-responding whose laws are dictated heteronomously under the name of dwelling, Heidegger describes it as the fourfold activity of "saving the earth, . . . receiving the sky . . . awaiting the divinities . . . initiating the mortals" (BDT 151). The ultimate significance of this quadruple performance is without doubts: to dwell "means at the same time to cherish and protect, to protect and care for" (BDT 147) the Fourfold.[16] But caring for the Fourfold can be accomplished only if mortals care for things, because things are the receptacle of the Fourfold. And things can be the receptacle only if they can be let be in their thinging.

The demand, which commands a different approach to things, finds its proper answer in the notion of *Gelassenheit,* a refined and sophisticated modification of the paesant woman's *Verlässlichkeit* in "The Origin of the Work of Art," which offers "the possibility of dwelling in the world in a totally different way" (DT 55). Neither indifference nor neglect, neither laxity nor permissiveness, but rather relinquishment of the metaphysical will to power, and therefore acting "which is yet no activity" (DT 61), *Gelassenheit* means to abandon oneself to things, to let things be in the alterity of their mirror-play which, expropriating the mortals, appropriates them to things. "To let be is to engage oneself with beings. . . . Such engagement withdraws in the face of beings in order that they might reveal themselves with respect to what and how they are and in order that presentative correspondence might take its standard from them" (BW 128), Heidegger writes. Only through this abandonment to things are mortals enabled to locate themselves within things, be appropriated by them, and ultimately be free, since "freedom manifests itself as exposure to the disclosedness of beings" (BW 128). In other words, mortals are committed to things by things themselves, which, through the mirror-play they host, in turn commit themselves to mortals—the relation is that of a mirrored commitment.

In *Discourse on Thinking,* Heidegger asserts that the relation between what he calls *die Gegnet,* that-which-regions, and *Gelassenheit,* as well as that between *die Gegnet* and the thing, "can be thought neither as ontic nor as ontological" (DT 76). What kind of relation is this relation, which, by extension, encompasses also the relation between *Gelassenheit* and things? Although Heidegger's word is silent, this relation could modestly be called ethics, if, as in Levinas, ethics is understood as the place of love for what remains and insists on remaining other. Things thus impose an imperative which comes close to an ethical demand. They request an act of love—ethics—which lets things be as things, and which therefore opens up a space for the hosting of the Fourfold. Heidegger, however, will never explicitly thematize the ethical character of such an act.

By welcoming things as things, mortals are welcomed within the things. How to enact the welcome which alone enables things to be in their alterity, and mortals to dwell by them? How to enact *Gelassenheit*? Neither Heidegger nor Levinas, when taken individually, provide their reader with a direct response: Levinas loves, but not things; Heidegger thematizes things, but does not love them enough. What neither can achieve separately, however, might perhaps be obtained through an exposure of one to the other—exposure which may contaminate the purity of their respective thought, but may also enable the thematization of an ethics of things that brings Levinas's thought farther, toward possibilities that, in a filial manner, are still his, yet impossible to him.

III ❖ The Ethics of Things: Tender Love, Festive Things

10 ❖ Prelude: Toward an Ethics of Things[1]

The confrontation between Heidegger and Levinas, in their encounter with things, is marked by a double truth. On the one hand, there are no things in Levinas, since things are for the same,[2] or for the Other,[3] but not for themselves. That is, in Levinas there is no alterity of things.[4] Conversely, there are things in Heidegger. For him, things are the place where the gathering of the Fourfold—the mortals, the gods, the earth, the sky—comes to pass, in an intimacy that is not fusion, but dif-fering. Each thing remains other in hosting the Fourfold in its peculiar way: other than the Fourfold and other than any other thing; other than the mortals, who can dwell by things in their thinging only if they can take care of things as things, if they can let them be in their alterity.

According to Levinas's suggestion, the place—which is not a place—where a relationship with the other can be achieved is ethics. Undoubtedly there is ethics in Levinas, even if his notion of ethics extends only to the other person (certainly the other man, hopefully also the other woman and child). Conversely, there is no ethics in Heidegger, at least according to the most common reading.[5] If the two thinkers are forced face to face in a confrontation that neither of them would advocate enthusiastically, the result is a chiasmatic structure,[6] whose branches connect a double negation—nonethics and nonthings—and a double affirmation—ethics and things.

Since Socrates, philosophy has walked the path of negation. If there is ethics, it is not of things; and if there are things, they are not ethical. The path of affirmation is a narrow strip, which has seldom been explored.[7] It leads to an ethics of things, where ethics cannot be traditional ethics in any of its formulations (utilitarian, deontological, virtue-oriented), and things cannot be traditional things (objects opposed to a subject). At the intersection between ethics and things, Levinas and Heidegger meet, as in "a contact made in the heart of a chiasmus."[8] The former offers the notion of a nontraditional ethics, the latter of non-traditional things.

Some remarks are in order with respect to the modality of the meeting. Despite the common rootedness in Husserl's phenomenology, the encounter between Heidegger and Levinas is not that of two Aristotelian friends; nor is the one the forerunner of the other; nor is the one in absolute opposition to the other. Levinas and Heidegger do not complement each other, either existentially or historically or philosophically (opposition being only the counterpart to complementation). They stand on their own as two separate, autonomous philosophical figures, one of whom, for chronological reasons, can exercise a sharp criticism of the other, which might be reciprocated, if chronology were to allow it. Their relation, which escapes friendship, enmity, complementarity, is better characterized by the Derridian notion of *supplement*. A complement comes from the interior of a common territory and aims at completion and enclosure. A supplement derives its authority from the exterior, opening the path for further development. Despite the evident differences the two philosophers exhibit, the legitimacy of the face to face between Levinas and Heidegger is grounded in such a notion of supplementarity entailing exteriority.

According to Derrida, two different meanings cohabit, oddly although necessarily, in the notion of the supplement.[9] The supplement is a surplus, an addition, a fullness that enriches another fullness. Yet the supplement is not only an excess. A supplement supplements. Its addition aims at replacement. It is as if it filled a void, an anterior default of a presence. It is compensatory and vicarious, "its place is assigned in the structure by the mark of an emptiness."[10] Neither Heidegger nor Levinas need each other. Yet, in both there is a remainder that is not described, that is forgotten in their meditation. In Heidegger it is ethics, in Levinas it is things. As supplementing each other, Levinas and Heidegger remain external, exterior, other, each not defined as the other than the same. But still as supplements, each of them offers the other that remainder that the other leaves unthought.

Besides preserving differences, the structure of supplementarity has one more, undeniable advantage: it relieves the burden of instituting an oppositional confrontation between Levinas and Heidegger. Criticism is not the weapon of the supplement, nor is it its goal. The absence of criticism also renders the need for an apology unnecessary. Supplementarity is not concerned with legal justice—who is right and who is wrong—but with metaphysical justice—how to think in a way that renders justice to the other. The appeal to justice comes neither from Levinas nor from Heidegger. Rather, it comes from things, as the alterity in need of a re-inscription within philosophical discourse. The ethics of things is the outcome of the supplementarity of Levinas and Heidegger when they are faced with their respective failures and desire.

Yet, why an ethics? And why of things? What is an ethics of things? How does this ethics relate to traditional ethics? How does it relate to the ethics of the other (person) that Levinas so vehemently advocates as the only, primary, originary form of ethics? Is there, can there be, an ethics of things? What is the meaning of the *of* connecting ethics to things?

The hermeneuticians of suspicion—Marx, Freud, Nietzsche, and not least Heidegger—have radically criticized the notion of value, thereby compromising irremediably the possibility of a "great" ethics in the Aristotelian, or even Kantian, sense of an ethical system able to give laws to reality by imposing norms and prohibitions to be respected. Yet far from disappearing, the ethical discussion seems to flourish. Medical ethics, legal ethics, environmental ethics, media ethics, not to speak of business ethics, crowd the contemporary ethical panorama. As the limitation in their names suggests, however, these are all forms of residual ethics, which, deprived of the possibility of a holistic approach to reality because God is dead, try to bridle at least that small part of reality within which they constitute themselves. Within the minimum realm in which they govern, they seek common values and principles able to give that part of reality order and rationality, upon which those who belong to the specific realm can ground their activity. Ethics becomes a *locus minimus.*[11]

The function and character of these ethics is necessarily limited, not only with respect to the domain in which they rule, but also in terms of credibility. The reality that "small" ethics tries to bridle by means of norms of behavior escapes their control. The rules they dictate are able neither to wonder over the infinite possibilities of good, nor to constitute a bulwark against the abyssal possibilities of evil reality manifests, as the factual event of Auschwitz suffices to prove beyond the disputability of any theoretical statement, since against its happening any kind of "small" ethics but also of traditional ethics collapses.[12] An ethics that may still be viable must take such a failure into account. It must be able to constitute itself as both a remedy and a hindrance to the repetition. Therefore, any ethics that wishes to be believable must renounce the claims normative ethics makes of being a practical guide, or a moral ought, or a science of mores, traditions, behaviors; of being able to posit rules and values as conditions for the development of human beings; of providing its followers with static sets of norms to direct moral actions. Ethics must renounce its normativity.[13]

What sense should ethics retain, then? According to the original meaning of *ethos,* ethics denotes "a dwelling place" (LH 233).[14] That is, ethics, as Levinas suggests, is a locative description, not a normative procedure. Ethics opens up a space. Rather than spatiality, the *locus* identifies spaciousness. Spatiality denotes the "safe space" in which, having accumulated and digested the notions coming from the past, one feels "at home"—that is, in the midst of one's possessions, living the present and awaiting the future. The encounter that takes place in ethical spaciousness is not with a fully unfolded presence—which would render possible adherence, but also its aberrations—but with what remains of the presence, with the other, with what escapes the digestive power of the same. Ethics does not deal primarily with being good, bad, or evil. Rather, it deals with how much of reality one is able to maintain—not necessarily the ontological reality available to human beings, but rather the metaphysical reality, the other reality subtracting itself to conceptualization. What is good is defined then in terms of what preserves the maximum of reality from destruction,[15] whereas what is bad is what works against reality, for its destruction and annihilation. The *metron* of ethics becomes not an abstract principle or value, but reality itself, its concreteness, the gravity of things.

In his project, Levinas welcomes the ancient meaning that has been so often forgotten. In his thought ethics is the place—which is not a place—where a distance is revealed, where a difference is maintained, where an encounter with the other can come to pass in such a way that the same is forced—with a force that is as spiritually authoritative as it is physically powerless—to become good, that is, moral. In other words, morality—as a set of rules—is subsequent to ethics, as the enactment, necessary but not originary, of what ethics means. In its being the transcendental ground for the normativity of morality, ethics transcends morality, without being per se either moral or immoral. The primacy of the good is ethical because it is metaphysical and not because it is moral. Even when the murder is committed of the metaphysical other, the I remains within the sphere of the ethical, despite the immorality of its action. What has made Western philosophy unethical is not the committing of the metaphysical murder, but the denial of the murdered and of the murderous act. Remaining within the range of Levinas's terminology, ethics can only be metaphysical. But, if we would rather adopt the phrasing of the postmetaphysical tradition which moves away from the hypostatization of essences Levinas himself wants to escape, ethics can legitimately said to be ontological.

The problem of whether to define ethics in terms of metaphysics or ontology, the nominal choice between a metaphysical ethics or an ontological ethics, is not merely a terminological question. Yet in the end it will dissolve into a terminological issue. The term *metaphysics* is charged by Heidegger with the accusation of ontotheology, closure, completeness, totalitarianism, violence, reduction to sheer presence, oblivion of the difference between being and beings. These charges are brought on behalf of a difference which is to be preserved in its ontological nature. Conversely, it is the term *ontology* that is denigrated by Levinas for its neutrality, anonymity, abstractness, concern with being rather than existing beings. Once again, the charges are brought on behalf of existing differences whose otherness is to be encountered in ethics. The term *metaphysics* is in turn rehabilitated by Levinas because of its understanding of reality in terms of distance, verticality, transcendence of reality to thought and being. Conversely, the term *ontology* is retrieved by Heidegger, in part at least, because of its understanding of reality in terms of the difference between being and beings. That is, reality can be explored in terms of the ultimate structures of being rather than its political, social, biological, moral constitutions, which are always ontic,[16] so that for Heidegger the ontological interpretation of reality would preserve the mobility that metaphysics—in the sense Heidegger criticizes—denies.

Both metaphysics and ontology, in the positive sense Levinas and Heidegger attribute to the two terms and not in the sense they criticize, are characterized by the same concern: the desire not to be oblivious to differences. What constitutes the difference is certainly crucial in differentiating Levinas from Heidegger. In Levinas, it is the difference between being and beyond being; in Heidegger, it is the difference between being and beings. The internal movement of the difference also shifts. For Levinas, the difference is transcendence; for Heidegger, if it is not properly immanence, it is not even transcendence. It is rather what, with a Derridian expression, one could call *différance,* the giving of itself of being, which can only give itself in beings, but always withdraws from them.[17] Despite the undeniable differences in the thought of the two philosophers, a similar—but not an identical—structure characterizes both. It is as if Levinas reproduced at a second order of reality what Heidegger enacts at a first order: horizontal verticality in Heidegger (the transimmanence of things), vertical verticality in Levinas.[18] But the structural movement remains the same. This structure could be appropriately called metaphysical: not in Levinas's sense (although close to it), not in the sense Heidegger criticizes, but in the sense Descartes suggests in the Third Meditation.

In his discussion of the idea of God, Descartes distinguishes between formal reality and objective reality. Following Levinas's (highly unusual) reading of Descartes, metaphysics could be considered as the difference between the two, between reality as it is and its perception, between the order of being and the order of knowing. Metaphysics is the fact that there is a reality that is bigger, or richer, than consciousness. Levinas applies this notion of metaphysics to the other as person, who is always the *idea* of the other, as the ego has the *idea* of God for Descartes. As Heidegger claims, however, given the structure of the Fourfold reality is greater than what can be grasped of it. Reality escapes perception, it escapes thought, even when reality consists of things rather than God (*pace* Descartes) or persons (*pace* Levinas). In this sense, ethics can be said to be metaphysical, whether it involves the relation with the beyond-being (Levinas) or with being (Heidegger). Metaphysics becomes transversal to the notions of transcendence, immanence, or *différance.* It describes what epistemology cannot achieve, what only the ethical dimension can approach.

Certainly a metaphysical ethics—as Levinas suggests—is an invitation to transcend oneself and the interiority of the same, and therefore, by opening up to the other, an invitation to go beyond one's limitations and become good. But precisely because it is metaphysical, ethics is more than a moral (pre)disposition of the individual to act in a certain way, characterized as good according to some external principle posed by that same subject who is supposed to follow the principle. It is more than a spontaneous benevolence destined to become aware of itself. A metaphysical ethics receives its orientation not from the subject, or from its formulation of values—which is the best life for human beings?—but from what epistemology cannot reach, from the other, as Levinas indicates, or from what Heidegger's ontological difference names, but does not describe ethically, from the other of the Other, from the things themselves. The ethical individual is a response to an appeal that does not proceed from the individual herself or himself, not even when such individuality is camouflaged under the universality of Kantian reason. This means that the ethical individual gives up the privilege of first action. To be free does not mean to claim authorship for oneself, to be autonomous, to be the archaic principle of one's life, but rather to respond (or not to respond) to an appeal coming from the exterior.[19] To transcend oneself means to give up this claim to be the absolute beginning; to release oneself to the authority of the other, and the other of the Other; to recognize that the I, although separated, is not alone.[20] The ethical imperative comes from otherness, from its right to existence as a form of reality. The only imperative is the injuction to let the other (of the Other) be.

By withdrawing from any claim to normativity, a metaphysical ethics recedes, by the same move, from the arrogance—exhibited by any "small" ethics—to define and delimit reality into categories always too narrow and constraining because artificial. Ethics is not in possession of reality, not even in the form of a prescription of how it ought to be.[21] What the I possesses is always a remainder of reality, what has been stiffened into the immobility of a still life. The truth of reality is always beyond its traces. In the object that the hand of the I grasps, there is no longer life. The object is a reject, the refuse of reality. It is what remains after the (Heideggerian) Fourfold has moved its abode somewhere else. It is not possible to possess that abode. Humans are not the only inhabitants of it. Other inhabitants offer a resistance to appropriative movements that is similar, in modes and shapes, to that offered by Levinas's Other. Not only humans and divinities, personal presences despite their substantial difference, dwell in the Fourfold. The earth and the sky inhabit it, too. And their resistance to domination and objectification is as strong as that of the (im)mortal other(s).[22]

It is not possible to possess the abode, unless a perversion of the nature of things—from things to objects. The impossibility of possession, however, does not legitimize irrationality, or any kind of negative theology of things. Far from preserving things in their mystery, irrationality ignores them. It is within the boundaries of reason that things must exercise their subversive power, forcing reason to recognize them as the *locus* where thought cannot proceed further, where consciousness cannot appropriate its origin, where the I cannot return to itself. If it is not possible to possess the abode of the Fourfold, it is possible, however, to inhabit it. The proper dwelling in it, that dwelling that respects the otherness of the codwellers, is ethics. Ethics resumes its ancient significance of dwelling place.

The relation with things (a relation that is alien to Levinas's meditation) becomes the place where the ethical reaches its broadest latitude. There, the locative character of ethics doubles itself. Things are the *locus* where the Fourfold dwells in its structure of alterity (Heidegger), and ethics—as the place where otherness can be encountered (Levinas)—is the *locus* where the *locus* of the Fourfold can be inhabited.

Why is the extension to things so important for ethical discourse? Why can ethics not be simply an ethics of the other person? Why, ultimately, does Levinas need to be supplemented by Heidegger? The main reason lies in the anthropologocentric partiality of Levinas's project. No discourse on otherness is genuine if it repeats in any of its parts those negative structures it aims to overcome. Not only the Other, but also the other of the Other, must become part of philosophical discourse for that discourse to achieve the level of metaphysicity it advocates.

Every philosophy is a quest for wholeness, insofar as it retraces principle(s) of explication/description able to account for the entire experience, and not only for part of it. The distinction among different philosophical projects—their being totalizing or not—lies in the methodology in which they engage to reach the wholeness they beseech. Traditional Western thought has pursued wholeness by means of reduction, integration, systematization of all its parts. Totality has replaced wholeness, and the result is a totalitarianism from which what is truly other escapes, revealing the deficiencies and fallacies of the attempted system. A philosophical discourse that aims to be metaphysical must still make the other the theme of its discourse. But it must do so by moving not from the same, but from the other, and not only the Other, but also the other of the Other, and, if that is the case, the other of the other of the Other. In this must, it must also be aware of the inescapable injustice embedded in any formulation of the other (of the other, of the Other) in terms of *logos,* so as to unsay the said in which the Saying of the other has been encapsulated by making of it the theme of its discourse.

An analogous quest for wholeness, then, marks both ways of philosophizing, those centered on autology and those directed by heterologies. They both share the same claim to inclusiveness. What a metaphysical ethics does, however, is to consider the other (of the other, of the Other) not as a presence (that can be possessed because of its full presence), but always as the trace of the presencing (therefore already gone, removed from the scene of discourse). And each trace is already a trace of the trace.[23] Thus, the claim to wholeness is always displaced, not as an instance of an eternal quest for a (bad) infinite, but as the structure of the infinite itself. If the process of de-flection (rather than re-flection) halts, philosophy decays into totalitarianism, wholeness into totality, ethics into morality, the other (of the other, of the Other) into object. According to Heidegger's description, things harbor in themselves the infinite movement of mirroring and deflection. It is necessary to include them in the philosophical discourse not so that philosophy becomes totalitarian, but (precisely because of its infinite desire for infinity) to avoid totalitarianism.

The play of deflection, of infinite mirroring, of the trace of the other that is never a presence, is not an illusion, a phantasy, a hallucination produced by a shrewd magician, or a mirage due to the productive imagination of the I. The trace is always of a presencing, never of an absence, even if it is the trace of a presencing that can never be grasped, unless residually. Behind the mirror there is not a void, but the fullness of the other. It is this same otherness that, as alterity, appeals from things. Things are neither illusionary nor noumenal, as Plato and Kant and many others in their mold would like. Things possess a reality in themselves that cannot be postponed or dislocated. Their materiality can be experienced, enjoyed, even accessed, if only through a specific modality of approach that comes into contact without possessing, so that access is never a totalization. This modality, to be fully thematized later, is the touching mode of tenderness. What cannot be possessed, what tenderness respects and preserves, is the fullness of the presencing. In other words, a thing is richer than the sound, the smell, the taste of it the I may—and does indeed—enjoy. It contains memories of an unreachable past, of the ancestral dance of the earth and the elements, of the eternal play of light and darkness, of being, but always as a beyond-being.

To escape totalitarianism, however, Heidegger's notion of things needs to be broadened. The hidden assumption underlying Heidegger's notion of things is that things have been, at one time or another, in contact with human beings. Even in the recesses and solitude of the

Schwarzwald, Heidegger remains a European, whose landscape, through the course of centuries, has been heavily shaped by the human hand. Conversely, in the formulation "ethics of things," the term "things," besides denoting all sorts of non-human entities as hosts of the interplay of the Fourfold, aims to include within its range of signification also beings that have never been reached by any human activity. Uncontaminated nature displays the same metaphysical structure that the jug, or the bridge or the domesticated animal does for Heidegger. Therefore, it participates in an ethics of things with the same dignity and according to the same modalities of the jug (or the bridge or the animal).

What does it mean for humans to be part of the Fourfold, when the Fourfold is hosted in a thing that has never received the imprint of human activity, not even in the form of a look the thing may have received? Heidegger's remarks on presence, which should always be understood as an interplay of presencing and absencing, together with the notion of preservation as the proper mode to inhabit the Fourfold, are crucial at this juncture. The presence of mortals in the uncontaminated thing is their becoming present to it through their activity of preserving the thing in its unspoiled reality. But mortals participate in the Fourfold of the uncontaminated thing also in another sense. Although from a distance, the uncontaminated thing has witnessed the mortal activities of innumerable human beings, which have gone by without imprinting their activity on it, as if the thing had outlasted them all. The thing bears thus their mark in the form of presenting the absence of any imprint. The uncontaminated thing will not only be preserved, but has been preserved in its most untouched being. Regardless of whether the accidentality of this preservation is the best way to inhabit the Fourfold, the thing is still inhabited by mortals. The Fourfold maintains its fourfold dimensionality even in the untouched thing.

In Levinas the exposure to things—if there were such an exposure, which is not the case—would subtend the prior exposure and subjection to the otherness of the other as person. For him, human ethics is archetypal.[24] There may be some degree of truth to Levinas's conviction that the relation to the other (person) represents the exemplar of ethics. The other person is what compels the same to ethics in the most authoritative way because it is more evident—with an evidence that is not epistemological, but ethical—to human beings.[25] The ethical authority of the Other, however, should not obliterate another form of alterity, which is different from the otherness of the other person, and whose presence is less apparent, less evident, less loud: the alterity of what Levinas's ethics neglects, things.

The exemplarity Levinas advocates, then, should not entail ontological primacy, or primacy of perfection, or transcendental primacy, in comparison to which every other instance of a similar case is derivative—human ethics as the *arche*. Exemplarity should not be genealogical. It should rather be a case where something surfaces in the clearest manner: a model, a paradigm, an illustration, but also a magnifier through which other othernesses may reverberate and voice their existence. The exemplarity of human ethics lies not in its being the prescriptive origin, but the descriptive model of ethics. As such a descriptive model, the ethics of the other person is to be broadened, because its paradigmacity does not (and cannot) provide, although it indicates it, the metaphysical access to the existence of other othernesses. In other words, a paradigm is not self-sufficient and all-inclusive. It depends on the existence of other cases that it describes, but does not exhaust. With respect to such cases, a paradigm performs a catalytic function: it brings them into the open in the power of their reality, disruptive of any attempt at fixation in a system (even an ethical system). Catalysis is not a mode of technological, or even genealogical, production, where willful creation by an agent occurs. Catalysis is the fecundity of an explosion in which the conflagration is independent of the catalytic elements, accidental, external to them in its origin and power. The ethics of things may take its move from the ethics of the other (person), but its truth is independent from the other (person). It lies in the reality of the things themselves. The ethics of things reaches further than Levinas's ethics, even if it may receive an inspiration from that ethics.

Some difficulties arise in the project of extending Levinas's notion of ethics to Heidegger's concept of things. The notion of metaphysics that has been adopted allows for a characterization of the ethics of things as metaphysical, cutting across the distinction between transcendence and immanence/*différance.* This distinction, which represents the difference between Jewish tradition and Greek philosophy, presents itself again in applying Levinas's ethical categories to the reality of things.[26] A torsion, which need not be a dis-torsion, is required. In Levinas, the voice of the ethical other comes from on high. The other is "what is positive enough to appeal to being and separate enough for it to order it imperatively."[27] The other is beyond being, is a break with being and ontology. In Heidegger, there is no height in things, although there is depth in them.

Things are not beyond being. If anything, they are in being, as the gift of being. Their depth, however, keeps open a space within the appearance of immanence with which they present themselves. In a way, it is a case of reversed immanence, which grants some form of transcendence: what Heidegger calls the ontological difference. Being is beyond the things in which it gives itself, so that what may appear as reversed immanence, what is not properly transcendence although is *différance,* is a circular ringing. As already shown, both height and depth are a form of metaphysics. The difference between metaphysical transcendence (Levinas) and metaphysical ringing (Heidegger), between height and depth, constitutes the difference between persons and things. The Other as person has height; the other as thing has the open circularity of differing. The difference between the two expressions of otherness does not indicate a lack on either side. It is rather a richness, as the supplementarity of Levinas and Heidegger is richness. Things and humans both entail the verticality of metaphysics, but each in its idiomatic way. Totality does not belong to ethics.

The opposition between transcendence and immanence—whatever form they may assume—should not be thought in terms of an antinomy. It is Levinas himself who has taught his readers to disregard oppositional, dichotomic ways of thinking in favor of differences. This means that in the differences there may be elements of similarity, without yielding to identity, but rather maintaining equivocity. As with the Other (person), despite the fact that things apparently do not stand on high, there is no reciprocity between the things and the I. The indifference with which things are charged—what Jean-Luc Nancy calls the "heart of stone" of things as opposed to the mobility and mobilitation of thinking[28]—speaks for their being located on a different level. The relationship remains asymmetrical. The presence of things appeals to the I in a way that goes beyond the I's understanding. It is not a matter of epistemological weakness, but rather, as Heidegger shows, of the inner structure of things. There is a sacredness that does not appeal from on high, but from below. The lowness is height, as the height of the Other (person) is also lowness in the destitution of the other. Things are both master—they obsess the I with the authority of a constant presence; they are always there—and hostage—they are frail, dependent on continuous protection; their existence is the frailty of a reality always in danger of being destroyed.

The metaphysicity of the transcendence of the Other and of the ringing of things is what draws persons and things close to each other, providing the ground for an ethical discourse concerning both. However, this ethics remains different in the two cases, thus preserving the difference of things and persons. The metaphysical structure remains the same: in both cases, it is an ethics. One is an ethics of otherness as person, the other is an ethics of alterity as things. The difference preserves a metaphysical ethics from totalitarianism. It is a desire for an infinite that is not exhausted in a same structural form.

The expression "ethics *of* things," as the result of the supplementarity of Levinas and Heidegger, acquires a double meaning: it is *of* things, as the place where things can manifest themselves in their reality as the guardians and the receptacle of the Fourfold, and from their receptivity can appeal to humans to dwell by them. But it is *of* things also in the sense that humans are compelled by things to respond to the demands placed upon them and shape their behavior in accordance to the inner mirroring of things. Things signify both a subject and an object for ethics. *Of* things means thus the directionality of a double movement: that which moves out from the things to reach the I and the other, and that which, in response to the first, moves from the I and the other to reach the things and to be concerned by them. The first movement is that of the demand or the appeal that things place on human beings by their mere impenetrable presencing there. It is the thingly side of the ethics of things. The second movement is that of tenderness, as the response to the demand and the properly human configuration of the ethics of things.

11 ❖ Things' Obsessive Appeal

Despite philosophy's millenary attempt to stabilize the thingness of things through their meticulous reinscription into intellectual categories, a fundamental truth presents itself to philosophy, every time anew, every time more radically, as the recurrent arising of the question "What is a thing?" throughout Heidegger's thought testifies: the truth that things are everywhere, in an ubiquity which legitimizes the undoing of the previous answer and the arising of the new questioning.

Endowed with a persistance which echoes with obsessiveness, things saturate the world with their presence. Wherever the I turns, there are things, and when it closes its eyes, they still haunt its imagination with the presentation of odors, sounds, tastes, almost imperceptible sensations through which things still pulse their vitality. But, after all, what if life were a dream? Even then, oniric states are populated by the presence of things, liberated from their material and causal connections, hovering and floating in the lightness of free associations. As Merleau-Ponty writes, "the world obsesses us even during sleep, and it is about the world that we dream."[1] In different ways, the theoretical experience narrated by Descartes in the *Meditations,* and the practice of life of the heremits testify that it is possible to avoid the other (person), to reject the encounter, to be solipsistic without condescendence, in an autism which isolates its bearer from socialization. Conversely, to exempt oneself from an encounter—any encounter—with things, as Socrates very well knew, is to die, and live the disembodied life of pure spirit. Yet, Socrates' death, the relinquishment from the obsessive presence of things, is still achieved through what Socrates seeks to reject. That hemlock which he so avidly drank, and which alone enabled him an early passage to the immortal life with the gods, is still, in an ironic countermove of things, a thing. From its inception to its conclusion, mortality is marked by the finitude of being conditioned, *bedingt,* as Heidegger says, by things (*Dinge*). As Levinas recognizes, sensibility, having a body, is not a moment of representative knowledge, an inferior, still self-unconscious mode of thought; it "does not belong to the order of thought, but to that of sentiment, that is, the affectivity wherein the egoism of the I pulsates" (TI 135). Sensibility is therefore to be exposed to things, where the body becomes the exposure. "To be a body is . . . to be *me* though living in the *other*" (TI 117).[2]

Phenomenologically, then, things pack and harrass existence in a variety of ways which determine the spectrum of not only bodily, but also spiritual, feelings and emotions. Things cheer, entertain, satisfy. Things intimidate, scare, hamper. Things embarass. Things depress. Things transform. Things escape. Things challenge and defy. Things embroider existence and make it empty. The technological approach, which, in its mastering attempt, diminishes things to objects of manipulation, is still an encounter, although perverted by the logic of powerfulness, with the obsessiveness of things. Although deprived of their thingly nature, technological objects impend obsessively over the existence of the I. The recycling of waste material, its re-admission into the exchange economy, does not extinguish its piling up at the periphery of the dwellings of the I. As in a self-fulfilling prophecy, dumps, the result of a fear response to the obsessiveness of things, turn into a new menace placed on the existence of the I. In a Hegelian spirit, the possession of objects by the I achieves its dialectical counterpart in the control of the I by its objects. The Hegelian proudly claims that the truth of the dialectical movement lies in its result. In the specific case, the truth of domination turns out to be being dominated.[3] Regardless of philosophical preferences and dissonances, the truth of the Hegelian result coincides with the truth of the non-Hegelian beginning. Despite and in its attempts at circumventing them, the I is inexorably exposed to things, obsessed by them, where "obsession is neither a modification nor a pathological exasperation of consciousness, but the very proximity of beings" (CPP 120).[4]

In the negative process that informs the Hegelian movement, if a truth has been conquered, another has been lost: the truth that obsessive exposure need not be an inspiration to war, but to peace; not to attacking, but to opening up; not to opposition, but to cooperation. Things need not be objects which try to dominate the I, from which the I must defend and protect itself by means of counterdomination, as if the best form of defense were the attack, as popular wisdom phrases it. As Levinas indicates in the opening pages of *Totality and Infinity,* the approach to the world which relates to it in terms of war and violence is vitiated by an ontological attitude aimed at the legitimation of that same violence thus enacted (TI 21ff). Oppositions lead to relations whose inner dynamics are developed in terms of power and force, winner and loser, stronger and weaker. The result of the dichotomic way of thinking, in its being shaped by the principle of noncontradiction imposing that opposites cannot coexist, rather than the establishment of peace, is inevitably a loss—the loss of the loser.

As Heidegger acknowledges, things stand in opposition only when their reality as things is denied. An object has only one surface: the one that confronts the I, and stands in opposition to it because of a primordial constituting activity that sees reality as a confrontation of subjects and objects. But, as Heidegger indicates in the later essays, besides being more originary, the structure of things is more intricate than that recognized to them by their interpretation in terms of objectivity—not only more complicated, but also more complex, that is, richer. In Heidegger's description, a thing has four directionalities. It is open toward the earth, toward the sky, toward mortals, and toward the divine. It includes corporeality as well as spirituality, rootedness as well as displacement, temporality as well as eternity. More fundamentally, to be in relation with things, to be able, as mortals, to be located within the open circularity they describe means to be in relation to them, not through opposition, but through what Heidegger has named *Gelassenheit:* an ontological attitude whose implications border on ethics in its recognition of the multilayeredness of things, and in its intimation to an act of listening, caring, attention to their alterity.

Ever since its first appearance on the scenes of being, in its bodily mortality the I, "body naked and indigent" (TI 127), is released to things, abandoned to the restlessness of their ubiquity. The movement of objectification and technological domination by which the I attempts a mastery of the restlessness of things, and which Heidegger sees as the loss of the thingness of things, the loss of the possibility of inhabiting the Fourfold, is already a response to a presence which cannot be ignored, unless at the cost of life—bodily life, to be sure. But, as Nietzsche remarks, such a life is the only existence human beings can be certain of. According to Levinas's analysis, the I is contraction into interiority, implosion of being that claims its own being for itself. Its story, together with a temporality which moves beyond the achronicity of being, begins at the moment of its upsurge into being (TO 51–57). Its movement possesses the unidirectionality of the emergence. What Levinas does not acknowledge, however, and what Heidegger seems to allow, although unthematized, is the truth that, even before the ontological constitution of any I, things are already there, and to be mortals means precisely to let oneself be placed at the crossroad where the thinging of things happens. Inscribed in the visible shape with which things present themselves to the world are traces of a past which, invisible, unrecognized as past, was there even before the movement of self-recognition accomplished by any I, and causing that acceleration of time with which temporality begins.

Inscribed in the visible form of things is thus preserved a story coming from a past more originary than that of any I, an immemorial past in which the earth and the sky, the divine but not these mortals, though maybe other mortals, have interwoven their existence, before these mortals, too, were allowed and welcomed within the open circle of the Fourfold. Even when produced by the most perverted technological manipulation, there is a sense in which things are never completely fabricated, a sense in which, in their materiality that is there before production, in their having been transformed—that is, before their consumption—they *come* to mortals, as in a gift, which is both unexpected and unreturnable, since the condition previous to the things' coming is unrestorable. In this sense, things bear in themselves not only traces of the finite and the infinite, of the mortal and the immortal, of time and eternity, but also of the temporal and the atemporal, of the archaic and the anarchic, in a coalescence of the synchronic, diachronic and the achronic.

It is this tension that, in its subtracting itself to the systematization in vain attempted by ontological procedures of thought, disrupts the I, causing it to resort to defensive positions—the work ethics through which the I, according to Levinas's description, subtracts the elemental to the anonymity of the *il y a* and inserts it into the identifiable world of things (TI 159ff). It is this origin in a past preceding any thematization and experience possible to the I, in what Levinas considers the nocturnal and mythical dimension of the *il y a,* that things bear hidden in the folds of their materiality. It is this past, guarded and preserved, and still lurking in the roughness of their apparent impenetrability to touch that allows things to have their own, idiomatic face. As Heidegger recognizes, what is encountered in things is not, as Levinas claims, an indeterminate *apeiron* which perfidiously "gives itself while escaping" (TI 141), "the reign of mythical gods" (TI 142), "faceless gods, impersonal gods to whom one does not speak" (TI 142). What is encountered is rather the configuration brought about by the ever new intertwining of the dimensions of the Fourfold, in which the Four achieve their own determination precisely through the relation they enter in things. In the thinging of the thing the Fourfold has always already a face—that of the thing in its thinging—that is, the thing's faciality.[5]

Philosophy, and Levinas among the other philosophers, has always resisted to the recognition to things of a faciality the significance of which goes beyond its biological meaning. If eyes, and with them the possibility of some faceness, are recognized, among all things, to animals, they are granted to them only as a manifestation of their animality, in its constitution of continuity and immanence. According to this line of interpretation, instinct, which properly characterizes animality, exhausts itself in the actions it promotes, in a coincidence of origins and goals which precludes any space for metaphysical discrepancy, for projection, for the difference between past, present, and future. However, such an interpretation retains its plausibility only if things, and with them animals, are understood in terms of essences rather than events, in terms of presences rather than the presencing of the Fourfold.

Anticipating a typical Levinasian theme—restricted by Levinas, however, (as Heidegger in a nonreferential comment indicates) to the description of the interpersonal relation—Heidegger suggests that "we tend to think of face to face encounter exclusively as a relation between human beings. . . . Yet being face to face with another has a more distant origin; it originates in that distance where earth and sky, the god and [the mortal] reach one another" (OWL 103-104). Granted, as Levinas shows, the uniqueness and specificity, not to be denied, of the human face to face relationship; nevertheless, Heidegger's different account of the origin of the face within the thing acknowledges the possibility that things too may be the source of an ethical encounter. The source is to be located not *in* the thing itself, which would make Heidegger liable to the accusations of ontologism moved against him by Levinas, but rather in the distance of the Fourfold that the thing maintains while bringing the Fourfold to a nearing.

It is from this distance that the possibility of a relation of face to face originates—a face to face not with humans, as Heidegger suggests, but with the faciality of the very things. Insofar as things maintain the distance—that is, insofar as they are let be as things and not reduced to objects—insofar as they display a structure of metaphysical depth interrupting the immanence of pure being, the persistence in being, they can be said to have a faciality. Not a human face, not human eyes, because the attempt to recognize such features in the nonhuman realm is a novel form of ethnological imperialism still assigning privileged status to the human entity, and failing thus to acknowledge fully the alterity of the nonhuman, but, nevertheless, a faciality that, ethically, refers to a beyond the being that the thing itself is. Silent, voiceless witnesses to our endeavors, things look at us and remind us, through the sheer expression of their pure presence, of another other, of another alterity—other than human, other than presence, other than being.

Double obsessiveness of things, then. On the one hand, things harass with the obsession of a perennial presence, which cannot be definitely resolved by its reabsorption into any dialectical or historical movement, because there are always more things. On the other hand, the presence of things comes from a *locus* in front of which thinking has to stop, a place where the earth and the sky are deprived of their solar element, since the Platonic sun, as Levinas's ethics demands, has remained beyond being. It is a place where there is no direct light, but only the reverberation of the light, a place which thinking cannot penetrate unless gropingly, because the presence of the Fourfold in things is rather a presencing, which maintains in itself the characters of an absencing.

Never fully developed, never fully unfolded, never completely transparent to thinking, the thingness of things retains something mysterious, separate, sacred. In *Being and Time,* Heidegger remarks how there exists a conspicuousness of things that reveals itself when things resist insertion in the self-referential economy of

Zeughaftigkeit. Rather than being constituted as a lack of equipmentality, such a resistance is ontologically primary. There is an opaqueness of things, which tradition has identified with their materiality, that subtracts itself to the penetration of thinking as well as to pragmatic manipulations by the hand. Such an impenetrability suspends the intentionality of the same, its lust for appropriation and possession. Despite all intellectual and physical manipulation, even in matter that has been reduced to its highest degree of transparency there exists a vibration of being, which fragments itself but does not totally submits itself, and which, as the waste material at the peripheries of town, always reappears to jeopardize and therefore challenge the supremacy of the I. Such an impenetrability suspends the power of domination on the side of the I, neutralizes the intentionality of its appropriative movements, and opens the I up to things in awe, admiration, and wonder. As Kant very well knew, two are the moments of inspiration filling the human heart with admiration: the moral law, whose source is, in an anti-Kantian move,[6] in the ethical Other of whom Levinas speaks; but also, in a Thaletian remembrance, the starred sky above, that which because of its distance cannot be grasped and possessed, like the things, which in their impenetrability always refer to a beyond of which there is no possession but traces in the very things.

And yet, as Heidegger's meditation on technology reveals, the glimmer into the beyond, which the locating of oneself in the space opened up by the Fourfold enables, is frail and endangered. The little opening onto the beyond that the opacity of things reveals is always in danger of closing itself up in the opacity of the refusal. Unlike the originary opacity of things, rather than disclosing the same to the alterity of things the opacity of the refusal rejects the same upon itself, upon what Levinas describes as the ontological constitution of the I. The thing then turns into an object, to which the same reacts with a lust for power and domination, whereas the originary opacity of things assumes the characters of its inexpressiveness—

that observed by those who claim, like the philosophical tradition, that things have no faceness.

From the ubiquity of things always referring further, to a beyond never completely transparent; from their altercity always on the verge of disappearing and yet never capable of pausing and resting upon itself; from their presenting themselves with a faciality through which the Fourfold expresses its determination comes the possibility of a call and demand that things place on mortals—the possibility that things, in their alterity, summon an appeal.

How do things appeal, however? How can they place demands on the I, when they seem to lack exactly the feature that enables the possibility of a communication of the appeal, namely, language? In Levinas, the appeal from the Other from which the ethical dimension originates occurs by means of its expression: first through the eyes of the Other, which, in the face, by looking at the I question his right to mastery, and then, as the thematization of the look, in language. But do things have a language?

Affectionate to an interpretation of human beings that defines them in terms of their having *logos,* in its double meaning of reason and language, the philosophical tradition has always been very reluctant to recognize a language to things. When it has admitted to such a possibility, it has done so by legitimating some versions of human language: animistic, religious, mathematical, in a translation that reinterprets things in terms of human needs and organization of actions. Even if impossibilitated to ignore, because of its commitment to the truth, the vocalization of instincts, passions, and feelings that shapes the animal world, philosophy has generally denied the legitimacy of their description as language. Rather, it has understood the articulation of such pulsions as sounds, not organizable in terms of a logical formulation and therefore not a language. "Because plants and animals are lodged in their respective environment but are never placed freely in the lighting of being which alone is 'world,' they lack language," writes Heidegger. He continues: "in its essence language is not the utterance of an organism; nor is it the expression of a living thing" (LH 206). In this scenario which denies things, whether artificial, mineral, vegetal, or even animal, a proper language, language becomes the exhaltation of the human, and humanly shaped, world, rather than the celebration of the mortals' relation with things.

Yet, the denial to things of a structured language need not work to the detriment of things. Rather, it might work toward their liberation from the context of a logocentric ethics, and toward the recognition of their difference and alterity. As Levinas acknowledges when recognizing the possibility to place an ethical demand even to the mute other, to the other deprived of words—that is, of the structuring of language that takes place in speech (BPW 167)—the lack of language is not equivalent to the impossibility of expression, and therefore intelligibility. As André Neher points out,[7] there are instances where the only occuring communication is, and must be, nonverbal, or even more radically, silenced. Such is the case of the Holocaust, where no language is dignified enough, and adequate, to describe the horrors of history without betraying the tragicity of the events. There are instances where silence, not a silence contoured by words, but the absolute silence of the impossibility of speech, is more expressive than words. On the other hand, in his meditations on language in *Being and Time,* Heidegger describes, under the category of "idle talk," situations where verbality does not convey any genuine communication at all (BT 211ff), where discourse "serves not so much . . . to keep being-in-the-world open for us in an articulated understanding, as rather to close it off, and cover up the entities within-the-world" (BT 213). Levinas himself admits that the expression is ethical before its formulation in words, since the appeal that demands from the I that she or he become good is an injunction that can be voiced in silence, as well as in sounds, as well as in gestures. That is, speech is not essential to the expression of things. To relinquish the necessity of a structured language for there to be an ethics of things means, simultaneously, to release such an ethics from any anthropologocentric suspicion and to recognize to things the possibility for an ethical demand.

Although in a way different from the logocentric tradition, things express themselves. They do so in the purest, most immediate form of expression: through their sheer eventuation. By being as things, they express the Fourfold that gathers in them. Their expression becomes thus their idiomatic voice, where language is, according to Heidegger's formulation, "the lighting-concealing advent of being itself" (LH 206). Since there are as many things as there are ways of eventuation, things express themselves in as many idioms as there are things,[8] to the effect that each idiom is particular to every single presencing of the thing. In compliance with the different ways in which the Fourfold's interplay occurs, and in accordance with the different *oikoi* thus established, the center of discourse, from logocentric, becomes decentered, pluricentric, and plurivocal, in a stereophony which mirrors the things' uniqueness and irreducibility to one another. In this sense, as the thingly world (whether artificial, mineral, vegetal, or animal) testifies, there is no unified language, no esperanto of things, but rather their symphony in an ecological, polyrhythmic song that each thing, separately and yet jointly, contributes to create.

The Babelic chaos of languages is the divine restoration of diversification and differences against the artificial unification created by human desire. In it, though, incommunicability reigns. Not so for things. The translation from one thingly idiom into the other is possible for mortals as inhabitants of the Fourfold, but only as an operation of deracination and transference into the different spaciousnesses different things disclose. To hear the language of things means to enter the spaciousness of things, to let them be as things, and thus to become thingly. Yet, because of the impossibility of a complete access to things given the alterity that, as Heidegger describes, the Fourfold implicates, no transference can ever be absolute coincidence, thus incapacitating the flattening of things into objects or presences ready for either intellectual or technological manipulation. To transfer into things means for mortals to enter, but without possession, into a relationship with things which respects and inhabits the spaciousness that the Fourfold display.

The lack of coincidence, the distance that is thus maintained, constitutes the ground for the possibility of difference: between mortals and things, and among things themselves. No unified gaze, which also means no normative approach to things, is ever allowed. All translations imply violation and betrayal, and thus the need of a different interpretation. As is the case for Abraham, to enter the spaciousness of things does not mean not to have a home, but to be willing and ready to abandon such an originary home. Only *via negationis* is the nomadic one who has no home; otherwise, she or he is the one who has not one, but many homes, even though without possessing any. Homelessness is not poverty; it is the possibility of infinite richness.

As Heidegger's meditation on the Fourfold pointed out, the space things delimit, which constitutes their form, erupts the boundaries of an enclosure, and reconstitutes itself as an open space in which the four dimensions meet. This is the thing's proper spatiality in the form of its spaciousness. The depth things reveal, in their spaciousness, also implicates a temporal depth, since each of the four components of the Fourfold enters the relation enabled by things endowed with a temporality of its own (the transcendent eternity of the divines, the finite temporality of the mortals, the immanent presencing of the earth and the sky). The traces of such multiple temporalities are, although hardly and only to the attentive ear, borne on the very things. To each of the Four, then, the thing tells the story of the other three, so that the narrative mode constitutes the temporal dimension of the thing. It is the narrative modality stratified in the layers of materiality of which each thing is made that enables things to have their own faciality. Faciality is given precisely by the wrinkling of the temporal stories on what traditional philosophy understands as the unidimensional surface of things.

At the limit between being and beyond being, things participate in being without being exhausted in and by it. Their facialities express the presencing of a beyond from which and to which the demand things place upon mortals originates. The form of the demand is the very presence of things, the obsessiveness of their gathering at the margins of human existence, of their impending over such an existence, which is, in its very essence, exposed and thrown to the mercy of things. The content of the demand is, primarily, an invitation to enter the spaciousness of the thing, that place where the Fourfold gathers. In this sense, the demand is a demand to come into contact, not in the modes of manipulation, but rather in the modes of a nearing that maintains the alterity of the Fourfold.

However, as Heidegger's meditation on "The Thing" illustrates, the place of the gathering cannot be penetrated without the danger of violating its nearing character. The possibility of an admission into it, then, must be renegotiated not as to penetrate, but as to be invited; not as to intrude, but as to be welcomed; not as to be the host, but as to be the guest; not as to be the master, but as to be the servant. The appeal things send out is an invitation to put down the dominating modes of thought, to release oneself to things, and only thus to let them be as things, rather than as objects of technical and intellectual manipulation.

The invitation by things to the approach contains already both an injunction and a prohibition. The injunction is to let things be the dwelling of the Fourfold, and the prohibition is to violate such an injunction. The invocation is to restrain the I's voracity, and the prohibition is to operate through practices which equate freedom with autonomy, unlimited power, and mastery. Ultimately, the demand things place on human beings is an appeal to remain faithful to their own mortality, a reminder of the finitude of subjectivity. Heidegger characterizes death as "the possibility of the absolute impossibility" (BT 294), whereas Levinas describes it as "an experience of the passivity of the subject" (TO 70), which foreshadows the greater, but less terminal passivity experienced by the I in her or his encounter with the other. In both cases, death is recognized as the ultimate trait characterizing subjectivity, whether as being-toward-death or as absolute passivity. In their exposure to things, it is not as humans, but as mortals that human beings are welcomed within the mirroring play of the Fourfold. By demanding from humans that they relinquish their lust for ontological power and domination, and by inviting them to enter into the place of the Fourfold through a releasement of themselves to things, things rejoin humans to the ultimate feature which characterizes them. They bestow humans the gift of mortality.

Mortality as blessing, and not as a limitation, is the gift things donate. To be mortals is to be within limits, to live an existence marked by the margins of birth and death. Yet, being within limits is not tantamount to being limited. The difference between the two concepts concerns the depth of their ontological semantics. Limit becomes limitation only when finitude drifts into fallenness, condemnation, sin, as in the Judeo-Christian, Neoplatonic tradition, which reinterprets existence in terms of fall, sin, and guilt, and therefore in need of salvation and redemption. Limitation implicates a constraint, a force that is repressed, blocked in the exercise of its expansive movement, and condemned to fold back upon itself, in a movement toward intimization whose features have been explored by Nietzsche in his analysis of *ressentiment.*[9] Conversely, the notion of limit is structurally exempt from any reactive connotation. The limit signifies the delimited area within which one is able to unfold one's own vitality, expand one's own energy, fulfill one's own destination. In the Athens conference, Heidegger describes the limit as "that through which something is gathered into what is most proper to it, so as to appear in all its fullness, to come into presence" (PA 368). Rather than a condemnation and a confinment, then, the delimited area is the area of one's proper location. To be delimited is to be placed somewhere, rather than everywhere, in a repudiation of the impossible ubiquity to which universal reason aspires. To be within limits is to be allowed the possibility of having a place, and therefore being welcomed within a home—the home of the Fourfold the thing hosts.[10] Only because they are within limits can mortals enter the place of gathering the thing is, the site of the encounter, the curved space of ethics. And yet, exactly because they are within limits, they can surpass their limits, and ethically respond to the appeal of things, thus inhibiting the transformation of their within-limits into a limitation.

The demand from things to enter the area delimited by the Fourfold is ultimately, for humans, an appeal to authenticity, a Nietzschean invocation to become what we are.[11] Only by being mortal—that is, only by being within limits—can one enter into the Fourfold. Only by being mortal can one encounter the thing. Being within limits, in its nuance of being located in one's proper place, also entails a dismissal of the attempt to usurp the place of others, and the recognition of one's own constitution in terms of such others. To be within limits means for the mortals to renounce the ontological lust for power and domination, to make oneself powerless while letting the divine be the divine, the earth be the earth, the sky be the sky, the things be things. The appeal from things is an appeal to mortality as powerlessness and passivity, or maybe patience—the patience which it takes to enter the place of the encounter with things.

Appeal to finitude as blessing, then, is the gift-giving virtue of things. Yet, such an appeal exceeds itself in that it resonates with more than the appeal to the limitness constituting the ontological dimension of mortals. The appeal is not simply a demand to remain faithful to mortals' most proper nature. The appeal from things is an appeal to ethics in the restricted sense of being an appeal to move within the place of an encounter. Furthermore, it is an appeal to ethics in the excessive sense of commanding mortals to transcend the limitness of their own ontological constitution, to exceed themselves.

If to be within limits means to be "implaced"[12] within

things as mortals, being within limits also implicates the sense of being at the limit, on the threshold, ready to cross the threshold and transcend oneself, to release oneself toward the alterity of the elements that encounter the mortals in the Fourfold. As is the case for Nietzsche's tightrope walker in *Thus Spoke Zarathustra,*[13] to be on the threshold is to be suspended: between finitude and infinity, between mortality and divinity, but also, because of the multidimensional structure of the Fourfold, which displaces all oppositional systems of relation, between the earth and the sky, floating between sameness and alterity, open to, because opened up by, that alterity with which the mortals are in a mirroring relation. Things appeal thus to a noncoincidence with oneself, to a subjectivity constituted in terms of noncorrespondence with oneself and of correspondence to others, which displaces one's proper being and forces it toward a beyond-being in which the alterity of the Fourfold, and hence of things, is maintained. The appeal from things is an appeal to abandon oneself to things, to give oneself to alterous relations, and therefore to make of oneself a gift, in absolute generosity, without any warrantee of a reward, of recognition, of return.

At the same time familiar and stranger, things simultaneously speak of belonging and deracination, of gathering and fragmentation, of being within limits and being at the limit, on the threshold. In this ambivalent significance, things enjoin simultaneously to leave ontological egoism and to submit to a metaphysical subjectivity in which the constitution of selfhood is relational rather than solipsistic, generous rather than retributively fair or just, ethical rather than legalistic—not with reference to humans, but to things. The appeal from things turns therefore into an invitation to the celebration of things, in pure loss and gratuitousness. How to celebrate things in their alterity becomes the ethical question waiting for an answer. Tenderness, as the mortals' response to the appeal of things, is the beginning of such an answer.

12 ❖ Touch, Attention, Tenderness

Heidegger's initial meditation on things in *Being and Time* offers a precious suggestion: the understanding of things in terms of *pragmata*—that is, in terms of a "concernful dealing" (BT 96) with them—discloses touch as the privileged mode of coming into a relation with things. His subsequent reflections on *techne* and technology in the following years, however, warn against the ambiguous nature of touch, a modality always on the verge of falling into the excesses of technological manipulation, depriving things of their thingly aspect. Yet, there is something fundamentally intriguing in Heidegger's original observation: the suggestion that, when it comes to the possibility of entering an ethical relation with things, touch retains a primacy unparalleled by any other sensory organ. Although in a context unrelated to things, the primacy of touch as a dimension of sensibility is acknowledged by Levinas when claiming that "touch is a pure approach and a proximity that is not reducible to the experience of proximity" (CPP 118).

The distinctiveness of touch over any other organ of perception had already been established by Aristotle, who in the *De Anima* devoted several pages to an analysis of such a mode of perception which "act[s] by contact" (423b3).[1] Against the Platonic interpretation of thinking as a mode of vision, Aristotle conceives of thought as analogous to perceiving, and establishes a comparison between the mind and the hand (432a1), going so far as to assert that "men are well or poorly endowed with intelligence in proportion to their sense of touch, and no other sense; for men of hard skin and flesh are poorly, and men of soft flesh well endowed with intelligence (*dianoia*)" (421a24ff). That is, the possibility of an access to things, which Aristotle identifies here with intelligence (of the *ousiai*), is a matter of sensitivity. The one who is more sensitive is also the one who has a greater understanding of the truth, which includes the truth of things in their alterity and the preservation of such an alterity as part of the truth. Even for Aristotle, the philosophical path on the way to the truth proceeds through ethics, as the place where an encounter (a contact, the characters of which still need to be explored) with things is allowed to happen, where the human sensitivity is allowed to flourish and be nourished by the obsessive appeal of things.

But why does touch retain such a privileged position? First of all, according to Aristotle, touch is primary because it determines the very essence of what it means to be mortal, in its double significance of being alive and being subject to death: "without touch an animal cannot exist" (435b17), but "the excess of tangible qualities . . . destroys the animal" (435b14). It is by touch that one lives, and by touch that one dies, Aristotle seems to say. Heralding both life and death, touch displays an ambiguous structure of activity and passivity: the one who touches is also the one who is touched, in a contact which may be mortiferous, but which is, in any case, exposure to the obsession of the encountered. Touching, subjectivity is exposed to that which is touched; its very activity makes it defenseless, powerless, vulnerable. Certainly subjectivity can revolt, rebel toward its own passiveness, and embrace the aggressivity of technological manipulation, as Heidegger is aware. But in its basic structure as portrayed by Aristotle's analysis, touch emerges as a modality at least capable to correspond to the obsessive appeal of things to enter the Fourfold by abandoning oneself to being conditioned (*be-dingt*) by things.

What is most puzzling to Aristotle, and hence most remarkable about touch, is the fact that touch alone, among all other senses, perceives by immediate contact. Whereas all other senses necessitate a medium, "we perceive tangible things not by a medium, but at the same time as the medium" (423b17). There is no external intermediary between that which touches and that which is touched—that is, there is no means between the toucher and the touched, since the flesh, which might appear as such a means, is itself felt upon contact.[2] That is, "in touch proximity is a special factor."[3] Again, the recognition of touch as a privileged mode to correspond to the appeal of things to enter the Fourfold, to become near, to come in contact finds here ground for support: direct proximity happens not through vision, smelling, or hearing, but only through touch.

The absence of any intermediary represents a crucial point in the constitution of ethical proximity (OBBE 81–98, CPP 109–26), and certainly a main point in favor of touch as the possibility of such proximity. As Levinas has acknowledged in many of his essays, a fundamental, devastating role in the perpetration of the ontology of violence characterizing Western philosophy is imputable to mediation (TI 44–45). The presence of a mediator amounts to the presence of a third perspective from which the relation between the I and the other can be overviewed from a common standpoint, and therefore bridged and totalized in the commonality of an encompassing embrace. The space that mediation seemingly maintains between the two terms to be mediated is, rather than a peaceful place of encounter, the space where arbitrariness, abuse, violence, "ontological imperialism" (TI 44) happens. In this sense, mediation, always ontological, never recuperable to ethical redemption, is the betrayal of the possibility of alterity. Where mediation is present, the other as Other disappears.

Two more features mark the suggestiveness of Aristotle's analysis of touch for the possibility of an ethics of things: the pervasiveness of touch, and the uniqueness of its intentional object. In his attempt to describe touch by analogy with the other senses, Aristotle is rather troubled by the fact that, in the case of touch, it is particularly difficult to locate the organ appointed to being "receptive of the form of sensible objects without the matter" (424a19). He even wonders whether there may be more than one of such an organ (422b20). Finally, the organ of touch is, although not specifically identified, at least located: "that which is perceptive of what is touched is within" (423b23)—that is, touch is the most inward sense, which acts in intimate connection with its means (the flesh) as the power of discerning sensations (*to meson kritikon*).[4] The impossibility of a unified location, and its intimacy with the flesh, which wraps the mortal body and constitutes it, conveys the pervasiveness of touch, which cannot be stripped from mortals without stripping them from their flesh, and hence from their mortality: "without touch an animal cannot exist" (435b17). Lived vulnerability thus becomes the pervasive dimension characterizing mortals as such, in a pervasiveness which turns ethics, as the place where the contact which makes one vulnerable occurs, into a primary dimension. To be vulnerably mortal, to be touching, to be within ethics—all these coincide.

The lived vulnerability of touch exposes the one who touches to a particular form of contact with what is touched, in a relation which retains at least the potentiality not to degenerate into more destructive forms of ontological violence neglectful of all alterity and otherness. Whereas sight synthetizes different objects or qualities of objects, gathering the visible into a common horizon which, through intellectual vision, enables the possibility of abstracting from such objects what is in common among them to construct notions of universality, touch encounters its intentional objects always one at a time, in their individuality and particularity, and never in the abstractness of their universality. Not only, as Aristotle notices, is the contact with things immediate, leaving neither the toucher nor the touched unaltered, but touch also entails an intimate commitment to the uniqueness of its object, and hence to the possibility of being addressed by its alterity or otherness.

Whether to caress or to violate, the hand that touches has to be directed and oriented by what it encounters in the contact, which, even when it gets destroyed, confronts what touches it with a resistance to assimilation coming from the toughness and impenetrability of its own materiality. Even when such a resistance is overwhelmed, no identity or assimilation is possible between the hand that touches and that which is touched, which maintains its alterity or otherness, although as a violated, fragmented, profanated other. No unity, fusion, assimilation is ever possible between the toucher and the touched. One cannot become the other through tactile experiences, in an exchange of identities which would annihilate the distance between them, would make each of them replaceable, and ultimately identical. What is touched remains compellingly exterior, so that touch is a contact without possession, without belonging, in difference. It remains an approach, a nearing, a contact without possibility for satisfaction and rest. Nonmediated, pervasive, vulnerable, touch constitutes for mortals the possibility to enter that place of an encounter with things that takes the name of an ethics of things. More than simply a mode of sensory perception, touch becomes a metaphor for how to enter such a place.[5]

As Heidegger very well knows, however, the purity of a nearing immune from dangers does not belong to touch, which in its constitution discloses a frailty analogous to that of the things with which it wants to enter a contact without possession. As Levinas phrases it, "contact can turn into palpation" (CPP 118), that is, into ontological cognition aimed at informing and transforming in profanation. Whereas ontology always retains the structure of an economy of violence, ethics does not offer any absolute guarantee of a successful move beyond violence. In the postmodern times of the death of God, all absolute certainties have been abandoned, and what is left is the challenge of a resistance which hopes to be ethical, but without self-assurances. Ambivalence has become the rule. Therefore, the dividing line that separates ethical touching from ontological grasping is tenuous: touching is always on the verge of drifting into grasping because of the ontological power of the concept, which aims at assimilating the other through its recomprehension within the structure of the system, and which, as Heidegger's meditations on *techne* reveal, finds its most evident instantiation in the aberrations of technological manipulation.

And yet, despite its tenuousness, the line of differentiation separating touching from grasping is clearly demarcated. Grasping occurs when, rather than being oriented by that which is to be touched, touch lets itself be determined by the needs of the one who touches. That is, the ethical possibilities of touch are betrayed when touch ignores the appeal from the other, in this case when it ignores the obsessive appeal from things. In so doing, touch betrays its own nature as described already by Aristotle, which is a nature made of vulnerability and exposure to what remains exterior to it. The betrayal of touch, and of the possibility of an ethical encounter with things, occurs every time touch forgets its vulnerability; that is, every time touch neglects to be declined in juncture with listening. Without engaging in an analysis of the modality of listening, to which both Heidegger and Levinas, in different ways, have devoted several pages of their works,[6] it suffices to say that to remain faithful to itself and to the possibility of the encounter with things which is in its power to enable, although not to grant, touch needs to be declined by the ad-tention paid to the appeal of things, it needs to ad-tend to them, to be ad-tentive.[7] Attention becomes an essential component of the human side of the ethics of things.

Analogous to touch, with which it shares several affinities, attention is structurally stretched between activity and passivity.[8] Ultimately, attention is an exercise in patience. In its ad-tending to something, in its concentrating itself on the object to which it wishes to devote itself, attention reveals the activity of busying oneself, of engaging oneself, of bustling about. Tenaciously and persistently, attention tends toward something. And yet, in such a fervor of activity, attention can be successful, can avoid falling into invasiveness only if it lets itself be directed by that toward which it tends, if it folds itself upon itself, hollows its activity out, and makes itself passive. The fervor of the activity comes from the degree of the passivity, it nourishes itself upon it.

In its being an exercise in patience, which strengthens and consolidates it, attention is, fundamentally, humility. Not the humbleness of servility, but the dignity of a deference that wishes to welcome and assert differences and othernesses characterizes attention. Attention waits for the other to make the first move, the first offer to which it will respond by being attentive. What is deferred in this movement of humility is, primarily, the power of a will that wants to modify, rather than being modified by, things. The move is one toward eccentricity, toward the periphery of the Fourfold (which mortals perhaps inhabit, but do not possess) because at the center are the things. Humility, then, is a centrifugal movement away from a notion of subjectivity constructed as the giver of meaning. It is disposition to the loss of meaning, to displacement, renunciation to being the archaic authority legislating reality. In humility, the light of reason, the Apollinian sun which proudly engages in its own systematization of the world and things through a process of individuation whose rules are endemic to the very reason that establishes them, has burnt out. It has been replaced by what Levinas suggestively names, although only in reference to the structure of desire displayed by the approach of the personally other, the "night of the erotic," a night where the path is oriented only by the touch which tentatively, and yet amorously, follows the uncertain and ever-differing silhouette of things. Humility is an act of love of the one who lets herself or himself be taken by hand and led by things. Not the erotic sensuality of passionality, but the more feeble and modest affection of tenderness is what constitutes such a love.

Again, like touch, attention can only be concerned with the particular, which, in its uniqueness and specificity, inspires and nourishes attention. And yet, attention retains an element of indeterminacy, which prevents its closure into the staticity of essences, and maintains its open and welcoming character.[9] Although always directed toward the particular, attention does not know, yet, what will inspire its being attentive. Attention occurs in the dimension of the *insomnia,* of the watch that waits for, without knowing what this "for" is which is to come, and for which one waits. As Heidegger writes, "waiting all right; but never awaiting, for awaiting already links itself with re-presenting and what is re-presented. . . . In waiting we leave open what we are waiting for" (DT 68). In its indeterminacy, attention is unconditioned welcoming, unconditioned letting oneself be guided by things.

Active and yet passive, humble and yet not servile, specific yet indeterminate, attention inhabits that narrow strip of land, perhaps the strip of land of the promise made to Abraham, where ethical separation between the terms can be maintained in the absolution of their relation. Subjectivity is not extinguished in the passivity of a mystical disappearance into the things it encounters, but is rather reaffirmed in its mortality as vulnerability. The alterity of things, far from being annihilated by the subject by which they are encountered, directs and guides the mortals and therefore leads them to a welcoming which is, first of all, a being welcomed within things themselves. When touch is declined by attention, grasping becomes caressing, whereas attention itself, from condition for the possibility of the encounter of mortals as mortals with things, changes into an ethical sentiment, and it becomes tenderness, that is, attentive touch.[10]

The derivation of tenderness from attention, which assimilates tenderness to a modality of touch, implies that its nature be analogous to that from which it originates, and to that which it declines. Like touch, tenderness is affected from the outside. Its motives are exterior to it, independent from it, acting on it. They lie in those things toward which tenderness exerts itself; they are directed by those things. Tenderness is to be ex-tended—that is, stretched—toward and by the outside. In this sense, tenderness is passivity, patience, susceptibility to what is other than itself and the subject in which it is experienced. To be tender is to be inspired. Yet, despite the affinities with the sensory modality of touch, tenderness is not ruled by the chaotic disorder of accidentality shaping sensations. Rather, in its active structure that brings it to be stubborn, tenacious, persistent, tenderness is endowed with the rigor and seriousness of reason; a reason oriented not by the self, but by the alterity of the things to which it applies, which give tenderness its planning forsightedness. In this sense, tenderness is void of the casuality, frivolity, and arbitrariness which inform sensations, because it possesses its own measure, its own directive criteria in the things themselves. A sentiment but not a psychological feeling, tenderness is rather a metaphysical horizon, a way of being which, aroused by the appeal of things, enables the move to the ethical place of their encounter.

Tenderness as a *Stimmung,* then—as a mood and attunement. As Heidegger has pointed out in the existential analysis of *Dasein* contained in *Being and Time*, attunement is not simply a psychological phenomenon. Rather, its nature is ontological, always disclosive and revelatory, insofar as it manifests "how one is, and how one is faring" (BT 173). Attunement is revelatory of one's *ethos,* of one's own place (according to the ancient meaning of the Greek word)[11] with respect to being.[12] But, as the analysis of the structure of things has disclosed, things reveal continuous displays of alterity which impede their interpretation in merely ontological terms. In things, there is some alterity; not simply being, things express a beyond being in the signification of their own depth. This in turn means that, despite Heidegger, and also despite Levinas, things possess a metaphysical dimension surpassing all ontology. In more Heideggerian terms, being does not exhaust itself in the beings by which it gives itself, or, in Levinas's more metaphysical terms, the Saying is never completely reducible to the said, although it is necessarily always reduced to it. The structure of being, which gives itself in things, because of the mirror-play of the Fourfold, which contains displacement and differing, always indicates beyond itself, toward a beyond being toward which tenderness is responsive. Rather than simply an ontological notion, centered around being, tenderness becomes a metaphysical concept because of the opening up of subjectivity toward the thinging of the thing which sustains its nature. Tenderness discloses an *ethos,* a place from which the place of the ethical encounter with things as things, and not as objects (as it would happen if tenderness were merely an ontological mood) can be entered. Insofar as it allows the encounter with things as things, tenderness moves beyond its ontological meaning, to access the vastness of the metaphysical dimension. In other terms, tenderness is the breaking point where the ontological structure is allowed to access its metaphysical beyond. It is, to employ the words of a lay thinker who uses a religious terminology, "the strait gate through which the Messiah might enter."[13] In the postmodern world devoid of all gods, tenderness becomes a secularized form of prayer.

Ontological because it reveals to mortals their own place, their own being, and yet metaphysical, because it opens them up to a beyond being of which the things carry the trace in the interplay of the Fourfold, tenderness lives in and on tensions, in and on ambivalences, which provide it with a richness precious in times of philosophical poverty deriving from the end of the great totalizing systems and, Heidegger says, of philosophy itself. As Nietzsche says, "one is *fruitful* only at the cost of being rich in contradictions."[14] In its constitutive ambivalences, tenderness, a notion always kept at the margins of philosophy, may have much to offer to a philosophical discourse that does not want to abandon things to the violations of ontological manipulation, violations which are the more serious the more rationally planned they are.

First of all, then, is the tension, inherited from attention, between activity and passivity, which makes tenderness firm, determined, obstinate, and yet inspired, oriented, ruled by that toward which it is tender. Then there is the tension, derived from the constitution of its intentional object, between ontology and metaphysics, which places tenderness in the privileged but onerous condition of being the pivot on which the destiny of things is played. More fundamentally, however, there is the tension of being stretched over the arch of time; not as an overarching modality, towering over the threefold temporal dimensions, as if a third point of view busy with the desperate and impossible task of a soteriological salvation of all events of history, as if in a messianic endevor, but rather as a structure whose very nature is interwoven with temporality.

Analogous to attention, tenderness is always tending to the particular thing which inspires it with the movement of its presencing. Therefore, tenderness is always in the present, occupied by the temporality of the instant in which it unfolds itself. Yet, in the appeal of the thing to which it tends, an immemorial past of lived experiences, expectations, and fears addresses itself to tenderness. Therefore, if tenderness is in the present, it is oriented also by that past which is borne inscribed in the roughness of the thing presenting itself, and from that past it derives nourishment and vitality. Exerted in the present, oriented by the past, tenderness looks at a duplicitous future. It looks at the future of things, which, with the strength of desperation coming from the awareness of the impossibility and impracticability of all holistic systems, tenderness still nobly attempts to preserve from the degeneration into objects of manipulation. And it also looks at the future of tenderness itself, since tenderness knows that no matter how promptly it comes to the scene, it is never promptly enough. Conversely, it is always, somehow, too late; something is already lost: the Fourfold has already abandoned the thing, so that the more tender tenderness is, the more tender it should in fact be, to allow for the fulfillment of that ethical encounter that is always displaced and postponed, because of the very structure of alterity revealing itself in the thing.

Stretched between the temporal dimensions, never fixed to any of them, since even the present, in which it is anchored, receives its determination from the past and the future which substantiate it, tenderness discloses an overflowing and floating consistency that enables it not to solidify into limits that soon become limitations. Not contour-less, but contour-free, tenderness continuously shifts into the different spaciousnesses described by the Fourfold in things, and lets itself be shaped by them. Incessantly moving and rearranging its boundaries, in its rigidity and yet mobility, tenderness is able to approach disparate things without ever losing the features that characterize it. Although always tending to a particular thing, tenderness can truly be applied to any thing; the realm of its action is in(de)finite.

Far from being indulgence, resignation, or acceptance of the status quo, tenderness' lack of discrimination toward its recipients is delivered from acquiescence. The flexibility and fluidification of its application signals the absence, in tenderness, of procedures of marginalization and exclusion which have brought about the assimilation and annihilation of the other, whether person or thing. As all readers of fairytales know, ogres, monsters, witches, even the devil have a face, albeit disfigured by the evil actions which have become their normal practice of life. The rationalistic philosophical tradition relegates the world of imagination to children's entertainment. It is Paul Ricoeur who, in *The Symbolism of Evil,* reminds the too rationalistically educated philosophical consciousness that "the symbol gives rise to thought. That sentence, which enchants me, says two things: the symbol gives; but what it gives is occasion for thought, something to think about."[15] Even the monsters created by a perverted technology ask for a tender gesture, whose expression, rather than going in the direction of their substantiation and nourishment, may assume the features of the isolation and neutralization not of their nature, which remains as a *memento* of the powerfulness of destruction, but of their destructive potentiality, since their destructiveness jeopardizes the possibility of the expression of other alterities and othernesses, and of more tenderness. The measure for the quantitative and qualitative practice of tenderness is not in the one who is tender, but in things themselves, in their ability to host, or not to host, the Fourfold. Ultimately, the measure of tenderness is in how thingly a thing is. Specific, insofar as it is oriented to the particular, and yet nondiscriminating, tenderness requires different applications in different circumstances. It is part of its nature that its practice cannot be narrowed down to the certainties derived from a table of codified principles, norms, or rules. Although tenderness is ethical, its ethicity cannot be fixated into a morality. Rather, tenderness is a challenge, the stake of which are things, and for mortals, the possibility of dwelling by the things, and thus being truly mortal.

Always inadequate, always belated, always uprooted because of its indefinite mobility, always tentative in the modalities of its own manifestation, tenderness exerts itself in trembling trepidation. But in tenderness, trepidation rids itself of the continuous frustration leading to neurosis characterizing the existential analysis of mortality. The trepidation of tenderness is not for the mortals, as if trepidation were a form of *Angst,* in which subjectivity concerns itself with being still understood as *its own* being. Tenderness trepidates for things. Its trepidation is not for the finite, but rather for the Infinite that discloses itself in things and to which all possibility of complete access is banned, because of the economy of violence in which the Saying necessarily becomes the said. Therefore, tenderness is never enough.

This is so, not because of a lack of power inherent in the I that enacts tenderness, nor because of a deficiency in the structure of tenderness which might be overcome by reversion to a different mode of touch. The vulnerability of tenderness, its precariousness and fragility correspond to the structure of things, which are themselves vulnerable, frail, always on verge of disappearing. And from this same vulnerability, precariousness, and fragility tenderness receives its strength and reinforcement. Since things are so frail and precarious, and hence precious, tenderness needs to be ever more tender. On the things' behalf, it needs to resist always ever more. But also, since tenderness itself is so belated, tenderness needs to always anticipate itself, and, again, make itself ever more tender. In the end, all tenderness is an occasion for ever new tenderness. For mortals, this implies an appeal to always be eccentered and excessive, beyond themselves, beyond their ontological being, altogether beyond being. Rather than a feeling or duty, tenderness proves itself to be a metaphysical dimension displacing mortals to the kingdom of the beyond—that is, tenderness is the access to the ethical place in which an encounter with things may happen.

13 ❖ Saddened Tenderness: Violence and Resistance

"Everyone will readily agree that it is of the highest importance, to know whether we are not duped by morality" (TI 21). This statement, with which *Totality and Infinity* begins, contains the enunciation of a problem that has become more and more urgent after Hegel's considerations on the vanity of an internal morality that does not translate into political activity, but also after Nietzsche's criticism of all forms of moralistic asceticisms sublating the faithfulness to the earth into the illusory promise of a kingdom of heaven in which all wrongs and unjustices will be mended and compensated. The urgency of the theoretical problem has been strengthened by the happening of the *Shoah*. In its face, as in the face of more recent tragedies constellating a historical horizon which, for Levinas, can never be exempt from some degree of ontological violence, ethics has not been able to pose itself as a bulwark against the advancing of destruction and evil.[1]

The problem Levinas formulates, which constitutes the crux of all moralities in this time of the death of all gods, is that of the potential illusoriness of morality, the risk of being mocked by morality when confronted with the structural violence which seems to characterize the economy of being. The danger, Levinas admonishes, is that morality, rather than working for the preservation of the good, may be inherently compromised in a project that, despite all ethical efforts, inevitably results into annihilation and havoc. How is tenderness, in its constitutive fragility, equipped to deal with the inevitable amount of violence with which the ontological self, but also the ethical subjectivity in its personal orientation as described by Levinas, may attempt to silence, neglect, deny the appeal of things, thus reducing them to objects of manipulation, enjoyment, labor? How is tenderness, in its inherent passivity and vulnerability, equipped to withstand and counteract violence at all?

Always amid the things to which it tends, tenderness is inter-ested in the preservation of their specific kind of being, which expresses itself in the continuous differal and interplay of the Fourfold. Ignorant of any form of universality, except as an abstraction, tenderness is burdened with the weight of its responsibility toward the things that it encounters and by which it is welcomed in its welcoming orientation. And yet, despite the specificity of its inter-est, tenderness is always dis-inter-ested, always disengaged from any particular thing, in its readiness to apply itself to any thing that places an appeal and a demand on it. Metaphysically interested but egologically—that is, ontologically—disinterested, tenderness is not an expression of the *conatus essendi* of the tender subject, but rather a response to the metaphysical configuration of the *conatus essendi* of the tended thing. Not itself beyond being, in its being a response rather than the *arche* to a demand to be let be, tenderness is nevertheless free of being, having devoid itself of the voluntaristic attitude characterizing even the best intentioned ethical self of the ontological tradition. In this sense, tenderness is lightness, delicacy, suspension of the weight, harshness, and aggressivity characteristic of the ontological economy of war, violence, and assault.

Yet, the lightness tenderness embodies can hardly be equated with the softness, gentleness, mawkishness that an ontological tradition too much inspired by belligerant values would, too promptly, ascribe to it. On the contrary, despite the lightness that characterizes it, tenderness is perseverance, firmness, and therefore strength deriving from the tenaciousness with which tenderness pursues its ethical project. The forcefulness characterizing tenderness comes from the very things, on the account of which tenderness is ready to resist. Resistance becomes thus the way by which tenderness confronts the ontological and metaphysical violence taking place in history.

There is always something, in things, which resists totalization, which escapes the constraining categories of manipulation by which the ontologically inspired subject has tried to bridle them, and legitimizes, even in times of technological domination, the ever new arising of the question, as in Heidegger, of "What is a thing?" It is in cor-respondence to the resistance of things, which is the resistance of the Fourfold in its structure of alterity, that the resistance tenderness enacts is exerted. Devoid of all egological connotations characterizing the notions of attack, assault, integration, the struggle in which tenderness engages in its corresponsive character receives its orientation from things, and from their demand to be as things, and not as objects. Therefore, such a struggle, enacted through modalities which remain themselves tender, attentive, nonviolent, serves not death, but life, in the plurality of its differentiations. Like philosophy in Levinas's reinterpretation of its meaning, tenderness enacts the "wisdom of love" (OBBE 162), of a love that loves life more than death, ambivalences more than determinations, alterities more than sameness.

Devoid of all cathartic, as well as soteriological, power, the resistance tenderness enacts is not capable of eliminating evil, from which violence stems. In its fragile firmness, tenderness has no power of imposing itself on the order of things, of which violence, in its perversive destructiveness, is still part. The ability to eliminate violence absolutely could only represent the renewal of a unilateral attempt on the side of the subject at instituting a different order of reality, not less totalizing than the ontological order, simply because of its being inspired by the good intentions of an ethical subjectivity. The ethical subject that has made herself or himself tender is the one who, through tenderness, endures even violence. Yet, rather than submitting, the tender subject resists it. Tenderness does not annihilate violence. Rather, its tenaciousness on behalf of things forces to think of different ways of dealing with violence. The purpose of tenderness, its responsiveness to the appeal of things, is the still very noble task of reducing the quantum of violence in the world, not through a counterviolence that would be different from violence only because of its opposite directionality, but through an isolation that places violence in the condition of not being able to harm any longer. In a way, the purpose of tenderness is that of a continuous adjournment of the destructive powers of evil in the hope that, thanks to its postponement, the violence which nourishes the destruction fades to the point of its disappearance.

Nietzsche's essays on morality remark how it is the self-control, and not the weakening and castration of passions, which proves itself the healthiest and more efficacious.[2] Therefore, it cannot be tenderness that redeems violence, but only, if anything, violence that redeems itself through its becoming responsive to the ethical demand of things. The only way to achieve this result in a manner that does not fall back into the modes of ontological egology, and hence in a manner that escapes the transitoriness of all ontological projects receiving their determination not from exteriority, but from the interiority of a will never resolute enough, is to be tender even toward what has made of violence its privileged weapon. Such is the tenderness of forgiveness, which offers a new beginning without being oblivious to the conditions that have motivated the necessity of a different scenario.

Committed to the future, by the possibility of which tenderness is oriented, engaged in the present as the temporality in which its resistance is enacted, tenderness has no power to undo what has been done, but only to welcome it in a tender embrace that consoles but does not heal, inspires but does not deny, preserves but does not mend. "Remain faithful to the earth, my brothers, with the power of your own virtue," invites Nietzsche's Zarathustra.[3] To such an invitation does tenderness remain faithful. If tenderness forgives, then, nevertheless it is a forgiveness that does not forget (that is, redeems) either the victim, or the perpetrator, or the very act of evil, which rather work as a motivation for the renewal of tenderness. The resistance of tenderness is thus delivered from reactive and oppositional motives. Ethical resistance is not dictated by the destructive events aimed at annihilating the alterity of things. If this were the case, if the resistance of tenderness were to receive its determination from that which it resists, its structure would not be any different than the dialectical movement of *ressentiment* outlined by Nietzsche in his *Genealogy of Morals*. That is, the resistance of tenderness would simply be a different, maybe more sophisticated version, of an ontological mood, and of a reactive form. Conversely, it is not evil that dictates the measure of the resistance of tenderness, but rather the ethical signification of the alterity that has been silenced and absenced.

The resistance tenderness enacts is oriented by the infinite alterity of the very things, by the interplay of the Fourfold which is welcomed in things as things. Therefore, the resistance in which tenderness engages is infinite as the things' resistance is infinite. It is ethical resistance, the resistance of the one who, and for that which, has no power and yet demands infinitely. Hence, tenderness allows for no resignation, release, truce, surrender. Its resistence is to infinity. The price of the ceasefire would be the irretrievable loss of things, which in their reduction to objects finds its most successful accomplishment. It would be, once again, as in the ontological tradition that Levinas's ethics does not completely dispel, the undisputed ruling of objectification.

Yet, despite the infinity of its ethical resistance, tenderness has no ultimate, apocalyptic means to grant the avoidance of the occurring of objectifying practices, or of practices of transformation that irreversibly alter the originary configuration of the Fourfold in things. When such events take place, even without reaching global dimensions, even when the transformative manipulation remains partial, occasional, perhaps unescapable; when things are denied the alterity of their configuration as things, tenderness is forced to modify itself and to turn into a different modality of ethical relation, for it to still correspond to the demand of things. Confronted with such adverse situations, tenderness turns into sadness, or into a saddened tenderness.

Like tenderness, of which it is a modification, sadness is not a psychological dimension, affecting subjectivity from the interiority of its perhaps unhappy consciousness. Rather, sadness is a metaphysical sentiment dictated, once again, by things in their exteriority and alterity. Not nostalgia for lost occasions, for possibilities that might have been but that the subject has not been able to seize because of the irreversibility and exclusiveness of any choice, which by choosing, necessarily discards other possibilities, sadness is not regret, remorse, guilt. Sadness is a tenuous and yet strenuous sentiment, an ineffable grief which accompanies the tender ethical subject and is motivated by the violation that has occurred in the configuration of things as things. Sadness is always for a loss. In this sense, sadness signifies in the face of death, of an evil that cannot be, and yet should have been, prevented. Rather than a negative, oppressive psychological feeling to be swept away, erased, concealed in the euphoric celebration of progress and happiness, in the naive conviction that the real is rational and the good will always win, sadness is a positive sentiment to be cherished and nurtured, because of the traces of alterity it harbors in itself even when all alterity is gone.

Whereas tenderness rejoices for the infinite possibilities of significations the interplay of the Fourfold expresses, for the alterity things display, sadness, as the couterpart of tenderness, mourns the mirroring structure of the Fourfold whose deferring existence has been abruptly interrupted, crushed, denied, impossibilitated to be. What is mourned by sadness is not the past that is no longer, that cannot be prolonged to eternity, because of an ephemeral present. What is lamented is rather the preciousness of alterity, which has gone lost. Sadness reminds that the present is not all that there is; that reality is always broader, in space, time, and concept, than the beings one encounters in everyday experience; that reality is never immanent and ontological, but rather transcendent and metaphysical; that reality always extends further than any subjectivity can reach, even further than the ethical relation to which tenderness offers some access. Like tenderness, sadness expresses the possibility of an opening up of ethical subjectivity.

Sadness is for tenderness the awareness of its fundamental vulnerability, the consciousness of its fundamental powerlessness, and hence the constant reminder of its necessity to be ever more tender, because no tenderness is ever enough. Farther from paralyzing the tender subjectivity in a practice of mourning and self-indugent commiseration, when it is oriented by the appeal of things that are no longer as things sadness spurs toward even more tenderness, toward the infinite desire for a more strenuous ethical resistance. Mourning, although serious and grave, as the loss of the alterity of things requires, can only be momentary, if it wishes to remain faithful to the things' invitation not to dwell on the temporal modality of presentification, and to rather open up to the transcendence of infinite significations. When the time of mourning is over, sadness takes over and becomes a constant accompaniment to all tender resistance in its offering the violated past all the caring attentions with which tenderness faces the things of the present in its resistance for the future. Sadness celebrates the remainders of the alterity of things, once their destruction as things has been consummed.

Although primarily oriented to and by the violated past, the temporality of sadness complicates itself in the present as well as in the future. Because of the intrinsic vulnerability of tenderness, sadness is a constant overtone accompanying tenderness in the display of its temporal expression. In the present, a saddened tenderness—that is, a tenderness constantly mindful of its own vulnerability—enables to halt the race toward the future, to pause, to consider which things are important, for which things it is worth to enact a more strenuous resistance, given that the soteriological power of a completely messianic redemption is precluded to tenderness. In the future, sadness enables tenderness to resist ever harder, ever more forcefully, on behalf of those things whose alterity demands to be preserved. Altogether, sadness nourishes and reinforces the resistance of tenderness on behalf of the alterity of things.

14 ❖ Festive Celebrations

As ethical attunement, and consequently void of the ontological power capable of the illusion of a soteriological act toward the things by which it is inspired, tenderness is a reflected sentiment. Therefore, tenderness belongs to the sphere of meditation. Its meditative character, however, does not inscribe it in the realm of speculation but rather, more consonant with the ancient Greek tradition, in that of philosophy as a practice of life. The reflection tenderness displays is, at least, threefold. As a response to that by which it is spurred (first reflection), tenderness, acknowledging the precariousness and vulnerability of things, folds itself on itself and its own need to become ever more tender (second reflection). But, since no tenderness is ever enough, tenderness turns into saddened tenderness—that is, into a tenderness which is aware of the loss it inevitably perpetuates (third reflection). A consciousness of guilt, conceived as the metaphysical inability to live up to the demand of the other, is not absent from tenderness.

The multilevelness of the reflection, which climaxes in the awareness of a loss, of an empty space no tenderness will ever be able to fill, subtracts tenderness from participation to what Heidegger has named the "metaphysics of the presence." It simultaneously isolates tenderness from the suspicion of being one more instance of a narcissistic self-reflection, the repetitive, egological circularity of which has been extensively criticized by Levinas. More than with ontological repetition, the movement of reflection of tenderness (in its never finding an ultimate ground on which to rest) reveals some affinities with the open circularity by which Heidegger describes the interplay of the Fourfold, in which presencing is never constrainable into the immanent flatness of complete presence, but rather directs to a configuration of ulteriority and beyond—a dimension of alterity. The fourth movement of reflection accompanying tenderness, preventing the reflection of tenderness from self-enclosure and conversely opening it up toward the dimension of the beyond is, paradoxically if compared with the role such a faculty performs in Hegel, or even Plato, that of memory.

In *Totality and Infinity*—that is, in this work explicitly devoted to exteriority—Levinas seems to dismiss the possibility that memory may be endowed with any sort of ethical power of resistance (especially TI 53–56), since memory "after the event assumes the passivity of the past and masters it" (TI 56). The reasons for the dismissal lie, mainly, in the fact that Levinas still very traditionally conceives of memory in terms of an ontological power of recollection able to control, and retrieve, what precedes it, and hence able to "ground myself after the event" (TI 56). His consideration, however, retains its validity only in the case of the possibility of a complete availability of the past that is to be retrieved. But such a condition is made impossible by the same structure of alterity constituting the Fourfold. The past is never totally present and transparent in things. What gleams through in things is rather traces of the past, hints, references to a temporal dimension that, although inscribed in the texture of things, cannot be recognized, identified, deciphered, let alone resurrected.

Given such a structure of withdrawal, memory can no longer be, as Plato, Hegel, and even Levinas believe, a victorious memory, the emperor's memory, according to Benjamin's image,[1] able to retain, or retrieve, all events of the past of things in itself, and therefore able to provide a secure foundation for the subject. Memory can only be finite memory, exposure to the powerfulness of the absencing of that which it would like to remember, passivity marked by the awareness that only traces of the past, but never the past in its entirety, can be preserved in tenderness. No redemptive power of restoration is entrusted to memory. As the knots on the handkerchief, the meaning of which has gone astray, memory can only (if anything, and even then without guarantees of success) choose to forget, but never to remember, despite Nietzsche's attempts to show otherwise, thus disclosing the powerlessness, vulnerability, and exposure of memory to the mark of things and to the tyranny of their fleeting temporality. That is, memory is oriented and determined not by the subject, but by that which it strives to remember, and which subtracts itself to it. Once again, the memorative structure reveals the absence of closure as its main characteristic.

Yet, like tenderness, like saddened tenderness, despite its vulnerability, memory has a difficult ethical obligation, entrusted to it by things in their continuous presenting themselves to memory: the obligation to resist on behalf of the alterity of things the vulnerability of which memory reflects in itself. The Hassidic tradition is rich in tales and narrations. Scholem relates a story, in which the finitude of memory, despite its limitations, still acts as a means of preservation: not of the past, which has irremediably gone lost, but of the traces of what that past can still achieve in the present. That is, memory can still be operative in the presencing of the past, and hence in the resistance on its behalf, since, as Benjamin very well knew, the future is nourished by "the image of enslaved ancestors rather than that of liberated grandchildren."[2]

Scholem writes:

> When the Baal Shem had a difficult task before him, he would go to a certain place in the woods, light a fire and meditate in prayer—and what he had set out to perform was done. When a generation later the "Maggid" of Meseritz was faced with the same task he would go to the same place in the wood and say: We can no longer light the fire, but we can still speak the prayers—and what he wanted became reality. Again, a generation later Rabbi Moshe Leib of Sassov had to perform this task. And he too went into the woods and said: We can no longer light a fire, nor do we know the secret meditations

> belonging to the prayer, but we do know the place in the woods to which it all belongs—and that must be sufficient; and sufficient it was. But when another generation had passed and Rabbi Israel of Rishin was called upon to perform the task, he sat down on his golden chair in his castle and said: We cannot light the fire, we cannot speak the prayers, we do not know the place, but we can tell the story of how it was done. And, the storyteller adds, the story which he told had the same effect as the action of the other three.[3]

The theme of Scholem's narration is that of the power of memory and its repetitions—not a repetition which presents itself as invariably identical to its past performances, not a repetition which coincides with the circularity of the eternal recurrence, which, in the eternal return of the same things, is the annihilation of becoming and alterity, but a repetition which is marked by an absencing: the absencing of that "immemorial past" (TO 43) of which memory means to speak. Tenderness guards in memory that past history which is inscribed in the crackings of the raw materiality of things, and which yet escapes its repetition in the articulation of rational discourse. A suggestion for accomplishing the possibility of such a memorative repetition, which tenderness wants to enact and which assumes the features of a recitation, comes from Benjamin, when he writes that "holidays . . . are days of remembrance."[4] It is in festivals that tenderness finds the ultimate way to enact a relation with things that respects, defers to, and honors their facialities. Why festivals, though? Because they reveal more than casual analogies with the modality of tenderness and with the structure of things. Ultimately, because they constitute the possibility of relating to things as to tendered facialities.

A privileged, although introductory, access to the significance of festivals in their ability to fulfill the requests of an ethic of things is offered through an analysis of the time of festivals, the structure of which is preserved in calendars. Clocks and watches offer a unidimensional, homogeneous account of time, which poses the temporal moments on a unilinear directionality corresponding to the advancement of progress in its different variations (reason, the Idea, the victory of the proletarians), thus instituting the modality of time as continuity. Conversely, calendars exhibit the notion of an interrupted temporality, in which each moment presents the possibility of multiple, innumerable, and therefore immemorial inscriptions the trace of which is, nevertheless, maintained in the citation of the date. Calendars measure time by the scansion of differences, othernesses, alterities. In such a scansion and articulation, each day marked by the calendar is a day of uniqueness and separation, as testified by the devotional tradition of attributing each day of the liturgical year to a diverse, distinct saint (and sometimes also to two different ones, who come to share a same day of commemoration, nevertheless without a collapse of their specific identity into one single agiography). In the commemoration of its own separation, every day, on calendars, becomes thus a day of celebration, a special day in which the flowing of time concentrates to the point of its explosion in a present which carries within itself memories of past events (first of all, the martyrdom of the saint), maybe lost forever to rational recollection but still, in their absence, operative in the recitation of the day.

In Büchner's *Lenz,* on January 20, the homonymous protagonist of the story walks in the mountains. In his walking only one thing seems inconvenient to him: not to be able to walk on his head.[5] As Paul Celan notes,[6] "he who walks on his head, ladies and gentlemen, who walks on his head, has heaven beneath him as an abyss."[7] January 20 is the date in which Lenz departs Strasbourg, a departure which will lead him to madness and death. Everyone has his or her own dates to remember, and on Lenz's calendar January 20 deserves special mention. But the significance of the date is not exhausted in the instantaneousness of its present occurrence, or in the private, personal experience which it commemorates. Rather, each date tells of other dates, of other stories, thus maintaining in its citation also other re-citations, in a complication of the moments of temporality that makes of calendars a place of gathering rather than of the unrollment of time. January 20, then, is also the date of the Wannsee Conference in 1942, a day in which the *Endlösung* of Judaism is decided. The abyss which Celan retraces in Lenz's walking also speaks of another abyss: that of the atrocities of the *Shoah,* the memory of which, in their evil magnitude that defies all possible speech, is not erased, but heightened in the multilayeredness of dates the temporality of calendars offers. Rather than a homogeneous, continuous conception of temporality, available and transparent to the clarity of reason, what calendars offer is the more complex, convoluted, tortuous but altogether richer image of time as an occasion for memory and celebration—that is, for festival, since, as Gadamer points out, celebration constitutes the time-experience of the festival.[8] That, on calendars, each day is a day of celebration implies thus the possibility of an everlasting festivity. It is in the celebration of things as in a festive day that the ethics of things finds its ultimate accomplishment. To celebrate things festively means to enter the relation with things in the time of festival—that is, in the discontinuous and nonhomogeneous time, in the sacred because consecrated time in which differences can be maintained.[9]

Such a sacred time, which allows for separation and alterities, is a faint image, a feeble memory, a trace, as Levinas would say, of the time of the origin. As Eliade points out, festivals offer the possibility to "re-enter . . . the *time of origin,* the time that "floweth not" because it does not participate in profane temporal duration, because it is composed of an *eternal present,* which is indefinitely recoverable."[10]

What escapes Eliade, however, is the fact that, as Levinas recognizes, no complete recovery of the origin is ever possible, since only traces of the origin reveal themselves. More fundamentally, though, what is missing from Eliade's consideration is the fact that, insofar as it is, as Levinas claims, always a passed time, the time of the origin cannot be the time of unity and repetition of the same in the eternity of the present. Rather, such a time is the time of a complication of differences and alterities which do not annihilate one another, the time of paradoxes and ambivalences which need not be resolved, because in its being located beyond being and the logic of noncontradiction ruling its existence, the origin is itself anarchic plurality, multiplicity, differentiation in the undifferentiated. Because of the anarchy of the origin, which, in its being passed, cannot provide any foundational ground, the celebration of festivals has to be repeated. And, because of the historical profane time in which it takes place, but also because of the structure of that origin which it thus repeats, it can only repeat itself differently, so that, as Gadamer acknowledges, its "own original essence [is] always to be something different (even when celebrated in exactly the same way)."[11]

When, in Plato's *Laws,* the Athenian stranger is asked how many festivals should there be in the ideal republic, his reply is without hesitations: "There shall be not less than 365."[12] When taken in isolation from the context of the Platonic agenda, such an answer might easily be mistaken as an invitation to an aesthetic life of endless parties, orgies, revelries, and dissolutions. Yet, in the rigorous context of an ethics of things, which shares Plato's ultimate concern with the realization of the Good, and in which festivity develops as a response to an ethical demand, the reply becomes rather the intimation to relate to things according to the temporality disclosed by festivals. Not to live a life of festivals, but to live the relation with things, in tenderness, as if it were a festival, in festivity; that is, to celebrate things festively is the suggestion provided by the Platonic text.

The difference between a life of festivals and a life in the time of festivals—a festive life—has ultimately to do with the structure of the origin to which festivals seek to provide access, whether such an origin is represented (and sought) under the modality of indifference or under that of differentiation and separation.

According to Georges Bataille, the meaning of festivals has to be retraced to a movement of transgression, "of deliberate violation of the most hallowed laws"[13] by which humankind has established its independence from animality. Through the interruption of "the course of an existence subordinated to ordinary ends," festivals contest the "lucid and voluntary servility" of the profane world by liberating the "animal forces" transfigured under the form of the sacred.[14] Bataille romantically emphasizes the impossibility of a complete coincidence with the origin, for "since man has uprooted himself from nature, that being who returns to it is still uprooted."[15] What is sought in festivals through the transgressive move is precisely a reunion with a "lost intimacy" which, however, is ridden with anguish because "what is intimate, in the strong sense, is what has the passion of an absence of individuality," so that "intimacy is violence, and it is destruction, because it is not compatible with the positing of the separate individual."[16] Festivals offer a solution to the anguished desire for lost intimacy because on the one hand, says Bataille, they constitute "the place and time of a spectacular letting loose." But on the other hand, by subordinating such a releasement of frenziness to the needs of the profane world, "there is a conservative prudence that regulates and limits [them]."[17] Festivals assume therefore a therapeutic value, the significance of which is however still determined by that for which they aim at being a therapy—ultimately, that animalistic origin which is void of all distinctions and differentiations. More than an "amicable reconciliation," as Bataille qualifies them,[18] festivals appear in his reading as resourceful palliatives for an orgiastic spirit which is too afraid of its own death to dare its union with an undifferentiated origin which is still as much desired as it is feared. Rather than constituting a moment of positive liberation, in their transgressive nature festivals betray thus an inhibitory, sublimatory character which makes of them moments of negation: both of the origin, which is desired and yet feared, and of the distantiation from the origin, which is detested and yet still desired (although for different reasons). In such a reconstruction, the excessive nature of festivals remains negative, and they result bound to unsatisfaction: the origin is not reaccessed, the economy of utilitarianism is reinstituted. Bataille's festivals, in their orgiastic, animalistic character, can only be temporary because of that undifferentiated origin which rules the dynamic of their institution.[19]

However, that festivals need not occur under the sublimated fear of an orgiastic melting of distinctions in "the intense heat of intimate life"[20] was evident already to Nietzsche, who in the *Birth of Tragedy* acknowledges the "immense gap which separates the Dionysian Greek from the Dionysian barbarian,"[21] gap which is comparable to the abyss separating animality (the bearded satyr borrowing its attributes from the goat) from divinity (Dionysus himself). According to Nietzsche, it is the barbarian Dionysian celebrations, which occur under the patronage of an animal, the satyr, that display, as for Bataille, a transgressive movement toward unity with nature understood as an undifferentiated force (all satyrs in this sense resemble one another). As Nietzsche writes, "in nearly every case these festivals centered in extravagant sexual licentiousness, whose waves overwhelmed all family life and its venerable traditions; the most savage natural instincts were unleashed, including even that horrible mixture of sexuality and cruelty which has always seemed to me to be the real 'witches' brew'."[22]

Conversely, Greek Dionysian festivals occur under the patronage of Dionysius—that is, a god with an already individuated identity—but also under the influence of a peace treaty established between Dionysius and Apollo, the god of order and individuation. This means that the unity with the origin sought in Greek festivals is an immersion in the everflowing, but still differentiated, multiplicity of existence. The unity which is sought is not undifferentiated unity, but richness and complication of differences. "If we observe how, under the pressure of this treaty of peace, the Dionysian power revealed itself, we shall now recognize . . . in the Dionysian orgies of the Greeks, as compared with the babylonian Sacaea with their reversion of man to the tiger and the ape, the significance of festivals of world redemption and days of transfiguration."[23] Festivals celebrate and foster multiplicity and separation, what Nietzsche qualifies as "the greatest exaltation of all . . . symbolic faculties,"[24]—that is, the ability to create ever-new constellations of existence. According to Nietzsche's insight, as for Bataille, festivals are transgressive. Yet, the transgression finds its rest in an origin already represented as differentiated and multiple—that is, nonorgiastic or animalistic, and therefore satisfactory. Therefore, festivals can become, as in Plato's suggestion, a dimension of everyday life. Festivals become a powerful assertion of the differentiation of existence.

Consequently, to live the relation with things festively comes to mean to let things flow, or better, overflow, to let them create ever-new configurations of the Fourfold which exhibit the play of differences and alterities. "A good whose nature is festive flows abundantly," writes Bataille.[25] Festivals, then, are moments of excess. What is excessive in them, though, is not the actions of a subject which break loose of all conventionalisms imposed by its desire for sovereignity over animality. What is excessive is the possibility of evernew significations of the very things, which subtract themselves to the order of exchange economy imposed by the subject to reenter the dimension of pure gift finding in itself its own meaning, its own *raison d'être.*

The significance of festivals, however, does not lie primarily in their being the occasion for a recitation of the past, albeit the past of the origin, the immemorial memory of which they retain in the repetition of calendars. According to Rosenzweig's phenomenology of festivals in *The Star of Redemption,*[26] festivals, and especially secular festivals, mark the "anniversaries on which mankind becomes conscious of its passage through time."[27] That is, in their unerasable interconnection not with the eternity of an immutable present, but with the flowing of a temporality pregnant with past, present, and future, festivals are for mortals a memento of their caducity, of their mortality and hence of their vulnerability and exposure to the exteriority of things. According to the Greek myths of the origins, it is the celebration of funeral rites that first gives spur to all great festivals. In conformity with Gadamer's description of play,[28] festivity, then, rather than a sheer exaltation of cheerfulness, becomes a serious affair. Similarly to things, which, in their disclosure as things rather than objects, recall human beings to their existential condition as mortals, festivals reassert the inevitability of such a mortality and, in their festive—that is, also joyous—aura, they invite to participate to a yes-saying to it.

The relevance of festivals finds thus its completion in the present. In the present, festivals are days of special significance, located at the margins of everydayness, which they interrupt and suspend, in a disclosure of its banality. It is their interruptive character that renders them the most appropriate situation through which the ethics of things can be fulfilled. In their being a suspension of the banality of the everydayness, festivals also suspend that everyday, nonfestive attitude which is prone to a consideration of things in terms of objects, and thus neglectful of the thinging of things. The day of festival is, altogether, a day of rest, of leave not from everydayness, but more radically from the preoccupations which busy everydayness: first of all, the preoccupations with sustenance, which lead to consider things as objects, in terms of their intentionality as a "so that" and "in-order-to." The festive day, in its being an event of loss of the utilitarian attitude, subtracts festivals and what is celebrated in them from the domination of calculative reason, therefore opening up a different space: the space of what is meaningful in itself, without reference and insertion into a previously constituted system.

In this sense, festivals disclose and offer the possibility for the manifestation of a richness, a surplus, an excess which escapes previous conceptualization.[29] Even in a situation of direst poverty, one still celebrates festivals. That is, even then things are allowed to escape the constriction of all ontological determinations, and stand unconditioned in the thinging of their thingness as a gift that cannot be exchanged but only donated. What is expressed in festivals is a love for things which maintains them in the separatedness of their alterity.

The moment of festival, the moment in which objects regain their character of things, the moment of liberation from the banality and routine of a life of repetitions which technological progress, with its infinite possibilities for reproduction, has contributed to spread on a planetary scale, is, according to Hegel and Schopenhauer, a "Sunday in life," an exceptional event owing its exceptionality exactly to its extraordinariness. As Bataille more recently writes, the festival coincide with "a cessation of work," a break which goes temporarily against the order, an interruption of the rules of everyday's work.[30] But, as Heidegger notices, existence corresponds to everydayness only for *das Man,* that is, only for a *Dasein* leading a life of inauthenticity and dispersion that, paradoxically, might assimilate it rather to a Kierkegaardian aesthetical individual than to a Levinasian ethical subject inspired by love for alterity. Festivity is not simply a work day made interesting and amusing; it is not boredom made exciting by entertainment and change. The aesthetic individual, and perhaps even *das Man,* are interested in the exploitation of objects to their own enjoyment, to the extent that for the aesthetic personality, always troubled by the agonizing search for pleasure turned almost into a job, the *dolce vita* with which it lulls himself or herself becomes a desperately unfestive affair. Conversely, as Chrysostom reportedly said, *ubi caritas gaudet, ibi est festivitas*[31]: where love rejoices (and only there, one might want to add), there is festivity. If, as in Levinas, love implies not a Platonic need for unity and return to the origin, but a desire for alterity that maintains separation (TO 86, but also OBBE 162), it is only where alterities are allowed to reveal themselves and flourish that festivity can be found. That is, tenderness toward things requires, rather than everydayness, a festive life in which the love for things expresses itself in a celebration of things in a festive manner. To be tender toward things means to celebrate them, and the memory of them, festively—festively because this dimension is capable of maintaining things in the separation of their alterity. Festivity becomes a constant practice of life, and not the filler for the days of laziness.

In a famous letter to D'Alembert, Rousseau elaborates an interesting account of the distinction which opposes theater and festivals. Whereas theater, by Rousseau considered as a symbol of the monarchy, offers an indirect communication of its content passing through the intermediary of the *mise en scène*—that is, of a representation that objectifies the event and creates an unabridgeable gap between spectator and actor—that is, between theory and practice, festivals "show nothing," because in them there is no eye of theory (the spectator) oriented toward an external object. Rather, it is the spectators themselves who, by renouncing the untouched and untouchable eye of theory and speculation, create, one for the other, public spaces constituted as intersubjective places of action and gathering nonmediated by concepts or rules. In their celebratory moments, festivals exhibit an articulation of differences which nevertheless come together in a proximity without mediation.[32] In their social character of convening the community around that originary place of gathering the very things are, festivals contribute a dimension of nonmediated publicness to the ethics of things, which is always, like all ethics, in danger of being confined to the sphere of private interiority and sentimentality.

The primary nature of festivals, which in this mirror and celebrate a movement structurally identical to that occurring in the thinging of things, is thus one of gathering. Although festivity is a matter of personal response, thus justifying Nietzsche's claim that "the trick is not to arrange a festival, but to find people who can *enjoy* it,"[33] the nature of festivals is primarily in their being social events, which in their occurrence bring together: the community,[34] but also the community and that which is meant to be celebrated, yet without mediation. The reason the Athenian stranger adduces in Plato's *Laws* to support its prescription of a yearround festivity is that through this institution it will be possible to sacrifice to one either of the gods or of the daemons every day. That is, the meaning of festivals is religious, where by religion, as in Levinas, one should understand "the bond that is established between the same and the other without constituting a totality" (TI 40).

Certainly, even in its religious dimension, what festivals celebrate is a gathering which occurs in the immanence of the here and now, even when the nature of its participants is not exhaustible in the pure immanence of the place and time. Rather than searching its fulfillment and redemption in the realization of another world which remains distant, alien, and, as Nietzsche has taught, always suspect of being a fiction of the imagination, festivity lives wordly. It lives among and within the things of this world, in a belonging to this world which Bonhoeffer, evoking Nietzsche, describes as not "the shallow and banal this-worldliness of the enlightened, the busy, the comfortable, or the lascivious, but the profound this-worldliness characterized by discipline and the constant knowledge of death and resurrection."[35] Rather than fleeing from life, festivity leads to a Nietzschean faithfulness to the earth, to a yes-saying to the world and the things of the world in which the gathering is celebrated. The main feature of such a yes-saying consists in the full appreciation of things as things; not the savoring which dissolves things in the instantaneousness of the aesthetic experience, and which opens the way to a conception of things as objects of consumption, but rather the appreciation that in the festive action subtracts objects from the purely utilitarian context and thus celebrates things as things, thus constituting itself as a response to the ethical demand placed by things themselves. Festivity, in its intimation of alterity, retains an ethical, not an aesthetic, modality of relation to the world.

Yet, the celebration of festivals has nothing to do with some unconditional approval of everything, that is, with an optimism that deprives reality of its tragic dimension. If festivals certainly celebrate joy, they also celebrate, as in their Greek origin, mourning, pain, death. The festive celebration of the events of pain and suffering, if on the one hand amounts to the affirmation of the reality of evil without mystifying, compromising, sublimating its nature into some higher purpose that ultimately reduces its character of radical scandal, on the other hand does not subscribe and legitimate its existence. Rather, through the commemoration of mourning, festivals invite resistance to the final destruction and annihilation deriving from the loss of all memory of evil.

In the celebration that takes place here and now, festivals are worldy events; yet, as the Athenian stranger points out in his answer, no festivities can properly be considered to be profane. Since the festive here and now is distinct from that of pure immanence, since festivals remind of the possibility of a reality different from that of the present, festive occurrences open up to the dimension of the beyond—what in the Athenian stranger's language appears under the name of gods and daemons, and what, in the post-Nietzschean, Levinasian language that necessarily must take into account the "strange rumours about the death of God or the emptiness of the heavens" (OBBE 5) could more properly be called the transcendence of alterity.

The religiosity contained in festivals is thus that of a lay sacredness, which takes seriously the process of secularization intervened in history, and yet does not renounce the possibility of a celebration of the transcending alterity of the beyond. Analogously to tenderness, which, in its ethical dimension, constitutes the possibility of an encounter with that place of gathering of alterities the very thing is, festivals celebrate an encounter that, conforming to the originary religious tradition from which festivals stem, takes the features of the gathering between incommensurable dimensions of existence.

Already in its traditional understanding as a religious event, the very nature of festivals rests on its bringing about the possibility of a communion with the transcendent, or with the divine event that the festival celebrates, on which the celebration of the festival itself depends. That is, analogously to tenderness, although the celebration of festivals lies entirely within the elements which it gathers, the nature of the festival receives its signification from the exterior. Its relevance is grounded on an alterity which constitutes it and forbids the return of the festival upon itself. Festivals cannot be imposed by a voluntaristic, subjectivistic activity of legislative institution. When this imposition happens, when festivals search for a foundation of their own origin within themselves, they betray their own character of response to the call of the events and become ceremonies, parades, masquerades at the service of regimes. That is, festivals lose their ethical component and turn into political ideologies, mythological creations of an ontological rationality rather than responses of an ethical subjectivity, exaltation of the orgy of feelings rather than celebration of the modesty of alterity.

Whereas human beings can arrange all ceremonies and processions, and therefore make the celebration, they cannot create what is to be celebrated, they cannot make the festive occasion and the cause for celebrating, if not through an ideological falsification of the festival that ultimately mystifies and distorts its being. Analogously, although mortals are invited and welcomed to enter the Fourfold and thus a relation with things as things, they cannot properly make, but only let things be in their thingness, since every attempt at constriction and manipulation turns things into objects. That is, in festivity there is the celebration of a pure gift: the gift of what gives itself in and by itself, unconditionally because it is unconditioned.[36] In festivity, things gratuitously give themselves to celebration and appreciation as things.

❖ Notes

Preface

1. For an account of the reception of the anecdote within Western philosophy, see Hans Blumenberg, *Das Lachern der Thrakerin. Eine Urgeschichte der Theorie* (Frankfurt: Suhrkamp, 1987). The anecdote is evoked by Hannah Arendt, *The Life of the Mind* (New York: Harcourt & Brace, 1978), vol. 1 82–83. On it, see Jacques Taminiaux, *The Thracian Maid and the Professional Thinker: Arendt and Heidegger*, trans. M. Gendre (Albany: SUNY Press, 1997).

2. This position is shared also by Heidegger, who makes the same claim in the opening pages of *What Is a Thing?*

3. Friederich Nietzsche, *Twilight of the Idols*, 4, 4; in *The Portable Nietzsche*, ed. W. Kaufmann (New York: Random House, 1954).

4. Nietzsche, *Twilight of the Idols*, 4, 1.

5. Nietzsche, *Twilight of the Idols*, 3, 5.

6. Interestingly enough, the part of Aristotle's *Poetics* which, after having defined man as an animal endowed with laughter, supposedly dealt with laughter, has been lost. On the theme of laughter, see Jean-Luc Nancy, "Laughter, Presence," in *The Birth to Presence*, trans. B. Holmes et al. (Stanford: Stanford University Press, 1993), 368–92.

7. Nietzsche, *Twilight of the Idols*, 4, 6.

8. The image is desumed from Francis Bacon, *De Dignitate et Augmentis Scientiarum*, 2, 2, in *Works*, ed. Spedding, Elkis, Hearth, vol. 4, 297. Bacon has Thales fall into mirroring water

as part of his own polemic against astronomy (as one of the *artes liberales*) and in favor of the *artes mechanicae,* thanks to which one can build mirrors and other optical devices.

9. See, for example, the very title of Heidegger's work "The End of Philosophy and the Task of Thinking," in TB 55–73. See also John Sallis, *Delimitations: Phenomenology and the End of Metaphysics* (Bloomington: Indiana University Press, 1994), especially with relation to the role played by imagination in relation to metaphysics.

10. Jean-François Lyotard, *The Postmodern Condition: A Report on Knowledge,* trans. G. Bennington and B. Massumi (Minneapolis: University of Minnesota Press, 1997), xxiv.

11. Jean-Luc Nancy, "You ask me what it means today . . . ," trans. P. Kamuf, *Paragraph* 16, 2 (1993), 108.

12. Friedrich Nietzsche, *The Gay Science,* trans. W. Kaufmann (New York: Random House, 1974), 3, 125.

13. See Theodor W. Adorno, *Negative Dialectics,* trans. E. B. Ashton (New York: Continuum, 1973).

14. See Adorno, *Negative Dialectics.* See also Edith Wyschogrod, *Spirit in Ashes: Hegel, Heidegger and Man-Made Mass Death* (New Haven: Yale University Press, 1985), in which the logic of the death event is traced back to pre-Socratic philosophy and to some mythological motifs recurring in Western thought.

15. See TI 11.

16. See especially Friedrich Nietzsche, *The Antichrist,* trans. W. Kaufmann, in *The Portable Nietzsche,* 568–656.

17. On the issue of Auschwitz which, according to Levinas, has revealed the very nature of evil, thus terminating, among other things, the possibility of traditional theodicy, see the essays "Nameless" in PN 119–23, and "Useless Suffering," trans. R. Cohen, in *The Provocation of Levinas: Rethinking the Other,* ed. R. Bernasconi and D. Wood (New York: Routledge, 1988), 161–64.

18. In *Totality and Infinity* Lingis writes that "with [Levinas's] permission, we are translating '*autrui*' (the personal Other, the you) by 'Other'" (TI 24fn.). Following this convention, I

will capitalize 'Other' when the term refers to the *other person* (*Autrui*) rather than to the generic other (*l'autre* or *Autre*).

19. The comparison was made in the course of a cycle of four lectures delivered in Bremen on the subject of technology. The quotation reads as follows: "Agriculture is now a motorized food industry, the same thing in its essence as the production of corpses in the gas chambers and the extermination camps, the same thing as blockades and the reduction of countries to famine, the same thing as the manifacture of hydrogen bombs." On the issue, see Philippe Lacoue-Labarthe, *Heidegger, Art and Politics,* trans. C. Turner (Cambridge: Blackwell, 1990), 31–40. On the reasons for Heidegger's silence on the theme of Auschwitz, see Jean-François Lyotard, *Heidegger and "the jews,"* trans. A. Michel and M. S. Roberts (Minneapolis: University of Minnesota Press, 1980). See also the collection of essays contained in *Martin Heidegger and the Holocaust,* ed. A. Milchman and A. Rosenberg (Atlantic Highlands: Humanities Press, 1996).

Chapter 1: Out of Love: The Break with Parmenides

1. Quoted in French in Richard Kearney, *Dialogues with Contemporary Continental Thinkers* (Manchester, UK: Manchester University Press, 1984), 58.

2. Levinas's position with respect to Kierkegaard is enunciated in "Kierkegaard: Existence and Ethics," and "A Propos of Kierkegaard vivant," both in PN 66–79. On Levinas's relation to Kierkegaard, see Mark Taylor, Altarity (Chicago: University of Chicago Press, 1987), 185–216. See also Merold Westphal, "The Transparent Shadow: Kierkegaard and Levinas in Dialogue," in *Kierkegaard in Post/Modernity,* ed. M. Matustik (Bloomington: Indiana University Press, 1995). Interesting remarks on the relation between Levinas, Kierkegaard, and Derrida, especially with respect to death and subjectivity, are contained in Hent De-Vries, "Adieu, à-dieu, a-Dieu," in *Ethics as First Philosophy,* ed. A. Peperzak (New York: Routledge, 1995), 211–30.

3. In opposition to "desire," which satisfies itself in "nourishment," in *Existence and Existents* Levinas describes "love" as characterized by "an essential and insatiable hunger," "voluptuousness" as "the pursuit of an ever richer compromise; it is

made up of an ever growing hunger which pulls away from every being," launching forth into "an unlimited, empty, vertiginous future" (EE 43–44), the intention of which is the Other. Although through a different terminology, this distinction prefigures the distinction operated in *Totality and Infinity* between the satiability of need and the insatiability of desire, in its opening up to metaphysical transcendence.

4. For a very clear and suggestive analysis of desire, a movement at the limit of phenomenology, see Fabio Ciaramelli, "Levinas e la fenomenologia del desiderio," in *Levinas: Filosofia e trascendenza,* ed. A. Moscato (Genova: Marietti, 1992), 143–67.

5. Levinas's individuation of the exceptional moments in which the possibility of transcendence is enunciated *within* the very ontological tradition he criticizes is fundamental because it enables him not to pose the biblical tradition as the only possible alternative to the unitarian tendency dominating Western philosophy. That is, it is possible not to be ontologists and still remain within Greek philosophy. A meditation on (the blind spots) of Levinas's reading of other philosophers can be found in Jacques Derrida, "Violence and Metaphysics," in *Writing and Difference,* trans. A. Bass (Chicago: University of Chicago Press, 1978). On Levinas's relation to the philosophical tradition, see also Brian Schroeder, *Altared Ground* (New York: Routledge, 1996).

6. See especially Adorno, *Negative Dialectics,* but also T. Adorno and M. Horkheimer, *Dialectics of Enlightenment,* trans. J. Cumming (New York: Seabury, 1972). On Levinas's relation to Adorno, see Wayne Floyd, "To Welcome the Other: Totality and Theory in Levinas and Adorno," *Philosophy and Theology* 4, 2 (1989), 145–70.

7. Levinas refers, as examples, to "the land that supports us and disappoints our efforts, the sky that elevates us and ignores us, the forces of nature that aid us and kill us, things that encumber us or serve us, men who love us and enslave us" (CPP 49).

8. Most of Michel Foucault's works explore precisely this dialectical move. See, for example, his *Madness and Civilization: A History of Insanity in the Age of Reason,* trans. R. Howard (New York: Vintage, 1973), where the confinement of clinical madness within the walls of mental hospitals clearly indicates the wish

not to cure, but to isolate, therefore to protect, defend, save oneself from the ineliminable presence (and threat) of another madness, cosmic madness.

9. Levinas considers Hegel as "the culmination of philosophy itself," because of his systematizing spirit for which "the spiritual and the reasonable always reside in knowledge" (EI 76). On Levinas's relation to Hegel, see Robert Bernasconi, "Levinas Face to Face—with Hegel," *Journal of the British Society for Phenomenology* 13 (1982), 267–76 and, by the same author, "Levinas and Hegel: The Possibility of Forgiveness and Reconciliation," *Archivio di Filosofia* 54 (1986), 325–46. See also Adriaan Peperzak, "Some Remarks on Hegel, Kant and Levinas," in *Face to Face with Levinas,* ed. R. Cohen (Albany: SUNY Press, 1986), 205–17, and Jean-François Lyotard, "Levinas' Logic," in *Face to Face with Levinas,* 117–58, where Lyotard writes that "Levinas struggles to escape the Hegelian persecution" (121) by attacking "Hegelian alterity so as to show that it is only a caprice of identity" (119).

10. Levinas acknowledges the superiority of Heidegger's ontological analysis in *Being and Time* over the previous tradition, which had neglected the "verbality" of being by reducing it to the presence of a noun (see EI 38–39). Even Heidegger, however, submits to the accusation of ontology Levinas places on the rest of Western philosophy, insofar as: a. Heidegger's *Dasein* maintains the structure of the Same that makes of it a totalitarian egology (see, for example, CPP 51–52); b. Heidegger conceives of being as the ultimate universal, making being a neutrum; c. although critical of the metaphysics of presence, Heidegger is unable to renounce it when describing being as coming into presence (see Emmanuel Levinas and Richard Kearney, "Dialogue with Emmanuel Levinas," in *Face to Face with Levinas,* 13–33). On Levinas's criticism of Heidegger, see Adriaan Peperzak, "Phenomenology—Ontology—Metaphysics: Levinas's Perspective on Husserl and Heidegger," *Man and World* 16 (1983), 113–27, and Luk Bouckaert, "Ontology and Ethics: Reflections on Levinas's Critique of Heidegger," *International Philosophical Quarterly* 10 (1970), 402–19. See also Robert Bernasconi, "Deconstruction and the Possibility of Ethics," in *Deconstruction and Philosophy,* ed. J. Sallis (Chicago: University of Chicago Press, 1987), 122–39, and Steven Gans, "Ethics or Ontology," *Philosophy Today* 16 (1972), 117–21.

11. Hegel's criticism of Schelling focuses precisely on this point. In Schelling, the negative is not incorporated as part of the process of knowing, which does not entail identity (Schelling), but identification (Hegel). To use Hegel's famous formulation, in Schelling, substance does not become subject.

12. Derrida, "Violence and Metaphysics," 152.

13. Whereas the notion of ambiguity lies at the chronological level of presence, ambivalence finds its place at the diachronic level of ethics. However, at times Levinas seems to use the terms interchangeably. On the notion of ethical ambiguity, see D. H. Brody, "Emmanuel Levinas: The Logic of Ethical Ambiguity in *Otherwise than Being or Beyond Essence*," *Research in Phenomenology* 25 (1995), 177–203.

14. The issue of the relation between Levinas's philosophy and the Greek tradition, as well as the problem of the origin of Levinas's philosophy itself have been variously discussed. Among others, see Derrida, "Violence and Metaphysics," which exposes the Greek character of Levinas's otherwise non-Greek philosophy; John Llewelyn, "Jewgreek or Greekjew," in *The Collegium Phenomenologicum: The First Ten Years,* ed. G. Moneta et al. (Dordrecht-Boston: Kluwer, 1988), 273–87; and Theodore De Boer, "Judaism and Hellenism in the Philosophy of Levinas and Heidegger," *Archivio di Filosofia* 53 (1985), 197–215. On the relation between Judaism and Hellenism, see also what Levinas himself says in AT 177–178.

15. On the Jewish roots of Levinas's philosophy, see Catherine Chalier, "The Philosophy of Emmanuel Levinas and the Hebraic Tradition," in *Ethics as First Philosophy,* 3–12, and Robert Gibbs, "Height and Nearness: Jewish Dimension of Radical Ethics," in *Ethics as First Philosophy,* 13–24.

16. In EE 63, footnote 1, Levinas himself refers to Maurice Blanchot, *Thomas l'Obscur* (Paris: Gallimard, 1941), especially chpt. 2, as to his source for the description of the *il y a.* See also *Ethics and Infinity,* where Levinas makes reference to Blanchot's later work, *The Writing of the Disaster* (Lincoln: University of Nebraska Press, 1986). On the relation between Levinas and Blanchot, see Paul Davies, "A Fine Risk: Reading Blanchot Reading Levinas," in *Re-Reading Levinas,* ed. Bernasconi and Critchley (Bloomington: Indiana University Press, 1991), 200–

226, and also, by the same author, "Difficult Freedom," *Research in Phenomenology* 18 (1988), 149–72.

17. On the notion of the *il y a,* see Jean-Luc Lannoy, "'Il y a' et phénoménologie dans le pensée du jeune Levinas," *Revue Philosophique de Louvain* 88 (1990), 369, 394, and Philip N. Lawton, "Levinas's Notion of the 'There is'," *Philosophy Today* 20 (1976), 69–76. See also Silvano Petrosino and Jacques Rolland, *La vérité nomade. Introduction à Emmanuel Levinas* (Paris: La Découverte, 1984), 19–25, and Edyth Wyschogrod, "Derrida, Levinas and Violence," in *Continental Philosophy* 2, ed. H. Silverman et al. (New York: Routledge, 1989), especially 183–86. The best discussions of the *il y a* offered by Levinas are contained in *Existence and Existents* and *Time and the Other.* On the connection between *il y a* and death, see Simon Critchley, "*Il y a*—A Dying Stronger than Death (Blanchot with Levinas)," *Oxford Literary Review* 15 (1993), 81–131.

18. See, for example, the essay "Transcendence and Evil," in CPP 175–86, in which one reads that "evil strikes me in my horror of evil, and thus reveals—or is already—my association with the Good" (CPP 183).

19. In "Violence and Metaphysics" Derrida refers to the passage in *Time and the Other* where Levinas invokes a break with Parmenides and reads it as if Levinas exhorted us to a second parricidium. On the issue, see John Protevi, "Repeating the Parricide: Levinas and the Question of Closure," *Journal of the British Society for Phenomenology* 23 (1992), 21–32.

20. The importance of the notion of creation (void of its physical-cosmological connotations) in Levinas's philosophy has been correctly understood and pointed out by O. Gaviria Alvarez, "L'idée de crèation chez Levinas: une archéologie du sens," in *Revue Philosophique de Louvain* 72 (1974), 509–38. For a discussion of the philosophical implications contained in the notion of creation, see also Silvano Petrosino, "L'idée de crèation dans l'oeuvre de Levinas," in *La différence comme non-indifférence,* ed. A. Münster (Paris: Kimé, 1995), 109–28, and Alberto Signorini, "L'idea di creazione ex nihilo e la libertà nel pensiero di E. Levinas," *Giornale di Metafisica* 11 (1989), 241–71.

21. On the gender identity of the child in Levinas, see Kelly

Oliver, *Family Values: Subjects Between Nature and Culture* (New York: Routledge, 1997), 211–15.

22. For a discussion of the title *Totality and Infinity* in its relation to the title of another fundamental work of Levinas, *Otherwise than Being or Beyond Essence,* see Jacques Rolland, "L'ambiguité comme façon de l'autrement," in *Emmanuel Levinas,* ed. J. Greisch and J. Rolland (Paris: Cerf, 1993), 428–31.

23. Levinas and Kearney, "Dialogue with Emmanuel Levinas," 21.

24. On the notion of Immemorial Past, see "Diachrony and Representation," in TO 111–14.

25. As already noticed, whereas ambiguity takes place at the ontological level of presence, and asks for its solution to avoid contradictions, ambivalence occurs at the diachronic level of ethics, and does not necessitate any relinquishment. As Nietzsche had already remarked, although within a different context, "one is fruitful only at the cost of being rich in contradictions;" Nietzsche, *Twilight of the Idols,* "Morality as Anti-Nature," 3.

26. Levinas and Kearney, "Dialogue with Emmanuel Levinas," 25.

27. As Peperzak suggestively indicates, Penelope, in her undoing of the tissue she weaves, should be the "patron of philosophy." See Adriaan Peperzak, "From Intentionality to Responsibility," in *The Question of the Other,* ed. A. Dallery and C. Scott (Albany: SUNY Press, 1989), 3–21.

Chapter 2: In Love: Ethics as the Meeting Place

1. On Levinas's confrontation with Descartes, from whom Levinas draws the resources for his critique of Western ontology, see Robert Bernasconi, "The Silent Anarchic World of the Evil Genius," in *The Collegium Phenomenologicum: The First Ten Years,* 252–72, and Anthony Beavers, *Levinas Beyond the Horizons of Cartesianism* (New York: Peter Lang, 1995).

2. See TI 48–50, 92–93, 210–11; see also *Emmanuel Levinas,* "God and Philosophy," in CPP 159–61, and "Philosophy and the

Idea of the Infinite," in CPP 53–54. On the latter essay, see Adriaan Peperzak, *To the Other: An Introduction to the Philosophy of Emmanuel Levinas* (West Lafayette: Purdue University Press, 1993).

3. In *Totality and Infinity,* at the end of the section titled "Metaphysics and Transcendence," Levinas emphasizes the originality of his notion of transcendence, which he opposes both to traditional philosophies of transcendence and to the philosophies of immanence. "Between a philosophy of transcendence that situates elsewhere the true life to which man, escaping from here, would gain access in the privileged moments of liturgical, mystical elevation, or in dying—and a philosophy of immanence in which we would truly come into possession of being when every 'other' (cause of war), encompassed by the same, would vanish at the end of history—we propose to describe, within the unfolding of terrestrial existence . . . a relationship with the other that does not result in a divine or human totality, that is not a totalization of history but the idea of infinity. Such a relationship is metaphysics itself" (TI 52).

4. For a discussion of Levinas's understanding of ethics as defying all forms of knowledge, and for an analysis of the peculiar notion of experience characterizing ethics, see Adriano Fabris, "Esperienza e etica," in *Levinas: Filosofia e trascendenza,* 199–230.

5. On Levinas's notion of desire in comparison to Hegel, see Brian Schroeder, "The (Non)Logic of Desire and War: Hegel and Levinas," in *Continental Philosophy* 7, ed. H. Silverman (New York: Routledge, forthcoming). See also Wendy Farley, "Emmanuel Levinas: Ethics as Damnation or Desire," in *Transitions in Continental Philosophy* ed. A. Dallery, S. Watson, and E. M. Bower (Albany: SUNY Press, 1994), 273–81.

6. That the meaning of space be not exhausted in transparency and ontology, but indicate an exposure to the outside of interiority is discussed by Levinas also in the context of his criticism of Kant's notion of space. See OBBE 179.

7. On the notion of the curvature of space, see César Moreno Marquez, "The Curvature of Intersubjective Space: Sociality and Responsibility in the Thought of Emmanuel Levinas," *Analecta Husserliana* 22 (1987), 343–52.

8. Because of its character of questioning, rather than providing answers, Bernasconi associates Levinas's ethics rather with the "contemporary suspicion of ethics than with the ethical tradition itself;" see Robert Bernasconi, "The Ethics of Suspicion," in *Research in Phenomenology* 20 (1990), 3–18.

9. The notion of the ethical intrigue as a key concept to understanding Levinas's philosophy has been discussed by Edvard Kovac, "L'intrigue ethique," in *Emmanuel Levinas,* 177–92.

10. On the relation between particularity and universality, see Fabio Ciaramelli, "Levinas's Ethical Discourse Between Individuation and Universality," in *Re-Reading Levinas,* 83–105.

11. A similar claim is made by Theodore De Boer, "An Ethical Transcendental Philosophy," in *Face to Face with Levinas,* 95; Robert Bernasconi, "Rereading Totality and Infinity" in *The Question of the Other,* 23–34 offers an insightful account and discussion of De Boer's article. On the issue of Levinas's transcendentalism, see also François Larouelle, " Au-delà du pouvoir: Le concept transcendental de la diaspora," in *Textes pour Emmanuel Levinas,* 111–25, which understands the transcendental as the unity of transcendence and immanence in the diaspora of the subject, and John Drabinski, "The Status of the Transcendental in Levinas' Thought," in *Philosophy Today* (1994), 149–58, which methodologically emphasizes the necessity of a transcendental grounding for Levinas's ethics as first philosophy.

12. A rejection of foundation as an architectonical notion connected to the world of the same is advanced by Levinas himself in DVI 141.

13. In this sense, ethics is a fact. Levinas reveals here some similarities with Kant. For Kant, too, the moral law is an indubitable fact, which cannot be questioned with respect to its ultimate ground. The Kantian inspiration of Levinas's ethics is an issue worth of attention. See the already mentioned Peperzak, "Some Remarks on Hegel, Kant and Levinas," and Lyotard, "Levinas' Logic," and Jere Paul Surber, "Kant, Levinas, and the Thought of the 'Other'," *Philosophy Today* 38 (1994), 294–316.

14. On the issue of transcendentalism, see Philip Maloney, "Levinas, Substitution, and Transcendental Subjectivity," *Man and World* 30 (1997), 49–64.

15. The separation is essential to avoid the "Nietzscheanism" of other French thinkers, such as Foucault, Lacan, Bourdieu, and Derrida, who bring to an extreme Nietzsche's criticism of subjectivity and call for the elimination of all notions of subjectivity. For the philosophical and political risks of such an elimination, see Luc Ferry and Alain Renault, "'Ce que a besoin d'être démontré ne vaut pas grand-chose'," in *Pourquoi nous ne sommes pas nietzschéens,* ed. A. Boyer et al. (Paris: Grasset, 1991). See also, by the same authors, *French Philosophy of the Sixties: An Essay on Antihumanism,* trans. M. Schnackenberg (Amherst: University of Massachussetts Press, 1990). For an assessment of the presence of Nietzsche's philosophy in contemporary continental thought, see Alan Schrift, *Nietzsche's French Legacy: A Genealogy of Poststructuralism* (New York: Routledge, 1995).

16. On the development of Levinas's notion of subjectivity, see G. Bailhache, *Le sujet chez E. Levinas: fragilité et subjectivité* (Paris: PUF, 1994).

17. An interesting analysis of the "here I am" as a performative is developed by Jan De Greef, "Skepticism and Reason," in *Face to Face with Levinas,* 171ff.

18. The anarchy of the two expressions is pointed out by Robert Bernasconi, "Levinas and Derrida: The Question of the Closure of Metaphysics," in *Face to Face with Levinas,* 189ff.

19. That is why, although one can speak of a "history of the face," this expression cannot mean that a face has a history, but that the face "ruptures history from within." Therefore it makes no sense to speak of an "end of history" or of an "end of philosophy" with respect to the face and ethics. See Bernasconi, "Levinas and Derrida," 195.

20. That love is a relation in which the separation of the I and the Other is maintained is argued by Luce Irigary, *I Love to You,* trans. A. Martin (New York: Routledge, 1996).

Chapter 3: My Love, Who Are You? The Face of the Beloved Other

1. On the issue of the other in Levinas, see William Large,

"On the Meaning of the Word 'Other' in Levinas," *Journal of the British Society for Phenomenology* 37 (1996), 36–52.

2. As Steven Smith, "Reason as One for Another," in *Face to Face with Levinas,* 63ff. notices, the *via negativa,* as an antiontology not dissociating itself from ontology, is merely a bad ontology. Therefore, it needs to be abandoned in favor of the *via eminentiae,* as Levinas does in his most recent philosophy.

3. In *Existence and Existents,* Levinas writes that the other "does not simply have another quality than me, but as it were bears alterity as a quality. . . . He is what I am not: he is the weak where I am the strong one. . . . What is essential is that he has these qualities by virtue of his very alterity" (EE 94–95). This excludes that there can be formed a collectivity grounded around something common, as it is the case for Heidegger's *Miteinandersein,* "a collectivity of the *with,*" formed around truth.

4. In *Ethics and Infinity,* Levinas writes that "ordinarily one is a 'character:' a professor at the Sorbonne, a Supreme Court justice, son of so-and-so, everything that is in one's passport, the manner of dressing, of presenting oneself . . . the meaning of something is in its relation to another thing. Here, to the contrary . . . You are you" (EI 86).

5. The notion of the face emerges first in the three essays "L'Ontologie est-elle fondamentale?" (1951), "Ethique et Esprit" (1952), and "Liberté et Commandement" (1953), to find its most significant elaboration in *Totality and Infinity* (1961). See Merold Westphal, "Levinas and the Immediacy of the Face," *Journal of the Society of Christian Philosophers* 10 (1993), 486–502.

6. The experience of the face is not, for Levinas, disclosure and unveiling (the reference is obviously to Heidegger), but rather revelation, expression of the one who presents himself or herself and signifies immediately, without mediation other than itself (TI 65–66).

7. Richard Cohen, "Absolute Positivity and Ultrapositivity: Husserl and Levinas," in *The Question of the Other,* 35–43 reads the immediacy of the face as the notion in whose name Levinas launches his attack on phenomenology.

8. On the notion of ethics as prophetic witness, see Ciaramelli, "Levinas's Ethical Discourse," in *Re-Reading Levinas,* 98ff. and also Catherine Chalier, "Singularité juive et philosophie," in *Emmanuel Levinas,* 78–98, especially on the notion of messianism.

9. See also EI 87, 89. On the centrality of language as the modality by which transcendence expresses itself, see E. Feron, *De l'idée de transcendance à la question du language. L'itinéraire philosophique de Levinas* (Grenoble: Millon, 1992), and also T. Wiemer, *Die Passion der Sagens. Zur Deutung der Sprache bei E. Levinas und ihrer Realisierung in philosophischen Diskurs* (Freiburg: Alber, 1988).

10. On the ontological powerlessness of the Other, which nevertheless turns into ethical power, see Jan De Greef, "Le concept du pouvoir éthique chez Levinas," in *Revue Philosophique de Louvain,* 68 (1970), 507–20.

11. The theme of the height of the Other is addressed especially in the essay "Transcendence and Height."

12. The asymmetry of the relation distantiates Levinas from all dialogical philosophies, and especially from Buber, who qualifies the ethical relation to the other as a relation of reciprocity. For Levinas's objections to Buber, see TI 68–69; for a broader appraisal of Levinas's appreciation of Buber, see the essays contained in *Proper Names* and *Outside the Subject,* specifically "Martin Buber and the Theory of Knowledge," in PN 17–35, "Dialogue with Martin Buber," in PN 36–39, "Martin Buber's Thought and Contemporary Judaism," in OS 4–19, and finally "Martin Buber, Gabriel Marcel and Philosophy," in OS 40–48.

13. On the figure of the stranger, see Jean Greisch, "Ethique et ontologie," in *Emmanuel Levinas,* 15–45.

14. Levinas and Kearney, "Dialogue with Emmanuel Levinas," 27–28.

15. For this discussion, see John Llewelyn, *The Middle Voice of Ecological Conscience: A Chiasmatic Reading of Responsibility in the Neighbourhood of Levinas, Heidegger and Others* (London: MacMillan, 1991), 54–56.

16. For an analysis of the idea of God in Levinas, see Jacques Rolland, "'Divine Comedie': La question de Dieu chez Levinas," in *La différence comme non-indifférence,* 109–27.

17. It is important to note, however, that it is not with reference to God's highness that the ethical heighness and mastery of the other are constituted; it is rather through the originary experience of the ethical highness and mastery of the other that the I can approach the idea of God. See the conference "Transcendence and Height." In Levinas and Kearney, "Dialogue with Emmanuel Levinas," one reads that "it is only in the infinite relation with the Other that God passes, that traces of God are to be found" (31).

18. On this topic, see Helen Chapman, "Levinas and the Concept of the Feminine," *Warwick Journal of Philosophy* 1 (1988), 65–83; Tina Chanter, "Feminism and the Other," in *The Provocation of Levinas,* 32–56, and Morny Joy, "Levinas, Alterity, the Feminine and Women—A Meditation," *Studies in Religion* 22 (1994), 463–85.

19. In this work, I will limit myself to indicate the figures of absence (woman, child) in Levinas's philosophy, in order to concentrate on the theme of things instead. Therefore, I leave to others (Chanter, Oliver, Irigaray among many) the important and urgent task of reconfiguring Levinas's philosophy from the perspective of an inclusion of such figures of absence. How would Levinas's philosophy change, if it were to be othered by women and children?

20. That such a description repeats traditional images of the feminine, and therefore obeys sexist stereotypes of the feminine was already argued by Simone de Beauvoir, *The Second Sex,* trans. H. Parshley (New York: Bentam Books, 1970), xvi, n. 3.

21. This suspicion dominates the essay by Craig Vasey, "Faceless Women and Serious Others: Levinas, Misogyny, and Feminism," in *Ethics and Danger,* 317–30.

22. On Levinas's relation to Buber, see Robert Bernasconi, "'Failure of Communication' as a Surplus: Dialogue and Lack of Dialogue Between Buber and Levinas," in *The Provocation of Levinas,* 100–135.

23. That Woman in Levinas's writing is viewed as a negative image of Man is argued by Luce Irigaray, "Questions to Emmanuel Levinas," in *Re-Reading Levinas,* 109–18.

24. Chalier, "Ethics and the Feminine," 122–23.

25. On this topic, see Tina Chanter, "Antigone's Dilemma," in *Re-Reading Levinas,* 130–35 and Irigaray, "Questions to Emmanuel Levinas," 109–118. On Levinas's notion of love, see also Jeffrey Bloechl, "How Best to Keep a Secret? On Love and Respect in Levinas' 'Phenomenology of Eros'," *Man and World* 29 (1996), 1–17.

26. See Luce Irigaray, "The Fecundity of the Caress: A Reading of Levinas, *Totality and Infinity,* section 4, B, 'The Phenomenology of Eros'," in *Face to Face with Levinas,* 231–56.

27. In this sense, fecundity fulfills Diotima's claim in Plato's *Symposium* that "reproduction . . . is what mortals have in place of immortality" (*Symp.* 207a).

28. On the problem of the relation between sexual difference and ethical difference (a problem opened up by the woman reader), see Jacques Derrida, "At This Very Moment in This Work Here I Am," in *Re-Reading Levinas,* 39ff. and "Violence and Metaphysics," 320–21, where Derrida clearly states that a woman could never have written *Totality and Infinity.* Some suspicions may however arise with respect to this statement, since it is a man who writes about the (non)being woman of another man.

29. Irigaray, "Questions to Emmanuel Levinas," 111. Irigaray's position with respect to Levinas is explored among others by Tina Chanter, *Ethics and Eros: Irigaray's Rewriting of the Philosophers* (New York: Routledge, 1995).

30. On the possibility that the son may be a daughter, see Oliver, *Family Values,* 211–15. See also Richard Cohen, "The Family and Ethics: The Metaphysics of Eros in Emmanuel Levinas's *Totality and Infinity,*" *Contemporary Philosophy* 15, 4 (1993), 1–7.

31. See T. Wright, P. Hughes, and A. Ainley, "The Paradox of Morality: An Interview with Emmanuel Levinas," 168–80, and the comments on it in Llewelyn, *The Middle Voice of Ecological Conscience,* 64–67.

32. See John Llewelyn, "Am I Obsessed by Bobby? (Humanism of the Other Animal)." Bobby is the name of the dog referred to by Levinas in the essay entitled "The Name of a Dog, or Natural Rights" and contained in *Difficult Freedom* (DF 151–53).

33. The term "anthropologocentrism" has been coined by analogy with Derrida's "phallogocentrism" to signify a metaphysical horizon constructed around the *logos* of the human being.

34. On the antihumanistic character of contemporary French philosophy, according to the authors a direct descendant of Nietzsche and Heidegger, see Ferry and Renaut, *French Philosophy of the Sixties*. The authors do not include Levinas in the group of antihumanistic thinkers.

35. The connection between the excesses of our history and the need for a different subjectivity is made evident in the dedication with which Levinas prefaces the work that more fundamentally elaborates such a notion of the ethical subject. "To the memory of those who were closest among the six million assassinated by the National Socialists, and of the millions and millions of all confessions and all nations, victims of the same hatred of the other man, the same anti-semitism" (OBBE V). On the importance of this dedication to understand the fundamental themes of *Otherwise than Being,* see E. Weber, *Verfolgung und Trauma: zu Emmanuel Levinas' "Autrement qu'être ou au-delà de l'essence"* (Vienna: Passagen Verlag, 1990). On Levinas's critique of antihumanist philosophies, see Peter Atterton, "Levinas's Skeptical Critique of Metaphysics and Anti-humanism," *Philosophy Today* 41 (1997), 491–506.

Chapter 4: Without Love: The Disappearance of Things

1. On Levinas's position on technology, see Adriaan Peperzak, "Levinas on Technology and Nature," *Man and World* 25 (1992), 469–82.

2. The term *alterity* will be reserved from here on to signify the peculiar form of otherness, distinct from human otherness, that this work aims to retrace in things.

3. On Levinas's reflection on art, see especially Levinas, "Reality and its Shadow," in CPP 1–13; "The Transcendence of Words: On Michel Leiris's *Biffures,*" in OS 144–50, and the section "On Maurice Blanchot," in PN 127–170. See also Edith Wyschogrod, "The Art in Ethics: Aesthetics, Objectivity, and Alterity in the Philosophy of Emmanuel Levinas," in *Ethics as*

First Philosophy, 137–48, and Jill Robbins, "Aesthetic Totality and Ethical Infinity: Levinas on Art," *L'Esprit Créateur* 35 (1995), 66–79.

4. On the topic of things in their relation to art, see Giampiero Comolli, "Il volto delle cose. Intorno alla questione dell'arte in E. Levinas," in *Aut-Aut* 209 (1985), 219–36.

5. The relation of Levinas to Heidegger is rather complex. However, for reasons explained in Part 3, chapter 10, of the present essay, it is not my interest here to dwell on the complications of the relation, which has been the theme of study of several excellent scholars. Among others, see Adriaan Peperzak, *Beyond: The Philosophy of Emmanuel Levinas* (Evanston: Northwestern University Press, 1997), chpts. 4, 6, and 14 especially.

6. A remarkable description of things is provided also by Merleau-Ponty. However, Merleau-Ponty's account remains within the context of a phenomenology of perception, whereas Heidegger's analysis, although labored, winding, and scattered along the entire course of his philosophical meditation, retains an unmistakenly ontological/metaphysical character. Hence, the preference accorded to Heidegger in the present work.

Chapter 5: The Question of Things

1. Johann Peter Hebel, quoted in DT 57.

2. Martin Heidegger, "Overcoming Metaphysics," in *The End of Philosophy,* trans. Joan Stambaugh (New York: Harper & Row, 1973), 85.

3. Martin Heidegger, "Hölderlin and the Essence of Poetry," in *Existence and Being,* 272.

4. Martin Heidegger, *What Is Philosophy?,* trans. J. Wilde and W. Kluback (New Haven: College and University Press), 43.

5. Heidegger, *What Is Philosophy?,* 77.

Chapter 6: Phenomenologically, Things

1. On the thematic issue of sciences, see what Heidegger writes in the "Postscript to 'What Is Metaphysics?'," in *Existence*

and Being, 353: "No matter where and however deeply science investigates what-is it will never find being. All it encounters, always, is what-is, because its explanatory purpose makes it insist at the outset on what-is. But being is not an existing quality of what-is, nor, unlike what-is, can being be conceived and established objectively."

2. For an analysis of Heidegger's first treatment of the ontological difference in *Basic Problems of Phenomenology,* see Graeme Nicholson, "The Ontological Difference," *American Philosophical Quarterly* 33 (1996), 357–74. On the ontological difference, see also what Heidegger says in *The Fundamental Concepts of Metaphysics,* 358ff.

3. Martin Heidegger, "My Way to Phenomenology," TB 82.

4. See Jacques Taminiaux, *Heidegger and the Project of Fundamental Ontology,* trans. M. Gendre (Albany: SUNY Press, 1991).

5. On Heidegger's understanding of phenomenology, see *Heidegger et l'idée de la phenomenologie,* ed. Franco Volpi (Dordrecht: Kluwer, 1988), and *Phénoménologie et metaphysique,* ed. Walter Biemel (Paris: PUF, 1984).

Chapter 7: Instrumental Modes of Disclosure

1. On Heidegger's subscription to phenomenology, see what he himself says in the essay "My Way to Phenomenology," TB 74–82.

2. For a detailed analysis of the notion of being-in-the-world, see Fernand Couturier, *Monde et être chez Heidegger* (Montreal: Presses de l'Université, 1971); Walter Biemel, *Le concept de monde chez Heidegger* (Louvain: Nauwelaerts, 1950) and, more recently, Hubert Dreyfus, *Being-in-the-World: A Commentary on Heidegger's Being and Time, Division 1* (Cambridge: MIT Press, 1991).

3. The opposition subject/object is what gives rise not only to metaphysical epistemology, but also to technology. In this sense the discussion of *Zeug* in terms of *Dasein's* being-in-the-world already repudiates the technological framework. But see Hubert

Dreyfus, "Between *Techne* and Technology: The Ambiguous Place of Equipment in 'Being and Time'," in *The Thought of Martin Heidegger,* ed. M. Zimmerman, Tulane Studies in Philosophy, 32 (1984), 23–35.

4. The expression "belongs" is however semantically incorrect, since *Dasein* does not properly *have* a world, but *is* in the world.

5. See Carl Friedrich Gethmann, "Heideggers Konzeption des Handelns in 'Sein und Zeit'," in *Heidegger und die praktische Philosophie,* ed. A. Gethmann-Siefert and O. Pöggeler (Frankfurt: Suhrkamp, 1988), 140–76, who speaks of a Heideggerian pragmatic program focused on the notion of the *Umgang* (handling). See also Richard Rorty, *Philosophy and the Mirror of Nature* (Princeton: Princeton University Press, 1979), 368 and passim.

6. On the impossibility of understanding the meaning of *phronesis* and *sophia* under the guiding line of the Kantian distinction between practical and theoretical reason, see Heidegger's *Plato's Sophist* (42ff.). On the issue of *phronesis,* see Robert Bernasconi, "Heidegger's Destruction of *Phronesis,*" in *Southern Journal of Philosophy* (supp.) 28 (1989), 127–47. The issue of the role of the Aristotelian virtues in Heidegger is complex. Beside Bernasconi's essay, see Jacques Taminiaux, "*Poiesis* and *Praxis* in Fundamental Ontology," *Research in Phenomenology* 17 (1987), 137–69; Franco Volpi, "Dasein comme *praxis,*" in *Heidegger et l'idée de la phénoménologie,* 1–41.

7. In *Being and Time* touch replaces the metaphysical (Platonic) supremacy of sight. Later it will be replaced by hearing, the postmetaphysical, posttechnological dimension adequate to an epoch that has reacted to the excesses provoked by all-encompassing manipulation. In *Being and Time,* however, technology, both as mass-production and mass-destruction, has not yet entered Heidegger's range of thought. On this topic, see Gerald Prauss, "Heidegger und die praktische Philosophie," in *Heidegger und die praktische Philosophie,* ed. A. Gethmann-Siefert and O. Pöggeler (Frankfurt: Suhrkamp, 1988), 177–90.

8. But see my article "On the Way to an Ontological Ethics: Ethical Suggestions in Reading Heidegger," *Research in Phenomenology* 24 (1994), 159–88, and the bibliography therein contained.

9. Note, on the other hand, the dis-interestedness that marks the encounter with the Other in Levinas. See especially OBBE 3–20, and 131–39.

10. The connection things/*pragmata*/concern emerges as early as the lectures on Plato's *Sophist* (see S 17). In the context of these lectures, Heidegger understands *praxis* not as producing (*poiesis*), but as acting (S 27), whereas producing is that toward which *techne* is oriented.

11. On Heidegger's still Platonic subordination of the sensible, of which things are an instantiation, to meaning, see John Sallis, "Twisting Free—Being to an Extent Sensible," in *Echoes: After Heidegger* (Bloomington: Indiana University Press, 1990), 76–96.

12. Hubert Dreyfus delineates a history of the *Zeug* in three stages: craftsmanship, the industrial age, and cybernetical planification. See Dreyfus, "Between *Techne* and Technology."

13. On the issue of the early Heidegger's (non)instrumentalist ontology, see Michael Zimmermann, *Heidegger's Confrontation with Modernity: Technology, Politics, Art* (Bloomington: Indiana University Press, 1990), 150–65.

14. Against Heidegger, Levinas thematizes the elemental as the realm of what cannot become the object of manipulation, the "non-possessable which envelops or contains without being able to be contained or enveloped." See, for example, TI 130ff.

15. On Heidegger's pragmatic attitude, see Mark Okrent, *Heidegger's Pragmatism: Understanding, Being, and the Critique of Metaphysics* (Ithaca: Cornell University Press, 1988).

16. The statement has been made central by most of the scholars who have engaged in a discussion of Heidegger's concept of nature. See John Llewelyn, *The Middle Voice of Ecological Conscience: A Chiasmic Reading of Responsibility in the Neighbourhood of Levinas, Heidegger and Others* (London: MacMillan, 1991), and Michel Haar, *The Song of the Earth: Heidegger and the Grounds of the History of Being,* trans. R. Lilly (Bloomington: Indiana University Press, 1993), 17.

17. The concept of nature as that which "stirs and strives" will be taken up later by Heidegger, especially in his essays on Hölderlin. See, for example, "Wie wenn am Feiertage...," in

Martin Heidegger, *Gesamtausgabe,* vol. 4 (Frankfurt: Klostermann, 1975–), 49–78, where nature appears as powerful because it is beautiful and omnipresent.

18. A similar experience of emptiness, in which things present themselves as indifferent occurs in the situation of profound boredom. "In this boredom the beings that surround us offer us no further possibility of acting and no further possibility of our doing anything" (FCM 139). Analogously to anxiety, profound boredom too discloses to Dasein something about its own being. The "telling refusal on the part of beings as a whole merely indicates indeterminately the possibilities of *Dasein,* of its doing and acting" (FCM 140). For an analysis of the fundamental mood of boredom, which thus parallels anxiety as a fundamental mood, see what Heidegger says in *The Fundamental Concepts of Metaphysics.*

19. Hence the charges of egoism moved against the existential analytic of *Dasein,* to which Heidegger replied by saying that such accusations arose from a primitive misunderstanding of his enterprise. See Martin Heidegger, *The Metaphysical Foundation of Logic,* trans. M. Heim (Bloomington: Indiana University Press, 1984), 186.

20. For a discussion of Heidegger's relation to Kant, see, for example, Charles Sherover, *Heidegger, Kant and Time* (Lanham: University Press of America, 1988), which shows a developmental unity between Kant's first critique and Heidegger's analysis of the categorical structure of human existence, and Frank Schalow, *The Renewal of the Heidegger-Kant Dialogue* (Albany: SUNY Press, 1992).

21. For a description of Heidegger's acceptance from Husserl of the notion of apriorism and transcendentalism, and of Heidegger's transmutation of such notions from the dimension of consciousness to "what is wholely different from man, namely the clearing of being," through existential phenomenology, phenomenology of historical *aletheia,* and finally topology of the event, see Reiner Schürmann, *Heidegger on Being and Acting: From Principles to Anarchy* (Bloomington: Indiana University Press, 1987), 64ff.

22. For an analysis of the proximity between Kant and Heidegger on the issue of idealism, see François Raffoul, "Heidegger

and Kant: The Question of Idealism," *Philosophy Today*, 40 (1996), 531–47.

23. Heidegger disclaims the accusation of a "subjective coloring" given to *Zeug* also in BT 101.

24. Heidegger, "What is Philosophy?," 81.

25. Werner Marx remarks how "Heidegger had to realize that it is first and foremost world and Being which 'give' and 'grant' to *Dasein* the fact that, and the way in which, entities appear in the light of their presence;" see Werner Marx, "The World in Another Beginning: Poetic Dwelling and the Role of the Poet," in *On Heidegger and Language*, ed. Joseph Kockelmans (Evanston: Northwestern University Press, 1972), 237–38.

Chapter 8: Artistic Modes of Disclosure

1. On Heidegger's discussion of art, see, among others, Joseph Kockelmans, *Heidegger on Art and Art Works* (The Hague: Nijhoff, 1985).

2. For an interesting discussion of animal life, see what Heidegger says in *Fundamental Concepts of Metaphysics*, 192–267.

3. For an interesting account of the notion of earth in Heidegger, see the essays contained in *Heidegger and the Earth*, ed. Ladelle McWhorter (Kirksville: Thomas Jefferson University Press, 1992).

4. Heidegger gives several examples of what is meant by the sheltering character of the earth, which remains undisclosed to scientific knowledge despite the precision of its measurements and calculations. "A stone presses downward and manifests its heaviness. But while this heaviness exerts an opposing pressure upon us it denies us any penetration into it. If we attempt such a penetration by breaking open the rock, it still does not display in its fragments anything inward that has been disclosed. The stone has instantly withdrawn again into the same dull pressure and bulk of its fragments. . . .Color shines and wants only to shine. When we analyze it in rational terms by measuring its wavelengths, it is gone. It shows itself only when it remains undisclosed and unexplained. Earth thus shatters every attempt

to penetrate into it. . . .The earth appears openly cleared as itself only when it is perceived and preserved as that which is by nature undisclosable, that which shrinks from every disclosure and constantly keeps itself closed up. . . .The earth is essentially self-secluding" (OWA 46–47).

5. See Travis Anderson, "Through Phenomenology to Sublime Poetry: Martin Heidegger on the Decisive Relation between Truth and Art," *Research in Phenomenology* 26 (1996), 198–229.

6. On this issue, see James Ward, "Poetic Dwelling: Homeland" in *Heidegger's Political Thinking* (Amherst: University of Massachussetts Press, 1995), 205–59.

7. On the shift in Heidegger's discussion from Van Gogh's painting to the Greek temple as a transition from representational to great art, see John Bruin, "Heidegger and Two Kinds of Art," *Journal of Aesthetics and Art Criticism* 52 (1994), 447–57.

8. See Hubert Dreyfus, "Heidegger and the Connection Between Nihilism, Art, Technology, and Politics," in *The Cambridge Companion to Heidegger*, ed. C. Guignon (Cambridge: Cambridge University Press, 1993), 289–316.

9. On the importance of Heidegger's confrontation with the poets in terms of the development of a notion of ethical responsibility, see Véronique Fòti, *Heidegger and the Poets: Poiesis, Sophia, Techne* (Atlantic Highlands: Humanities Press, 1992).

10. See Werner Marx, *Is There a Measure on Earth?*, trans. T. J. Neman and R. Lilly (Chicago: University of Chicago Press, 1987).

Chapter 9: Ethical Disclosure? The Faciality of Things

1. An earlier version of this chapter has been published as "The Face of Things: Heidegger and the Alterity of the Fourfold," *Symposium* 1 (1997), 5–15.

2. Heidegger asserts that the thing's being produced does not belong to its essence any more than the material of which it has been produced does (T 169).

3. Martin Heidegger, "Language," in *On the Way to Language,* referred to as L.

4. Excluded from the self-emerging domain of *physis,* divinities and mortals are reintroduced in the economy things institute, and thereby brought one near to another.

5. On the distinction between the Same and the Identical, analogous to that between oneness and unity, see Martin Heidegger, *Identity and Difference,* trans. John Stambaugh (New York: Harper & Row, 1969), 45ff.

6. The cluster of issues entailed in the technical term "Fourfold" have been discussed, at various length, by Vincent Vycinas, *Earth and Gods* (The Hague: Nijhoff, 1961); Otto Pöggeler, *Der Denkweg Martin Heideggers* (Pfullingen: Neske, 1963), William Richardson, *Heidegger: Through Phenomenology to Thought* (The Hague: Nijhoff, 1963), Joseph Kockelmans, *On the Truth of Being* (Bloomington: Indiana University Press, 1984).

7. Thus, Heidegger remarks, a country bridge gathers differently than a city bridge, which in turn gathers differently than the highway bridge. "The bridge *gathers* to itself in *its own* way earth and sky, divinities and mortals" (BDT 153).

8. Martin Heidegger, ". . . Poetically Man Dwells. . . ," in PLT.

9. Martin Heidegger, *Die Kunst und der Raum* (St. Gallen: Erker Verlag, 1969), 11.

10. Although in a different context, Nancy writes that "a world . . . is the way we exist together . . . not the time of an origin, nor the origin of time: it is the spacing of time." It is in this sense indicated by Nancy that things open up a world through the institution of a vicinity. See Nancy, *The Birth to Presence,* 163–64.

11. On the notion of the nearing, see Krzysztof Ziarek, *Inflected Language: Toward a Hermeneutics of Nearness* (Albany: SUNY Press, 1994).

12. See Derrida, *Writing and Difference,* 145: "the solicitation of the Site and Land is in no way, it must be emphasized, a passionate attachment to territory or locality, is in no way a provincialism or particularism . . . . The thinking of Being thus is not a pagan cult of the Site, because the Site is never a given proximi-

ty but a promised one." On the notion of space, see Maria Villela-Petit, "Heidegger's Conception of Space," in *Critical Heidegger,* ed. C. Macann (London: Routledge, 1996), 134–57.

13. In the essay "Language," it is the falling of the snow and the tolling of the vesper bell that, among other things, gather by themselves the earth and the heavens, the mortals and the gods (L 199).

14. Being-toward-death, which somehow had placed *Dasein* in a solitary universe, is now replaced by Heidegger with a dimension of ontological community, "of mutual belonging." (T 173).

15. When this happens, the Fourfold is denied its place. As Heidegger exemplifies it, when the hydroelectric plant is installed in the current of the river Rhine, challenging the river to unlock and store up the energy concealed in it, the presencing of the Fourfold is blocked; the river as thing has lost its alterity. See Martin Heidegger, *The Question Concerning Technology.*

16. This is done "in this way, that mortals nurse and nurture the things that grow, and specially construct things that do not grow" (BDT 151). The notion of building, which in its relation to *techne* and technology had concerned Heidegger in several occasions, is now recomprised as part of the activity of dwelling, which also reinterprets the being-in-the-world that characterized *Dasein* in *Being and Time.*

Chapter 10: Prelude: Toward an Ethics of Things

1. An earlier version of this chapter has been published as "Of Things Face-to-Face with Levinas Face-to-Face with Heidegger," *Philosophy Today* 40 (1996), 132–41.

2. As already seen, the section of *Totality and Infinity* devoted to "Interiority and Economy" offers Levinas's broadest account (confirmed in subsequent works and interviews) of a phenomenology of things.

3. In *Otherwise than Being* the world—and the things—are "extended by the sense of alterity, which takes form and becomes a phenomenon in the face of another." See Alphonso Lingis, "The Sensuality and the Sensitivity," in *Face to Face with Levinas,* 227.

4. One should note that in *Otherwise than Being* color and sonority are seen as a manifestation of a certain independence of the things, which is stabilized in art. Independence does not entail alterity, however. Moreover, the qualities of the things are not the things themselves.

5. On the possibility of retracing an ethical dimension in Heidegger, see Joanna Hedge, *Heidegger and Ethics* (New York: Routledge, 1995), and François Raffoul, "Responsabilité et Altérité chez Heidegger et Levinas," *Symposium* 1 (1997), 49–64.

6. A similar project of an *Auseinandersetzung* between Heidegger and Levinas but not specifically on the issues of ethics and things is attempted by Llewelyn, *The Middle Voice of Ecological Conscience.* Reference to the figure of the chiasmus is made by Levinas himself—with respect to Derrida—in "Wholly Otherwise," in *Re-Reading Levinas,* 6–8. Derrida too has employed the same trope to describe deconstructive reading. See, for example, Jacques Derrida, *Positions,* trans. A. Bass (Chicago: University of Chicago Press, 1971), 70.

7. The path of affirmation has been suggested, although in a very peculiar way, by Spinoza. His description of thought and extension as the two parallel attributes of the unique substance as well as his definition of ethics as the free attunement to the necessary geometrical structure of substance might lead to an ethics of things where, in order to think freely—that is, adequately—thought should adequate itself to the inner structure of things. Whether this structure were to allow for alterity seems improbable, given the rationalist framework of Spinoza' *Ethics.* Levinas associates Spinoza with Parmenides and Hegel in their privileging unity over separatedness and alterity. See TI 102. But, as Jean-Luc Nancy remarks, Spinoza is the only one to offer explicitly a "thought-thing." See Jean-Luc Nancy, *Une pensée finie* (Paris: Galilée, 1990), 205.

8. The expression is Levinas's, who uses it with respect to Derrida in "Wholly Otherwise," 8.

9. Supplementarity is discussed by Derrida in *Speech and Phenomena, and Other Essays on Husserl's Theory of Signs,* trans. D. Allison (Evanston: Northwestern University Press, 1973), 88–104, in a chapter explicitly devoted to the "Supplement of Origin."

10. Jacques Derrida, *Of Grammatology,* trans. G. C. Spivak (Baltimore: Johns Hopkins University Press, 1976), 144–45.

11. See Ugo Perone, *Modernità e memoria,* 91.

12. See Dietrich Bonhoeffer, *Ethics,* trans. N. H. Smith (New York: MacMillan, 1964), 5.

13. See Heidegger's appropriate criticism of ethics when this notion is meant in the reductivistic sense of morality, for example in BT 16, or in IM 16, 197–99, or in the "Letter on Humanism," 232–35.

14. See also Charles Scott, *The Question of Ethics: Nietzsche, Foucault, Heidegger* (Bloomington: Indiana University Press, 1990), 143–47.

15. Note what Heidegger says with respect to the verb "to save" (*retten*), which should be taken "in the old sense still known to Lessing. Saving does not only snatch something from a danger. To save really means to set something free [*freilassen*] into its own essence" (BDT 328).

16. Although Heidegger is critical of the usage of the term *ontology,* he writes that "we can also take the word 'ontology' in the 'broadest sense,' 'without reference to ontological directions and tendencies' (see *Sein und Zeit,* p. 11 top). In this case 'ontology' signifies the endeavor to make being manifest itself, and to do so by way of the question 'How does it stand with being?' (and not only with the essent as such)" (IM 41).

17. *Différance* is the (ontological) difference in its differing from itself and therefore de-ferring itself. In this sense *différance* is neither a word nor a concept. See Derrida, *Speech and Phenomena,* 129–60, but also the lecture delivered to the Société française de philosophie, and titled *La Différance;* now in *Margins of Philosophy,* trans. A. Bass (Chicago: University of Chicago Press, 1982), 1–27. One should note, however, that Derrida's *différance,* given its poststructuralist character, is entirely "horizontal," whereas the reference to the "ontological" dimension in Heidegger introduces "verticality." That is, the affinity, although legitimate, cannot be a ready assimilation.

18. Notice what is said in *Otherwise than Being* with respect to the amphibology of being and beings (Heidegger) and the ne-

cessity of a reduction to another amphibology, that of the Saying and the said (Levinas). See OBBE 51ff.

19. On the heteronomy of freedom, see Levinas's essay "Freedom and Command," in CPP 15–23, where Levinas writes that "to command is then to do the will of the one who obeys."

20. In *Otherwise than Being* Levinas identifies the freedom of the ethical subject with its infinite subjection, its passivity, its vulnerability, its exposure to the Other. See especially OBBE 121–29.

21. See Levinas and Kearney, "Dialogue with Emmanuel Levinas," 29–30.

22. In *Totality and Infinity* Levinas criticizes Heidegger's notion of the Fourfold—and inhabiting the Fourfold—as one more case of ontological affirmation and domination. Levinas calls it "an ontology of nature" (TI 46). What escapes Levinas, and what our interpretation of the Fourfold retrieves, is the nonexhaustibility of such dwelling, the fact that the Fourfold can never be possessed. Therefore, Heidegger is immune from Levinas's criticism on this point.

23. On the notion of the trace, see Edward Casey, "Levinas on Memory and the Trace," in *The Collegium Phenomenologicum: The First Ten Years,* 241–55.

24. Levinas says that "vegetarianism, for example, arises from the transference to animals of the idea of suffering. The animal suffers. It is because we, as humans, know what suffering is that we can have this obligation [not to make an animal suffer needlessly]," T. Wright, P. Hughes, and A. Ainley, "The Paradox of Morality," 172.

25. This statement contains the danger of a folding back of the ethical relationship upon itself, of a return of ethics to itself guided by the light of humanity or human suffering, of a self-reflection that retains a narcissistic flavor (both Narcissus and the river are reflected, this time). The I and the other return to themselves as to a two (rather than a one), delimiting a common territory (that of human ethics) that includes what is human in the "relation without relation," but excludes what is not human. In other words, the return of self-consciousness to itself is duplicated by its transformation into the dual relation between the I

and the other. The Third that keeps the relation open still moves within the common territory of human ethics.

26. See Llewelyn, *Jewgreek or Greekjew,* 282–86.

27. See Lingis, "The Sensuality and the Sensitivity," 227.

28. Nancy, *The Birth to Presence,* 171.

Chapter 11: Things' Obsessive Appeal

1. Merleau-Ponty, *Phenomenology of Perception,* 293.

2. An interesting account of the interaction between the body and things is offered by Alphonso Lingis within the context of a discussion of Merleau-Ponty's phenomenology of perception. See Alphonso Lingis, "The Competent Body," in *Foreign Bodies* (New York: Routledge, 1994), especially 4–12.

3. The literature on this topic is vast. Among others, see E. Marcuse, *One-Dimensional Man: Studies in the Ideology of Advanced Industrial Society* (Boston: Beacon Press, 1964); Lucien Goldmann, *Die Aufklärung und die Moderne Gesellschaft.*

4. For an inspiring phenomenology of things, see Alphonso Lingis, *The Imperative* (Bloomington: Indiana University Press, 1998), especially chpt. 5.

5. On the distinction between faces and facialities, see the Preface.

6. But note that also Kant's categorical imperative signifies independently of the proofs for the existence of God and the immortality of the soul that are furnished by reason. See OBBE 129.

7. André Neher, *L'exil de la parole. Du silence biblique au silence d'Auschwitz* (Paris: Ed. du Seuil, 1970).

8. Nancy, *Une pensée finie,* 211.

9. Friedrich Nietzsche, *Genealogy of Morals,* trans. W. Kaufmann and R. J. Hollingdale (New York: Random House, 1967), II.

10. On the philosophical "urge to be at home everywhere," and

the consequent description of philosophy as "homesickness," see FCM 8.

11. See Friedrich Nietzsche, *Ecce Homo,* trans. W. Kaufmann (New York: Vintage, 1989).

12. For such an expression, see Edward Casey, *Getting Back into Place: Toward a Renewed Understanding of the Place-World* (Bloomington: Indiana University Press, 1993).

13. Friedrich Nietzsche, *Thus Spoke Zarathustra,* "Preface," in *The Portable Nietzsche,* 131.

Chapter 12: Touch, Attention, Tenderness

1. More recently, a fundamental analysis of touch and the tactile experience has been provided by Maurice Merleau-Ponty in *Phenomenology of Perception,* trans. C. Smith (New York: Routledge, 1989), 315–17. It is in Aristotle, however, that the first description of the experience of touch can be found, and it is to Aristotle that Heidegger's own analysis in *Being and Time* is indebted. On Merleau-Ponty's understanding of touch, see among others Emmanuel Levinas, "Intersubjectivity: Notes on Merleau-Ponty," in *Ontology and Alterity in Merleau-Ponty,* ed. G. A. Johnson and M. Smith (Evanston: Northwestern University Press, 1990), 55–60.

2. Marleau-Ponty speaks of a "veritable touching of the touch, when my right hand touches my left hand while it is palpating the things, where the 'touching subject' passes over to the rank of the touched, descends into the things, such that the touch is formed in the midst of the world and as it were in the things;" Maurice Merleau-Ponty, *The Visible and the Invisible,* trans. A. Lingis (Evanston: Northwestern University Press, 1968), 133–34. Along similar lines of thought Nancy remarks that touch "*feels itself feeling itself,* since it only touches by touching also itself, touched by what it touches *and* because it touches," Jean-Luc Nancy, *The Muses* (Stanford: Stanford University Press, 1996), 17. See also Jacques Derrida, "*Le toucher:* Touch/To Touch Him," trans. P. Kamuf, *Paragraph* 16, 2 (1993).

3. The expression is taken from Edith Wyschogrod, "Doing before Hearing: On the Primacy of Touch," in *Textes pour Em-*

manuel Levinas, 194. To such an essay are the following comments deeply indebted. On the primacy of touch in Aristotle, see also Stanley Rosen, "Thought and Touch: A Note on Aristotle's 'De Anima,'" in *The Quarrel Between Philosophy and Poetry* (New York: Routledge, 1988), 121ff.

4. Somewhat analogously Merleau-Ponty remarks that "it is not the I who touch, it is my body;" *Phenomenology of Perception,* 316.

5. Nancy describes touch as "proximate distance;" Nancy, *The Muses,* 17.

6. See, for example, *Otherwise than Being,* where Levinas speaks of "the eye that listens to the resonance of silence" (OBBE 30), and of "the listening eye" (OBBE 37) that eventually turns into obedience.

7. The prefix *ad-*, which enters the composition of the word *attention* and its derivations, in Latin indicates the movement of a tending toward. That is, a movement toward some other is part of the etymological root of the word itself.

8. A history of the concept of attention is offered by Merleau-Ponty, *Phenomenology of Perception,* 26–51. However, Merleau-Ponty limits his analysis to a consideration of attention as a cognitive, epistemological modality.

9. Merleau-Ponty defines attention as "that 'empty' but already determinate intention;" *Phenomenology of Preception,* 28.

10. The notion of tenderness is Levinasian. In *Totality and Infinity* Levinas develops the concept of tenderness in connection to the feminine, and describes it as both the passivity of vulnerability, like the sensitivity of the skin, and the activity of responsive treatment of another. It is to such a treatment, and to the "femininity" of such a notion, that the present essay is indebted.

11. See Scott, *The Question of Ethics,* 142–47.

12. On the notion of attunement, see Heidegger's analysis in *The Fundamental Concepts of Metaphysics.*

13. Walter Benjamin, "Thesis on the Philosophy of History," in *Illuminations,* trans. H. Zohn (New York: Harcourt, Brace & World, 1968), 266.

14. Nietzsche, *Twilight of the Idols,* "Morality as Anti-Nature," 3.

15. Paul Ricoeur, *The Symbolism of Evil,* trans. E. Buchanan (Boston: Beacon Press, 1967), 348.

Chapter 13: Saddened Tenderness: Violence and Resistance

1. For a prophetic description of the inability of all ethical systems to oppose the evil of the *Shoah,* see Bonhoeffer, *Ethics,* 5.

2. See Nietzsche, *Twilight of the Idols,* "Morality as Anti-Nature" and "The Improvers of Mankind."

3. Nietzsche, *Thus Spoke Zarathustra,* 1, 22.

Chapter 14: Festive Celebrations

1. Walter Benjamin, "Reflections on the Works of Nikolai Leskov," in *Illuminations,* 97.

2. Walter Benjamin, "Theses on the Philosophy of History," in *Illuminations,* 262.

3. Gershom Scholem, *Major Trends in Jewish Mysticism* (New York: Schocken Books, 1961), 349–50.

4. Benjamin, "Theses on the Philosophy of History," 263.

5. Georg Büchner, *Lenz,* in *Gesammelte Werke* (Munich: Desch, 1963).

6. On Paul Celan, see Levinas's essay "Paul Celan: From Being to the Other," in PN 40–46.

7. Paul Celan, *Der Meridian,* in Gesammelte Werke (Frankfurt: Suhrkamp, 1983), vol. 3, 195.

8. For a description of the peculiar temporality of festivals, see Hans Georg Gadamer, *Truth and Method* (New York: Crossroad, 1982), 110–11.

9. On the notion of the festival as a way of actualization of sa-

cred time, see Mircea Eliade, *The Sacred and the Profane* (New York: Harcourt Brace & World, 1959), 69–70, 85–91, 104–5.

10. Eliade, *The Sacred and the Profane*, 88.

11. Gadamer, *Truth and Method*, 110.

12. Plato, *Laws* 828b1.

13. George Bataille, *The Accursed Share*, trans. R. Hurley (New York: Zone Books, 1993), vol. 2–3, 93. See also the account of transgression offered in George Bataille, *Eroticism*, trans. M. Dalwood (San Francisco: City Lights Books, 1986). On Bataille, see Michael Richardson, *George Bataille* (New York: Routledge, 1994), which challenges the assimilation of Bataille to postmodernism.

14. Bataille, *The Accursed Share*, 92–93.

15. Ibid., 90.

16. George Bataille, *Theory of Religion*, trans. R. Hurley (New York: Zone Books, 1992), 50–51.

17. Ibid., 54.

18. Ibid., 55.

19. In *The Gift of Death*, commenting on Jan Patocka, Derrida writes of the "heightening and recrudescence of the orgiastic" that technological civilization brings with itself; see Jacques Derrida, *The Gift of Death*, trans. D. Wills (Chicago: University of Chicago Press, 1995), 36. By breaking free of the technological relationship toward things, the ethic of things aims at a disruption also of the possibility of the orgiastic and its mysterious undifferentiation, since as Levinas writes, "the mystery of things is the source of all cruelty with regard to humans;" see Emmanuel Levinas, "Heidegger, Gagarin and We," in DL 301.

20. Bataille, *Theory of Religion*, 54.

21. Friedrich Nietzsche, *The Birth of Tragedy*, trans. W. Kaufmann (New York: Random House, 1967), 2.

22. Ibid., 2.

23. Ibid., 2.

24. Ibid., 2.

25. Bataille, *The Accursed Share,* 40.

26. Franz Rosenzweig, *The Star of Redemption,* trans. W.H. Hallo (Notre Dame: Notre Dame University Press, 1985), 358ff.

27. Ibid., 368.

28. Gadamer, *Truth and Method.*

29. The lack of conceptualization is denied by Bataille, who attributes to festivals a more limited, ambivalent role when claiming that "the festival . . . is itself integrated as a link in the concatenation of useful works;" see Bataille, *Theory of Religion,* 55.

30. Bataille, *The Accursed Share,* 90. The opposition between life's profane and sacred aspects lies at the core of much of Bataille's thinking.

31. Quoted in Louis de Thomassin, *Traité des festes de l'Eglise. Traités historique et dogmatique* (Paris 1683), vol. 2, 21.

32. See Jean-Jacques Rousseau, *Politics and Arts,* trans. A. Bloom (Ithaca: Cornell University Press, 1968), 126, where Rousseau writes: "What then will be the objects of [festivals]? What will be shown in them? Nothing, if you please. . . . Plant a stake crowned with flowers in the middle of a square; gather the people together there, and you will have a festival. Do better, yet; let the spectators become an entertainment to themselves; make them actors themselves; do it so that each sees and loves himself in the others so that all will be better united."

33. Friedrich Nietzsche, *Aufzeichnungen aus den Jahren 1875/79. Gesammelte Werke* (Munich: Musarion Ausgabe, 1922), vol. 9, 480.

34. See Emile Durkheim, *The Elementary Forms of Religious Life,* trans. K.E. Fields (New York: Free Press, 1995), 386–87.

35. Dietrich Bonhoeffer, *Letters and Papers from Prison* (New York: MacMillan, 1967), 193. It is the letter Bonhoeffer wrote on July 21, 1944.

36. On the notion of the gift, see especially Derrida's considerations at different points of his works. We cite Jacques Derrida, *Given Time: I. Counterfeit Money,* trans. P. Kamuf (Chicago: University of Chicago Press, 1992), and *The Gift of Death.*

❖ Bibliography

The following bibliography makes no claims to exhaustivity. It simply indicates essays that have been helpful in the completion of the present work.

1. Works by Levinas

La théorie de l'intuition dans la phénoménologie de Husserl. Paris: Vrin, 1963. Trans. A. Orianne, *The Theory of Intuition in Husserl's Phenomenology.* Evanston: Northwestern University Press, 1973.

De l'existence à l'existant. Paris: Fontain, 1947. Trans. A. Lingis, *Existence and Existents.* The Hague-Boston: Nijhoff, 1978.

Le Temps et l'Autre. Montpellier: Fata Morgana, 1979. Trans. R. Cohen, *Time and the Other.* Pittsburgh: Duquesne University Press, 1987.

"L'ontologie est-elle fondamentale?" *Revue de Métaphysique et de Morale* 59 (1954): 193–203. Trans. P. Atterton, "Is Ontology Fundamental?" *Philosophy Today* (1989): 121–29.

Totalité et Infini. Essai sur l'extériorité. The Hague: Nijhoff, 1961. Trans. A. Lingis, *Totality and Infinity: An Essay on Exteriority.* Pittsburgh: Duquesne University Press, 1969.

"Transcendence et hauteur." *Bulletin de la Societé Française de Philosophie* 56 (1962): 89–111. "Transcendence and Height," in *Emmanuel Levinas: Basic Philosophical Writings,* ed. A. Peperzaak, S. Critchley and R. Bernasconi, 11–31. Bloomington: Indiana University Press, 1996.

Difficile Liberté. Essais sur le judaisme. Paris: Albin Michel,

1963. Trans. S. Hand, *Difficult Freedom: Essays on Judaism.* Baltimore: Johns Hopkins University Press, 1991.

En découvrent l'existence avec Husserl et Heidegger. 2nd edition. Paris: Vrin, 1949. Trans. R. Cohen, *Discovering Existence with Husserl.* Bloomington: Indiana University Press, 1988. Trans. A. Lingis, "Philosophy and the Idea of Infinity;" "Phenomenon and Enigma;" "Language and Proximity," in *Collected Philosophical Papers,* 47–73; 109–26. The Hague-Boston: Nijhoff, 1987. Trans. A. Lingis, "The Trace of the Other," in *Deconstruction in Context: Literature and Philosophy,* ed. Mark Taylor, 345–59. Chicago: University of Chicago Press, 1986.

Quatre leçons talmudiques. Paris: Ed. de Minuit, 1968. Trans. A. Aronowicz, in *Nine Talmudic Readings.* Bloomington: Indiana University Press, 1990.

Humanisme de l'autre homme. Montpellier: Fata Morgana, 1972. Trans. A. Lingis, "Humanism and Anarchy;" "No identity," in *Collected Philosophical Papers,* 127–51. The Hague-Boston: Nijhoff, 1987.

Autrement qu'être, ou au-delà de l'essence. The Hague-Boston: Nijhoff, 1974. Trans. A. Lingis, *Otherwise Than Being or Beyond Essence.* The Hague-Boston: Nijhoff, 1981.

Noms propres. Montpellier: Fata Morgana, 1975. Trans. M. Smith, *Proper Names.* Stanford: Stanford University Press, 1996. Trans. S. Critchley, "Wholly Otherwise," in *Re-Reading Levinas,* ed. R. Bernasconi and S. Critchley, 3–10. Bloomington: Indiana University Press, 1991.

Sur Maurice Blanchot. Montpellier: Fata Morgana, 1975. Trans. M. Smith, *Proper Names,* 127–70. Stanford: Stanford University Press, 1996.

Du sacré au saint. Cinq nouvelles talmudiques. Paris: Ed. de Minuit, 1977. Trans. A. Aronowicz, in *Nine Talmudic Readings.* Bloomington: Indiana University Press, 1990.

L'au-delà du verset. Lectures et discours talmudique. Paris: Ed. de Minuit, 1982. Trans. G. Mole, *Beyond the Verse.* Bloomington: Indiana University Press, 1994.

De Dieu qui vient à l'idée. Paris: Vrin, 1982. Trans. B. Bergo, *Of*

God Who Comes To Mind. Stanford: Stanford University Press, 1998.

De l'evasion. Montpellier: Fata Morgana, 1982.

Ethique et Infini. Paris: Fayard, 1982. Trans. R. Cohen, *Ethics and Infinity*. Pittsburgh: Duquesne University Press, 1985.

Transcendance et Intelligibilité. Geneva: Labor et Fides, 1984, in *Emmanuel Levinas: Basic Philosophical Writings,* ed. A. Peperzaak, S. Critchley, and R. Bernasconi, 149–60. Bloomington: Indiana University Press, 1996.

Hors sujet. Montpellier: Fata Morgana, 1987. Trans. M. Smith, *Outside the Subject*. Stanford: Stanford University Press, 1994.

A l'heure des nations. Paris: Ed. de Minuit, 1988. Trans. M. Smith, *In the Time of Nations*. Bloomington: Indiana University Press, 1994.

Entre Nous: Essais sur le penser-à-l'autre. Paris: Grasset, 1991. Trans. M. Smith and B. Harshav, *Entre Nous: On Thinking-of-the-Other*. New York: Colmbia University Press, 1998.

La mort et le temps. Paris: Editions de l'Herne, 1991.

Dieu, la mort et le temp. Paris: Grasset, 1993.

Altérité et Transcendence. Paris: Fata Morgana, 1995. Trans. M. Smith, *Alterity and Transcendence*. New York: Columbia University Press, 1999.

2. Works by Heidegger.

Gesamtausgabe. Frankfurt: Klostermann, 1975–.

GA 2 *Sein und Zeit,* ed. F. von Herrmann (1977). Trans. J. Macquerrie and E. Robinson, *Being and Time*. New York: Harper & Row, 1962.

GA 4 *Erläuterungen zu Hölderlin Dichtung,* ed. F. von Herrmann (1982). Trans. D. Scott, "Remembrance of the Poet;" "Hölderlin and the Essence of Poetry," in *Existence and Being,* ed. Werner Brock, 243–91. Chicago: Henry Regnery Co., 1949.

GA 5 Holzwege, ed. F. von Herrmann (1977). Trans. A. Hofstadter, "The Origin of the Work of Art;" "What Are Poets For?," in *Poetry, Language, Thought.* New York: Harper & Row, 1971. Trans. W. Lovitt, "The Age of the World Picture," in *The Question Concerning Technology.* New York: Harper & Row, 1977.

GA 7 Vorträge und Aufsätze. Trans. W. Lovitt, "The Question Concerning Technology," in *The Question Concerning Technology.* New York: Harper & Row, 1977. Trans. J. Stambaugh, "Overcoming Metaphysics," in *The End of Philosophy.* New York: Harper & Row, 1973. Trans. A. Hofstadter, "Building, Dwelling, Thinking;" "The Thing;" ". . . Poetically Man Dwells . . .," in *Poetry, Language, Thought.* New York: Harper & Row, 1971.

GA 9 Wegmarken, ed. F. von Herrmann (1976). Trans. J. Sallis, "On the Essence of Truth;" trans. F. Capuzzi, "Letter on Humanism," in *Basic Writings,* 113–41; 189–242. New York: Harper & Row, 1977. Trans. T. Sheehan, "On the Being and Conception of *Physis* in Aristotle's *Physics* B, 1." *Man and World* 3 (1976): 219–70.

GA 12 Unterwegs zur Sprache, ed. F. von Herrmann (1985). Trans. A. Hofstadter, "Language," in *Poetry, Language, Thought.* New York: Harper & Row, 1971. Trans. P. Hertz, *On the Way to Language.* New York: Harper Row, 1971.

GA 13 Aus der Erfahrung des Denkens, ed. H. Heidegger (1983). Trans. T. Sheehan, "Why Do We Remain in the Province?" *Listening* 12 (1977): 122–25.

GA 19 Platon: Sophistes, ed. I. Schüßler (1992). Trans. R. Rojcewicz and A. Schuwer, *Plato's Sophist.* Bloomington: Indiana University Press, 1997.

GA 20 Prolegomena zur Geschichte des Zeitbegriffs, ed. P. Jaeger (1979). Trans. T. Kisiel. *History of the Concept of Time: Prolegomena.* Bloomington: Indiana University Press, 1985.

GA 24 Die Grundprobleme der Phänomenologie, ed. F. von Herrmann (1975). Trans. A. Hofstadter, *The Basic Problems of Phenomenology*. Bloomington: Indiana University Press, 1988.

GA 29/30 Die Grundbegriffe der Metaphysik. Welt-Endlichkeit-Einsamkeit, ed F. von Hermann (1983). Trans W. McNeill and N. Walker, *The Fundamental Concepts of Metaphysics: World, Finitude, Solitude*. Bloomington: Indiana University Press, 1995.

GA 40 Einführung in die Metaphysik, ed. P. Jaeger (1983). Trans. R. Manheim, *An Introduction to Metaphysics*. New Haven: Yale University Press, 1959.

GA 41 Die Frage nach dem Ding: Zu Kants Lehre von den transzendentalen Grundsätzen, ed. P. Jaeger (1984). *What is a Thing?* Chicago: Regnery, 1970.

"Die Herkunft der Kunst und die Bestimmung des Denkens," in *Distanz und Nähe, Reflexionen und Analysen zur Kunst der Gegenwart*, ed. P. Jaeger and R. Luke. Königshausen and Neumann, 1983. Trans. J. Chrétien and M. Reifenrath, "La provenance de l'art et la destination de la pensée," in *Cahier de l'Herne: Heidegger*, ed. Michel Haar, 365–80. Paris: Ed. de l'Herne, 1983.

Die Selbstbehauptung der deutschen Universität, ed. H. Heidegger. Frankfurt: Klostermann, 1983. Trans. K. Harries, "The Self-assertion of the German University." *Review of Metaphysics* 38 (1985): 467–80.

Gelassenheit. Pfullingen: Neske, 1960. Trans. J. Anderson and E. Freund, *Discourse on Thinking*. New York: Harper & Row, 1966.

3. Other Works

Adorno, Theodor W. *Negative Dialectic*. Trans. E. B. Ashton. New York: Seabury Press, 1973.

Adorno, Theodor W. and Horkheimer, Max. *Dialectic of Enlightenment*. Trans. John Cumming. New York: Seabury Press, 1972.

Allemann, Beda. *Hölderlin und Heidegger*. Freiburg: Atlantis, 1954.

Alvarez, Gaviria O. "L'idée de crèation chez Levinas: une archéologie du sens." *Revue Philosophique de Louvain* 72 (1974): 509–38.

Anderson, Travis. "Through Phenomenology to Sublime Poetry: Martin Heidegger on the Decisive Relation Between Truth and Art." *Research in Phenomenology* 26 (1996): 198–229.

Aristotle. *De Anima,* in *The Complete Works of Aristotle,* ed. Jonathan Barnes. Princeton: Princeton University Press, 1984.

Atterton, Peter. "Levinas's Skeptical Critique of Metaphysics and *Anti*-humanism." *Philosophy Today* 41 (1997): 491–506.

Bailhache, G. *Le sujet chez Levinas: fragilité et subjectivité*. Paris: PUF, 1994.

Bataille, George. *Eroticism*. Trans. M. Dalwood. San Francisco: City Lights Books, 1986.

———. *Theory of Religion*. Trans. R. Hurley. New York: Zone Books, 1992.

———. *The Accursed Share*. Trans. R. Hurley. New York: Zone Books, 1993.

Beaufret, Jean. "En chemin avec Heidegger," in *Cahier de l'Herne: Heidegger,* ed. Michel Haar, 220–27. Paris: Ed. de l'Herne, 1983.

Beauvoir, Simone de. *The Second Sex*. Trans. H. M. Parshley. New York: Vintage, 1974.

Beavers, Anthony. *Levinas Beyond the Horizons of Cartesianism*. New York: Peter Lang, 1995.

Benjamin, Walter. *Illuminations*. Trans. H. Zohn. New York: Schocken Books, 1986.

Bernasconi, Robert. "Levinas Face to Face—with Hegel." *Journal of the British Society for Phenomenology* 13 (1982): 267–76.

———. "Levinas and Derrida: The Question of the Closure of Metaphysics," in *Face to Face with Levinas,* ed. Richard Cohen, 181–203. Albany: SUNY Press, 1986.

———. "Levinas and Hegel: The Possibility of Forgiveness and Reconciliation." *Archivio di Filosofia* 54 (1986): 325–46.

———. "Deconstruction and the Possibility of Ethics," in *Deconstruction and Philosophy,* ed. J. Sallis, 122–39. Chicago: University of Chicago Press, 1987.

———. "'Failure of Communication' as a Surplus: Dialogue and Lack of Dialogue Between Buber and Levinas," in *The Provocation of Levinas,* ed. R. Bernasconi and D. Wood, 100–135. New York: Routledge, 1988.

———. "The Silent Anarchic World of the Evil Genius," in *The Collegium Phenomenologicum: The First Ten Years,* ed. G. Moneta et al., 257–72. Dordrecht-Boston: Kluwer, 1988.

———. "Rereading Totality and Infinity," in *The Question of the Other,* ed. A. Dallery and C. Scott, 23–34. Albany: SUNY Press, 1989.

———. "Heidegger's Destruction of *Phronesis.*" Southern Journal of Philosophy (supp.) 28 (1989): 127–47.

———. "The Ethic of Suspicion." *Research in Phenomenology* 20 (1990): 3–18.

Bernasconi, Robert, and Wood, David, ed. *The Provocation of Levinas. Rethinking the Other.* New York: Routledge, 1988.

Bernasconi, Robert, and Critchley, Simon, ed. *Re-Reading Levinas.* Bloomington: Indiana University Press, 1991.

Biemel, Walter. *Le concept du monde chez Heidegger.* Louvain: Nauwelaerts, 1950.

———. "Elucidations of Heidegger's Lecture 'The Origin of Art and the Destination of Thinking'," in *Reading Heidegger,* ed. John Sallis, 370–82. Bloomington: Indiana University Press, 1993.

———, ed. *Phénoménologie et métaphysique.* Paris: PUF, 1984.

Blanchot, Maurice. "Our Clandestine Companion," in *Face to Face with Levinas,* ed. Richard Cohen, 41–50. Albany: SUNY Press, 1986.

———. *The Writing of the Disaster*. Lincoln: University of Nebraska Press, 1986.

———. *The Infinite Conversation*. Trans. S. Hanson. Minneapolis: University of Minnesota Press, 1993.

Bloechl, Jeffrey. "How Best to Keep a Secret? On Love and Respect in Levinas' 'Phenomenology of Eros'." *Man and World* 29 (1996): 1–17.

Blumenberg, Hans. *Das Lachern der Thrakerin. Eine Urgeschichte der Theorie*. Frankfurt: Suhrkamp, 1987.

Boer, Theodore De. "Judaism and Hellenism in the Philosophy of Levinas and Heidegger." *Archivio di Filosofia* 53 (1985): 197–215.

———. "An Ethical Transcendental Philosophy," in *Face to Face with Levinas,* ed. Richard Cohen, 83–115. Albany: SUNY Press, 1986.

Bonhoeffer, Dietrich. *Ethics*. Trans. N. H. Smith. New York: MacMillan, 1964.

———. *Letters and Papers from Prison*. New York: MacMillan, 1967.

Bouckaert, Luk. "Ontology and Ethics: Reflections on Levinas' Critique of Heidegger." *International Philosophical Quarterly* 10 (1970): 402–19.

Brody, D. H. "Emmanuel Levinas: The Logic of Ethical Ambiguity in *Otherwise than Being or Beyond Essence*." *Research in Phenomenology* 25 (1995): 177–203.

Bruin, John. "Heidegger and Two Kinds of Art." *Journal of Aesthetics and Art Criticism* 52 (1994): 447–457.

Büchner, Georg. *Lenz,* in *Gesammelte Werke*. Munich: Desch, 1963.

Casey, Edward. "Levinas on Memory and the Trace," in *The Collegium Phenomenologicum: The First Ten Years,* ed. G. Moneta et al., 241–55. Dordrecht-Boston: Kluwer, 1988.

———. *Getting Back Into Place: Toward a Renewed Understanding of the Place-World.* Bloomington: Indiana University Press, 1993.

Celan, Paul. *Gesammelte Werke,* ed. B. Allemann and S. Reichert. Frankfurt: Suhrkamp, 1983.

Chalier, Catherine. *Figures du féminin: Lecture d'Emmanuel Levinas.* Paris: La Nuit surveillée, 1982.

———. *Levinas: L'Utopie de l'humain.* Paris: Albin Michel, 1993.

———. "Ethics and the Feminine," in *Re-Reading Levinas,* ed. R. Bernasconi and S. Critchley, 119–29. Bloomington: Indiana University Press, 1991.

———. "Singularité juive et philosophie," in *Emmanuel Levinas,* ed. J. Greisch and J. Rolland, 78–98. Paris: Cerf, 1993.

———. "The Philosophy of Emmanuel Levinas and the Hebraic Tradition," in *Ethics as First Philosophy,* ed. A. Peperzak, 3–12. New York: Routledge, 1995.

Chalier, Catherine, and Abensour, Miguel, ed. *Cahier de l'Herne: Levinas.* Paris: Ed. de l'Herne, 1991.

Chanter, Tina. "Feminism and the Other," in *The Provocation of Levinas,* ed. R. Bernasconi and D. Wood, 32–56. New York: Routledge, 1988.

———. "Antigone's Dilemma," in *Re-Reading Levinas,* ed. R. Bernasconi and S. Critchley, 130–35. Bloomington: Indiana University Press, 1991.

———. *The Ethics of Eros: Irigaray's Rewriting of the Philosophers.* New York: Routledge, 1995.

Chapman, Helen. "Levinas and the Concept of the Feminine." *Warwick Journal of Philosophy* 1 (1988): 65–83.

Chrétien, Jean-Louis. "La réserve de l'être," in *Cahier de l'Herne: Heidegger,* ed. Michel Haar, 233–59. Paris: Ed. de l'Herne, 1983.

Ciaramelli, Fabio. *Transcendence et éthique: Essai sur Levinas.* Brussels: Ousia, 1989.

———. "Levinas' Ethical Discourse Between Individualism and Universality," in *Re-Reading Levinas,* ed. R. Bernasconi and S. Critchley, 83–105. Bloomington: Indiana University Press, 1991.

———. "Levinas e la fenomenologia del desiderio," in *Levinas: Filosofia e trascendenza,* ed. A. Moscato, 143–67. Genoa: Marietti, 1992.

Cohen, Richard, ed. *Face to Face with Levinas.* Albany: SUNY Press, 1986.

———. "Absolute Positivity and Ultrapositivity: Husserl and Levinas," in *The Question of the Other,* ed. A. Dallery and C. Scott, 35–43. Albany: SUNY Press, 1989.

———. "The Family and Ethics: The Metaphysics of Eros in Emmanuel Levinas's *Totality and Infinity.*" *Contemporary Philosophy* 15, 4 (1993): 1–7.

Comolli, Giampiero. "Il volto delle cose. Intorno alla questione dell'arte in E. Levinas." *Aut-Aut* 209–210 (1985): 219–36.

Courtine, Jean-François. "Phenomenology and/or Tautology," in *Reading Heidegger,* ed. John Sallis, 241–57. Bloomington: Indiana University Press, 1993.

Couturier, Fernand. *Monde et être chez Heidegger.* Montreal: Presses de l'Université de Montréal, 1971.

Critchley, Simon. *The Ethics of Deconstruction: Derrida and Levinas.* Oxford: Blackwell, 1992.

———. "*Il y a*—A Dying Stronger than Death (Blanchot with Levinas)." *Oxford Literary Review* 15 (1993): 81–131.

Dallery, Arlee B., and Scott, Charles, ed. *Ethics and Danger: Essays on Heidegger and Continental Thought.* Albany: SUNY Press, 1992.

Davies, Paul. "Difficult Freedom." *Research in Phenomenology* 18 (1988): 149–72.

———. "A Fine Risk: Reading Blanchot Reading Levinas," in *Re-Reading Levinas,* ed. R. Bernasconi and S. Critchley, 200–226. Bloomington: Indiana University Press, 1991.

Derrida, Jacques. *Positions.* Trans. Alan Bass. Chicago: University of Chicago Press, 1971.

———. *Speech and Phenomena, and Other Essays on Husserl's Theory of Signs*. Trans. David Allison. Evanston: Northwestern University Press, 1973.

———. *Of Grammatology*. Trans. Gayatri C. Spivak. Baltimore: Johns Hopkins University Press, 1976.

———. "Violence and Metaphysics: An Essay on the Thought of Emmanuel Levinas," in *Writing and Difference*. Trans. Alan Bass, 79–153. Chicago: University of Chicago Press, 1978.

———. *Margins of Philosophy*. Trans. Alan Bass. Chicago: University of Chicago Press, 1982.

———. "At This Very Moment in This Work Here I Am," in *Re-Reading Levinas,* ed. R. Bernasconi and S. Critchley, 11–48. Bloomington: Indiana University Press, 1991.

———. *Given Time: I. Counterfeit Money*. Trans. P. Kamuf. Chicago: University of Chicago Press, 1992.

———. "*Le toucher*: Touch/To Touch Him." *Paragraph* 16, 2 (1993).

———. *The Gift of Death*. Trans. D. Willis. Chicago: University of Chicago Press, 1995.

Descartes, René. *Philosophical Writings*. Trans. E. Anscombe and P. T. Geach. New York: MacMillan, 1971.

DeVries, Hent. "Adieu, à-dieu, a-Dieu," in *Ethics as First Philosophy,* ed. A. Peperzak, 211–30. New York: Routledge, 1995.

Drabinski, John. "The Status of the Transcendental in Levinas' Thought." *Philosophy Today* (1994): 149–58.

Dreyfus, Hubert. "Between *Techne* and Technology. The Ambiguous Place of Equipment in 'Being and Time'," in *The Thought of Martin Heidegger,* ed. M. Zimmerman. Tulane Studies in Philosophy, 32 (1984): 23–35.

———. *Being-in-the-World: A Commentary on Heidegger's Being and Time, Division 1*. Cambridge: MIT Press, 1991.

———. "Heidegger and the Connection Between Nihilism, Art, Technology, and Politics," in *The Cambridge Companion to Heidegger,* ed. C. Guignon, 289–316. Cambridge: Cambridge University Press, 1993.

Durkheim, Emile. *The Elementary Forms of Religious Life.* Trans. K. E. Field. New York: Free Press, 1995.

Eliade, Mircea. *The Sacred and the Profane.* New York: Harcourt Brace & World, 1959.

Fabris, Adriano. "Esperienza e etica," in *Levinas: Filosofia e trascendenza,* ed. A. Moscato, 199–230. Genoa: Marietti, 1992.

Farley, Wendy. "Emmanuel Levinas: Ethics as Damnation or Desire," in *Transitions in Continental Philosophy,* ed. A. Dallery, S. Watson, and E. M. Bower, 273–81. Albany: SUNY Press, 1994.

———. *Eros for the Other.* University Park: Pennsylvania State University Press, 1996.

Farrell-Krell, David. "Daimon Life, Nearness and Abyss: An Introduction to Za-ology." *Research in Phenomenology* 17 (1987): 23–53.

Farwell, Paul. "Can Heidegger's Craftsman Be Authentic?" *International Philosophical Quarterly* 31 (1989): 77–90.

Feron, E. *De l'idée de transcendence à la question du language. L'itinéraire philosophique de Levinas.* Grenoble: Millon, 1992.

Ferry, Luc and Renaut, Alain. *French Philosophy of the Sixties: An Essay in Antihumanism.* Trans. M. Schnackenberg. Amherst: University of Massachussetts Press, 1990.

———. "'Ce que a bisoin d'être démontré ne vaut pas grand-chose'," in *Pourqoui nous ne sommes pas nietzschéens,* ed. A Boyer et al. Paris: Grasset, 1991.

Finkielkraut, Alain. *La Sagesse de l'amour.* Paris: Gallimard, 1984.

Floyd, Wayne. "To Welcome the Other: Totality and Theory in Levinas and Adorno," *Philosophy and Theology IV* 2 (1989): 145–70.

Foltz, Bruce. *Inhabiting the Earth: Heidegger, Environmental*

Ethics, and the Metaphysics of Nature. Atlantic Highlands: Humanities Press, 1995.

Forthomme, Bernard. *Une philosophie de la transcendence. La Métaphysique d'Emmanuel Levinas.* Grenoble: Jérome Millon, 1992.

Fòti, Véronique M. *Heidegger and the Poets: Poiesis/Sophia/Techne.* New Jersey: Humanities Press, 1992.

Foucault, Michel. *Madness and Civilization. A History of Insanity in the Age of Reason.* Trans. Richard Howard. New York: Pantheon Books, 1965.

Froment-Meurice, Marc. "L'art moderne et la tecnique," in *Cahier de l'Herne: Heidegger,* ed. Michel Haar, 305–29. Paris: Ed. de l'Herne, 1983.

Gadamer, Hans Georg. *Truth and Method.* New York: Crossroad, 1982.

Gans, Steven. "Ethics or Ontology." *Philosophy Today* 16 (1972): 117–121.

Gethmann, Friedrich. "Heideggers Konzeption des Handelns in 'Sein und Zeit,'" in *Heidegger und die praktische Philosophie,* ed. A. Gethmann-Siefert and O. Pöggeler, 140–76. Frankfurt: Suhrkamp, 1988.

Gibbs, Robert. "Height and Nearness: Jewish Dimension of Radical Ethics," in *Ethics as First Philosophy,* ed. A. Peperzak, 13–24. New York: Routledge, 1995.

Gilligan, Carol, *In a Different Voice.* Cambridge: Harvard University Press, 1982.

Girard, René. *Violence and the Sacred.* Trans. P. Gregory. Baltimore: Johns Hopkins University Press, 1977.

Greisch, Jean. "Ethique et ontologie," in *Emmanuel Levinas,* ed. J. Greisch and J. Rolland, 15–45. Paris: Cerf, 1993.

Greef, Jan De. "Le concept du pouvoir éthique chez Levinas." *Revue philosophique de Louvain* 68 (1970): 507–20.

———. "Skepticism and Reason," in *Face to Face with Levinas,* ed. Richard Cohen, 159–80. Albany: SUNY Press, 1986.

Haar, Michel. "La biographie réleguée," in *Cahier de l'Herne:*

Heidegger, ed. Michel Haar, 21–29. Paris: Ed. de l'Herne, 1983.

———, ed. *Cahier de l'Herne: Heidegger*. Paris: Ed. de l'Herne, 1983.

———. *The Song of the Earth: Heidegger and the Grounds of the History of Being*. Trans. R. Lilly. Bloomington: Indiana University Press, 1993.

Hand, Seán, ed. *Facing the Other: The Ethics of Emmanuel Levinas*. Richmond: Curzon Press, 1996.

Hedge, Joanna. *Heidegger and Ethics*. New York: Routledge, 1995.

Hegel, G. W. F. *Phenomenology of Spirit*. Trans. A. V. Miller. New York: Oxford University Press, 1977.

Irigaray, Luce. "The Fecundity of the Caress," in *Face to Face with Levinas*, ed. Richard Cohen, 231–55. Albany: SUNY Press, 1986.

———. "Questions to Emmanuel Levinas: On the Divinity of Love," in *Re-Reading Levinas*, ed. R. Bernasconi and S. Critchley, 109–18. Bloomington: Indiana University Press, 1991.

Johnson, Galen, and Michael Smith, ed. *Ontology and Alterity in Merleau-Ponty*. Evanston: Northwestern University Press, 1990.

Joy, Morny. "Levinas, Alterity, the Feminine and Women—A Meditation." *Studies in Religion* 22 (1994): 463–85.

Kant, Immanuel. *Critique of Practical Reason*. Trans. Lewis White Beck. Indianapolis: Bobbs-Merrill, 1956.

Kearney, Richard. *Dialogues with Contemporary Continental Thinkers*. Manchester, UK: Manchester University Press, 1984.

Kockelmans, Joseph. *On the Truth of Being*. Bloomington: Indiana University Press, 1984.

———. *Heidegger on Art and Art Works*. The Hague: Nijhoff, 1985.

Kovac, Edvard. "L'intrigue éthique," in *Emmanuel Levinas,* ed. J. Greisch and J. Rolland. 177–92. Paris: Cerf, 1993.

Lacoue-Labarthe, Philippe. *Heidegger, Art and Politics.* Trans. Chris Turner. Cambridge: Blackwell, 1990.

Lannoy, Jean-Luc. "'Il y a' et phénoménologie dans le pensée du jeune Levinas." *Revue Philosophique de Louvain* 88 (1990): 369–94.

Large, William. "On the Meaning of the Word 'Other' in Levinas." *Journal of the British Society for Phenomenology* 37 (1996): 36–52.

Laroulle, François. "Au delà du pouvoir: Le concept transcendental de la diaspora," in *Textes pour Emmanuel Levinas,* ed. F. Laruelle, 111–25. Paris: Ed. Jean-Michel Place, 1980.

Lawton, Philip N. "Levinas' Notion of the 'There is.'" *Philosophy Today* 20 (1976): 67–76.

Levinas, Emmanuel, and Kearney, Richard. " Dialogue with Emmanuel Levinas," in *Face to Face with Levinas,* ed. Richard Cohen, 13–33. Albany: SUNY Press, 1986.

Lingis, Alphonso. "The Sensuality and the Sensitivity," in *Face to Face with Levinas,* ed. Richard Cohen, 219–30. Albany: SUNY Press, 1986.

———. "The Elemental Imperative." *Research in Phenomenology* 18 (1988): 3–21.

———. *The Imperative.* Bloomington: Indiana University Press, 1998.

Llewelyn, John. "Jewgreek or Greekjew," in *The Collegium Phenomenologicum: The First Ten Years,* ed. G. Moneta et al., 273–87. Dordrecht-Boston: Kluwer, 1988.

———. "Am I Obsessed by Bobby? (Humanism of the Other Animal)," in *Re-Reading Levinas,* ed. R. Bernasconi and S. Critchley, 234–45. Bloomington: Indiana University Press, 1991.

———. *The Middle Voice of Ecological Conscience: A Chiasmic Reading of Responsibility in the Neighbourhood of Levinas, Heidegger and Others.* London: MacMillan, 1991.

———. *Emmanuel Levinas: The Genealogy of Ethics.* London: Routledge, 1995.

Löwith, Karl. "Zu Heideggers Seinsfrage: Die Natur des Menschen und die Welt der Natur," in *Aufsätze und Vorträge, 1930–1970.* Stuttgart: Kohlhammer, 1971.

Lyotard, Jean-François. "Levinas' Logic," in *Face to Face with Levinas,* ed. Richard Cohen, 117–58. Albany: SUNY Press, 1986.

———. *Heidegger and "the jews."* Trans. A. Michel and M. S. Roberts. Minneapolis: University of Minnesota Press, 1980.

Maloney, Philip. "Levinas, Substitution, and Transcendental Subjectivity." *Man and World* 30 (1997): 49–64.

Marcuse, Ernst. *One-Dimensional Man: Studies in the Ideology of Advanced Industrial Society.* Boston: Beacon Press, 1964.

Marquez, César Moreno. "The Curvature of Intersubjective Space: Sociality and Responsibility in the Thought of Emmanuel Levinas." *Analecta Husserliana* 22 (1987): 343–352.

Marx, Werner. "The World in Another Beginning: Poetic Dwelling and the Role of the Poet," in *On Heidegger and Language,* Joseph Kockelmans ed., 235–59. Evanston: Northwestern University Press, 1972.

———. *Is There a Measure on Earth?,* trans. T. J. Neman and R. Lilly. Chicago: University of Chicago Press, 1987.

McWhorter, Ladelle, ed. *Heidegger and the Earth.* Kirksville: Thomas Jefferson University Press, 1992.

Merleau-Ponty, Maurice. *Phenomenology of Perception.* Trans. C. Smith. London: Routledge, 1962.

———. *The Visible and the Invisible.* Trans. A. Lingis. Evanston: Northwestern Univeristy Press, 1968.

Milchman, A., and Rosenberg, A., eds. *Martin Heidegger and the Holocaust.* Atlantic Highlands: Humanities Press, 1996.

Nancy, Jean-Luc. *Une pensée finie.* Paris: Galilée, 1990.

———. "Laughter, Presence," in *The Birth to Presence*. Trans. B. Holmes et al., 368–92. Stanford: Stanford University Press, 1993.

———. *The Muses*. Stanford: Stanford University Press, 1996.

Neher, André. *L'exil de la parole. Du silence biblique au silence d'Auschwitz*. Paris: Ed. du Seuil, 1970.

Nicholson, Graeme. "The Ontological Difference." *American Philosophical Quarterly* 33 (1996): 357–74.

Nietzsche, Friedrich. *The Antichrist*, in *The Portable Nietzsche*. Trans. W. Kaufmann. New York: Random House, 1954.

———. *The Birth of Tragedy*. Trans. W. Kaufmann. New York: Random House, 1967.

———. *The Gay Science*. Trans. W. Kaufmann. New York: Random House, 1974.

———. *On the Geneology of Morals*. Trans. W. Kaufmann. New York: Random House, 1967.

———. *Twilight of the Idols*, in *The Portable Nietzsche*. Trans. W. Kaufmann. New York: Random House, 1954.

Okrent, Mark. *Heidegger's Pragmatism: Understanding, Being, and the Critique of Metaphysics*. Ithaca: Cornell University Press, 1988.

Oliver, Kelly. *Family Values: Subjects Between Nature and Culture*. New York: Routledge, 1997.

Ouaknin, Marc-Alain. *Méditations érotiques: Essai sur Emmanuel Levinas*. Paris: Balland, 1992.

Peperzak, Adriaan. "Phenomenology, Ontology, Metaphysics: Levinas' Perspective on Husserl and Heidegger." *Man and World* 16 (1983): 113–27.

———. "Some Remarks on Hegel, Kant and Levinas," in *Face to Face with Levinas*, ed. Richard Cohen, 205–17. Albany: SUNY Press, 1986.

———. "From Intentionality to Responsibility," in *The Question of the Other*, ed. A. Dallery and C. Scott, 3–21. Albany: SUNY Press, 1989.

———. *To the Other: An Introduction to the Philosophy of Emmanuel Levinas.* West Lafayette: Purdue University Press, 1993.

———, ed. *Ethics as First Philosophy: The Significance of Emmanuel Levinas for Philosophy, Literature and Religion.* New York: Routledge, 1995.

———. *Beyond: The Philosophy of Emmanuel Levinas.* Evanston: Northwestern University Press, 1997.

Perone, Ugo. *Modernità e memoria.* Turin: SEI, 1986.

Petrosino, Silvano. "L'idée de crèation dans l'oeuvre de Levinas," in *La différence comme non-indifférence,* ed. A. Münster, 97–108. Paris: Kimé, 1995.

Petrosino, Silvano, and Rolland, Jacques. *La vérité nomade. Introduction à Emmanuel Levinas.* Paris: La Découverte, 1984.

Poirié, Fançois. *Emmanuel Levinas: Qui êtes-vous?* Lyon: La Manufacture, 1987.

Pöggeler, Otto. *Der Denkweg Martin Heideggers.* Pfullingen: Neske, 1963.

Prauss, Gerald. *Erkennen und Handeln in Heideggers "Sein un Zeit."* Freiburg-Munich: Alber, 1977.

———. "Heidegger und die praktische Philosophie," in *Heidegger und die praktische Philosophie,* ed. A. Gethmann-Siefert and O. Pöggeler, 177–90. Frankfurt: Suhrkamp, 1988.

Protevi, John. "Repeating the Parricide: Levinas and the Question of Closure." *Journal of the British Society for Phenomenology* 23 (1992): 21–32.

Raffoul, François. "Heidegger and Kant: The Question of Idealism." *Philosophy Today* 40 (1996): 531–47.

———. "Responsabilité et Altérité chez Heidegger et Levinas." *Symposium* 1 (1997): 49–64.

Reed, Charles W. "Levinas' Question," in *Face to Face with Levinas,* ed. Richard Cohen, 73–82. Albany: SUNY Press, 1986.

Richardson, William. *Heidegger: Through Phenomenology to Thought.* The Hague: Nijhoff, 1963.

Ricoeur, Paul. *The Symbolism of Evil.* Trans. E. Buchanan. Boston: Beacon Press, 1967.

Robbins, Jill. "Aesthetic Totality and Ethical Infinity: Levinas on Art." *L'Esprit Créateur* 35 (1995): 66–79.

Rolland, Jacques. "L'ambiguité comme façon de l'autrement," in *Emmanuel Levinas,* ed. J. Greisch and J. Rolland, 428–31. Paris: Cerf, 1993.

———. "'Divine Comedie': La question de Dieu chez Levinas," in *La différence comme non-indifférence,* ed. A. Münster, 109–27. Paris: Kimé, 1995.

Rosen, Stanley. "Thought and Touch: A Note on Aristotle's 'De Anima'," in *The Quarrel Between Philosophy and Poetry,* 119–26. New York: Routledge, 1988.

Rosenzweig, Franz. *The Star of Redemption.* Trans. W. H. Hallo, Notre Dame: Notre Dame University Press, 1985.

Rousseau, Jean-Jacques. *Politics and Arts.* Trans. A. Bloom. Ithaca: Cornell University Press, 1968.

Sallis, John. *Echoes. After Heidegger.* Bloomington: Indiana University Press, 1990.

———. "Deformatives: Essentially Other Than Truth," in *Reading Heidegger,* ed. John Sallis, 29–46. Bloomington: Indiana University Press, 1993.

———, ed. *Reading Heidegger.* Bloomington: Indiana University Press, 1993.

———. *Delimitations: Phenomenology and the End of Metaphysics.* Bloomington: Indiana University Press, 1994.

Scherer, Réné. "Le dernier des philosophes," in *Heidegger ou l'experience de la pensée,* ed. R. Scherer and A. L. Kelkel. Paris: Ed. Seghers, 1973.

Scholem, Gershom. *Major Trends in Jewish Mysticism.* New York: Schocken Books, 1961.

Schrift, Alan. *Nietzsche's French Legacy: A Genealogy of Poststructuralism.* New York: Routledge, 1995.

Schroeder, Brian. *Altared Ground.* New York: Routledge, 1996.

———. "The (Non)Logic of Desire and War: Hegel and Levinas," in *Continental Philosophy VII,* ed. H. Silverman. New York: Routledge, forthcoming.

Schürmann, Reiner. *Heidegger on Being and Acting: From Principles to Anarchy.* Bloomington: Indiana University Press, 1987.

Schuwer, André. "Nature and the Holy: On Heidegger's Interpretation of Hölderlin's Hymn 'Wie wenn am Feiertage . . . .'" *Research in Phenomenology* 7 (1977): 225–37.

Scott, Charles. *The Question of Ethics: Nietzsche, Foucault, Heidegger.* Bloomington: Indiana University Press, 1990.

Serres, Michel. *Le contrat naturel.* Paris: Ed. Bourin, 1990.

Sheehan, Thomas, ed. *Heidegger: The Man and The Thinker.* Chicago: Precedent Publishing, 1981.

Signorini, Alberto. "L'idea di creazione *ex nihilo* e la libertà nel pensiero di E. Levinas." *Giornale di metafisica* 11 (1989): 241–71.

Smith, Steven G. "Reason as One for Another: Moral and Theoretical Argument," in *Face to Face with Levinas,* ed. Richard Cohen, 53–72. Albany: SUNY Press, 1986.

Stambaugh, Joan. *The Finitude of Being.* Albany: SUNY Press, 1992.

Surber, Jere Paul. "Kant, Levinas, and the Thought of the 'Other'." *Philosophy Today* 38 (1994): 294–316.

Taminiaux, Jacques. "L'essence vraie de la technique," in *Cahier de l'Herne: Heidegger,* ed. Michel Haar, 263–84. Paris: Ed. de l'Herne, 1983.

———. "*Poiesis* and *Praxis* in Fundamental Ontology." *Research in Phenomenology* 17 (1987): 137–69.

———. *Heidegger and the Project of Fundamental Ontology,* trans. M. Gendre. Albany: SUNY, 1991.

———. "The Origin of 'The Origin of the Work of Art'," in *Reading Heidegger,* ed. John Sallis, 392–404. Bloomington: Indiana University Press, 1993.

Taylor, Mark. *Altarity*. Chicago: University of Chicago Press, 1987.

Thiele, Leslie P. *Timely Meditations: Martin Heidegger and Postmodern Politics*. Princeton: Princeton University Press, 1995.

Valevicius, Andrius. *From the Other to the Totally Other: The Religious Philosophy of Emmanuel Levinas*. New York: Lang, 1988.

Vasey, Craig R. "Faceless Women and Serious Others: Levinas, Misogyny and Feminism," in *Ethics and Danger*, ed. A. B. Dallery and C. Scott, 317–30. Albany: SUNY Press, 1992.

Villela-Petit, Maria. "Heidegger's Conception of Space," in *Critical Heidegger*, ed. C. Macann, 134–57. London: Routledge, 1996.

Volpi, Franco. "Dasein comme *praxis*," in *Heidegger et l'idée de la phénoménologie*, 1–41. Dordrecht: Kluwer, 1988.

———, ed. *Heidegger et l'idée de la phénoménologie*. Dordrecht: Kluwer, 1988.

Vycinas, Vincent. *Earth and Gods*. The Hague: Nijhoff, 1961.

Ward, James. *Heidegger's Political Thinking*. Amherst: University of Massachussetts Press, 1995.

Weber, E. *Verfolgung und Trauma: zu Emmanuel Levinas' "Autrement qu'être ou au-delà de l'essence."* Wien: Passagen Verlag, 1990.

Westphal, Merold. "Levinas and the Immediacy of the Face." *Journal of the Society of Christian Philosophers* 10 (1993): 486–502.

———. "The Transparent Shadow: Kierkegaard and Levinas in Dialogue," in *Kierkegaard in Post/Modernity*, ed. M. Matustik. Bloomington: Indiana University Press, 1995.

Wiemer, T. *Die Passion des Sagens. Zur Deutung der Sprache bei E. Levinas und ihrer Realisierung in Philosophischen Diskurs*. Freiburg: Alber, 1988.

Wright, T., Hughes, P., and Ainley, A. "The Paradox of Morality: An Interview with Emmanuel Levinas," in *The Provoca-*

tion of Levinas, ed. R. Bernasconi and D. Wood, 168–80. New York: Routledge, 1988.

Wyschogrod, Edith. *Emmanuel Levinas: The Problem of Ethical Metaphysics.* The Hague: Martinus Nijhoff, 1974.

———. "Doing Before Hearing: On the Primacy of Touch," in *Textes pour Emmanuel Levinas,* ed. F. Laruelle, 179–203. Paris: Ed. Jean-Michel Place, 1980.

———. *Spirit in Ashes: Hegel, Heidegger, and Man-Made Mass Death.* New Haven: Yale University Press, 1985.

———. "Derrida, Levinas and Violence," in *Continental Philosophy II,* ed. H. Silverman et al. New York: Routledge, 1989.

———. "The Art in Ethics: Aesthetics, Objectivity, and Alterity in the Philosophy of Emmanuel Levinas," in *Ethics as First Philosophy,* ed. A. Peperzak, 137–48. New York: Routledge, 1995.

Ziarek, Krzysztof. *Inflected Language: Toward a Hermeneutics of Nearness.* Albany: SUNY Press, 1994.

Zimmerman, Michael. "Toward a Heideggerian *Ethos* for Radical Environmentalism." *Environmental Ethics* 5 (1983): 99–131.

———. "Implications of Heidegger's Thought for Deep Ecology." *Modern Schoolman* 64 (1986): 19–43.

———. *Heidegger's Confrontation with Modernity: Technology, Politics, Art.* Bloomington: Indiana University Press, 1990.

Index

F

G

H

I

K

L